ALL WE NEED IS A BODY

"I think you're lying," Detective Doris said heatedly. "I think you killed Dewilde. Not only that, I think you killed your business partner. I think you killed your mother."

Blaikie recoiled with a look of shock. And with that the Brighton detectives ended the questioning and watched an extremely nervous-looking suspect trudge out of the room.

"He killed him, all right," Moran said.
"Yeah," Detective Doris said. "All we need is a body. . . ."

"An intriguing story of foul play in a high place. . . reveals the shaky financial structure of a prominent family . . .a powerful argumet for changes in the law governing life insurance beneficiaries. . .As it stands we are all easy marks for killers." —— Darcy O'Brien, author of *Murder in Little Egypt*

WILLIAM SONZSKI is a freelance journalist whose reporting has appeared in such publications as *Time* and *People* magazines as well as the *Chicago Sun Times* and the *Boston Globe*. He lives in Boston.

FATAL AMBITION

GREED AND MURDER IN NEW ENGLAND

William Sonzski

AN ONYX BOOK

ONYX
Published by the Penguin Group
Penguin Books USA Inc., 375 Hudson Street,
New York, New York 10014, U.S.A.
Penguin Books Ltd, 27 Wrights Lane,
London W8 5TZ, England
Penguin Books Australia Ltd, Ringwood,
Victoria, Australia
Penguin Books Canada Ltd, 2801 John Street,
Markham, Ontario, Canada L3R 1B4
Penguin Books (N.Z.) Ltd, 182–190 Wairau Road,
Auckland 10, New Zealand

Penguin Books Ltd, Registered Offices:
Harmondsworth, Middlesex, England

First published by Onyx, an imprint of New American Library,
a division of Penguin Books USA Inc.

First Printing, September, 1991
10 9 8 7 6 5 4 3 2 1

In memory of James Droney,
reporter extraordinaire

Raskolnikov said: "I wanted to find out then and quickly whether I was a louse like everybody else or a man. Whether I can step over barriers or not, whether I dare stoop to pick up or not, whether I am a trembling creature or whether I have the *right* . . ."

"To kill? Have the right to kill?" Sonia clasped her hands.

Crime and Punishment
Fyodor Dostoevsky

Contents

I

DEATHS

And the doors shall be shut in the streets . . .
and all the daughters of music shall be brought low.

Ecclesiastes 12:4

Chapter 1

WALTHAM, MASSACHUSETTS
August 14, 1973

The old former mill town ten miles northwest of Boston awakened with most of New England to yet another dog day. A pall of gray clouds hung over a withering Charles River valley, and the annual siege of tropical air showed no sign of ending.

On the east side lay Warrendale, one of the city's neat and tree-lined neighborhoods. Easily the setting of a cheery television sitcom, the one-time farmland bore the poetic street names of Byron, Longfellow and Tennyson. At the corner of Whitman and Fairfax a charming Cape Cod-style house was distinguished by a rose-covered lattice archway at the head of the walk.

In the basement, a single bullet was fired.

If anyone on the quiet street that dreary morning heard the shot, no one reported it.

Called Eden Vale by English settlers three and a half centuries before, Waltham was a resurgent working-class city of 60,000 souls. It was home to Brandeis University on the wooded heights above the Charles. Further north of the river, Bentley College occupied a hundred forested acres. Among the trees on the western outskirts of town, sleek new buildings housed a burgeoning world-class center of high technology.

Although growing, the city of Waltham could not be considered prosperous. Near the weathered limestone city hall and its golden-domed clock tower, old shops and stores were just getting by. On the Charles embankment, a massive brick mill was a silent monument to the city's former textile greatness.

Across the river at the Waltham *News-Tribune,* reporter Thomas J. Neville was at his desk, looking over his byline feature. Scheduled to run the following morning, it was a nostalgia piece observing the hundredth anniversary of Waltham's first waterworks.

Nothing of news interest came over the crackling police scanner at the nearby city desk until 11:07 A.M., when a Waltham police dispatcher called for an ambulance.

He said a woman on Whitman Road had called about a possible death in a neighbor's house.

Tom Neville listened up. The street was near the house where he had grown up. He dialed the police department for any additional information they might have.

Minutes later, a Waltham police cruiser pulled up to the Whitman Road address and a portly young man rushed from the house. His cherubic features were frozen in an expression of grief as he neared the two uniformed officers.

After introducing himself as James Blaikie, he nodded in the direction of the corner house and apparently struggled to get his words out. "I found my mother in the basement. She shot herself, and I think she's dead."

As one patrolman reached into the cruiser to radio headquarters, his partner followed Blaikie across the small front lawn and into the one-and-a-half–story house.

Appearing overwrought, Blaikie remained upstairs as the officer hustled down a wooden stairway to the basement.

In the laundry area the plump sixty-four-year-old woman was lying face down on the concrete floor, wedged headfirst into a corner.

Wearing a diamond-patterned white cotton smock

and tan moccasins, bare-legged Alma Blaikie looked as though she had toppled forward from a curtsy.

Her left shoulder was pressed against a wall, and the left side of her face was lodged against the wide-open wooden door of a cabinet under a laundry sink. Her left leg was doubled under her torso and her right arm stretched back across her slightly bent right leg. On the floor, below her right hand and the crook of her right knee, lay a handgun pointing away from her.

Kneeling beside her, the patrolman left the .38-caliber revolver undisturbed and felt the wrist dangling above it. He found no pulse, only flesh no warmer than the dank basement air.

In the short reddish-gray hair behind her right ear a coaster-size patch of blood coagulated around a bullet wound. A trail of blood had trickled down the right side of her face and formed a pool about her head and chest. The blood verged on a slick of water that surrounded the body, apparently a spill from the open top-loading washing machine to the right of the sink and the body.

On the floor to the right of her head a pair of eyeglasses lay upside-down with the earpieces unevenly crossed. Forward of her head, a slightly crumpled piece of note-sized paper lay near the base of the open sink cabinet.

Crouching, the patrolman could make out the two lines of handwritten script near the top:

I can't stand how I
am anymore

He was joined by his partner and another patrolman, whose arrival was followed by the appearance of an emergency medical technician. He confirmed what the police knew—Alma Blaikie had apparently died of a gunshot wound behind her right ear.

With a police confirmation of a death on Whitman Road, Tom Neville left the weathered brick *News-Tribune* building at 11:20 A.M. and set out on the two-mile drive to Warrendale. He recalled James Blaikie as one of the people he had known as a young boy living on Whitman Road. Jim, a year behind him in public school, had been the only child of a retired military man and his wife.

Tom had not known Jim well but remembered him as a jovial kid tagging along after Tom and his older crowd. Jim had been a nonstop talker, forever laughing as though enjoying some private joke.

When Neville reached 89 Whitman Road, the ambulance and several police cruisers parked confirmed his fears. Whatever had happened, it had happened in the Blaikie house.

Tom looked around and then waited in vain for a police officer or EMT who might fill him in on the incident. Vaguely recalling that Jim had graduated from college and married, Tom assumed his boyhood neighbor no longer lived at home.

He was correct, but did not know that Jim was inside the house. If the neighbor in her hasty emergency call to police had said Jim was around, the police department had not mentioned it.

Tom dimly remembered Mrs. Blaikie from some long-distant afternoon. She had been standing at the front door, gently calling Jim in from play. Her son, like any other kid, had reluctantly obeyed. Jim's father escaped Tom's memory entirely and he could not remember the last time he had seen Jim.

He did recall that Jim had worked just about the most enviable summer job a youngster could hope for, hawking refreshments at Fenway Park. To attend Boston Red Sox home games and get *paid* for it had seemed to Tom Neville and his friends the greatest good fortune anyone could have.

Jim had graduated from Waltham High School in 1963, a year after Tom. More recently, Tom remembered hearing something of James Blaikie's work as an official in George McGovern's presidential campaign. From the sound of things the neighborhood kid with a perpetual grin had done all right for himself.

Several youngsters were inching close to the house,

but the emergence of a Waltham police officer from the front door sent them scurrying back to the sidewalk. Tom Neville walked up to the officer and asked what had happened. The succinct reply was, "The lady of the house, Mrs. Blaikie, committed suicide." Police were giving out no additional information.

Tom felt a twinge of sorrow for her and for Jim and his father, if the elder Blaikie were still alive.

The *News-Tribune,* like other newspapers, did not report suicides unless they had been committed by public figures or by ordinary persons in a public way. Tom anticipated that the death of Alma Blaikie would be handled by an obituary writer and the cause of death would not be noted. His work done there, he decided to linger awhile in case Jim Blaikie did come along. The least Tom felt he could do was offer his condolences.

By noon, half an hour after arriving, he still had seen nothing of his former acquaintance and dejectedly returned to his car for the drive back to the newspaper.

Early in the afternoon, Waltham deputy police chief John Rooney was joined in the basement of the Blaikie house by the local medical examiner, Dr. Nathaniel Brackett, and a state police detective from the district attorney's office.

After color photos of the decedent had been taken by a police photographer, a ballistician lifted the gun from the floor just behind her body.

The eight-inch–long revolver was literally a bastard. Its six-inch barrel had the stamp of a .38-caliber Smith & Wesson, but the imprint on the frame under the cylinder read "H & R," Harrington & Richardson. The two Massachusetts gun manufacturers had once had corporate ties.

The five-shot cylinder contained three live .38-caliber rounds and one empty case.

Hunkered down beside the body, Dr. Brackett observed the bullet hole behind the woman's right ear was a close-contact entry wound. With an assistant he gently turned the body onto its back. The blood on the forehead and right side of the face had flowed from the entry wound. There was no exit wound.

The medical examiner scanned the six-by-nine-inch sheet of paper on the floor near Alma Blaikie's head and read the brief message written with a blue ballpoint pen: "I can't stand how I am anymore."

Like the police before him, Dr. Brackett found no sign of a struggle.

Jim Blaikie called the nearby St. Jude's Roman Catholic Church and soon after a priest arrived and administered last rites. He spoke of Mrs. Blaikie as a regular parishioner, a convert to her husband's faith. As a high schooler, Jim had been a member of the local Catholic Youth Organization.

Upstairs the police had a talk with the son of Alma Blaikie.

Two days shy of his twenty-eighth birthday, a gloomy James Blaikie told of arriving at the house around nine o'clock that morning from Brookline, the Boston suburb where he and his wife shared an apartment.

"I had a cup of coffee with my mother till about nine-thirty," he said. "I was going to do some chores for her in the attic and she was going to visit a friend on Longfellow Road." He gave the name of a woman on the next street, and said, "I went up to the attic to clean out a closet. I came down about an hour later and made myself a cup of coffee."

Asked what time that was, he replied it was between ten-thirty and ten-forty-five.

"When she didn't get back by about eleven o'clock, I looked for her and went into the basement," he said. "I saw her on the floor. I grabbed her shoulder and called to her, but she didn't react." In a distraught voice he said he then ran to the neighbor's house, told of his discovery, and asked her to telephone for an ambulance.

Blaikie insisted that he had not heard the shot.

The officers exchanged glances. The attic was only two floors up from the basement and a .38 bullet had a plenty loud report.

When asked to identify the weapon, Jim said he didn't recognize it but he added that his father, an Army veteran, was a gun owner.

The seventy-two-year-old James F. Blaikie, Sr. was in the Veterans Administration Hospital in Bedford, ten miles north of Waltham. Jim mentioned that his father had frequently been a patient there since suffering a stroke five years before. Mrs. Blaikie, Jim said, had suffered a heart attack in the spring and had been on medication, including tranquilizers. He gave police the name of her doctor in nearby Weston.

Jim also indicated to the police that in the previous few weeks his mother had been especially despondent about her impaired health and the steadily deteriorating medical condition of her husband.

Asked what he did for a living, Jim said he was a partner in the Bacon and Blaikie Insurance Agency on Commercial Wharf in Boston. Actually, the agency was registered with the state under the name of its founder, Edwin C. Bacon, a prominent Boston social figure. Blaikie was currently sharing office space there. Until the previous spring, he had been sharing commissions too, but Bacon had put an end to the arrangement, citing lack of performance on Blaikie's part as the reason. As things stood, Jim would be lucky to make a thousand dollars at the agency this year.

Police determined later in the day that neighbors knew of no problems between Blaikie and his parents. He had no history of violence or criminal convictions.

Demonstrating extreme grief, Jim called on a friend from the McGovern campaign to help with funeral arrangements.

August 15, 1973

The lead story of the Waltham *News-Tribune* reported that President Richard M. Nixon was going on the air that night, trying once again to stem the rising tide of Watergate, the national rubric for the scandal plaguing his presidency. Former White House counsel John

Dean was accusing Nixon himself of covering up the 1972 break-in at Democratic headquarters in Washington's Watergate complex.

On page six a three-paragraph obituary on Alma J. Blaikie appeared. About her death it stated simply that she had "died suddenly Tuesday morning at her home."

At the funeral home in Waltham, word spread among those paying their respects that Mrs. Blaikie had shot herself.

However, James Blaikie told some associates at the Bacon Insurance Agency in Boston that his mother had died of a heart attack.

August 22, 1973

The state police report on Alma Blaikie's death summarized Jim's account of finding his mother dead in the basement of her house. According to the report, Mrs. Blaikie's physician confirmed her son's statement that she had been the recent victim of a heart attack. She had been on a regimen of Valium, a mild tranquilizer, and Digoxin, a derivative of digitalis that strengthens heart contractions.

The report, incorporating findings of state and Waltham authorities, concluded:

> After careful consideration of the available evidence, it was determined that the deceased had met her death as a result of a self-inflicted gunshot wound, and a post-mortem examination was not necessary.

The Alma Blaikie case was officially closed.

Jim and Kathleen, his strikingly attractive wife of five years, had a sailboat waiting at its mooring in Boston Harbor. Purchased for $15,700 two months before his mother's death, the thirty-foot sloop was a welcome transport for the Blaikies, who invited friends aboard for pleasure cruises on Massachusetts Bay.

It seemed to many in their circles that Jim doted excessively on twenty-six-year-old Kathleen. Some assumed the nondescript husband feared losing a beautiful wife. Others heard from her of a difficult life, beginning with her birth to Japanese parents on war-ravaged Okinawa, and viewed Jim's attentions as efforts to lift her spirits.

Jim found her given to depressions, which he attributed to a troubled relationship with her adoptive father. A U.S. serviceman, he had strenuously objected to Kathleen's marriage, once nearly coming to blows with the prospective groom.

In any event, Jim lavished the former Kathleen Goodrow with gifts. At Christmas he presented her with a sporty new blue car. To top off the holiday cheer he gave her a white fur jacket, and she modeled it for him and his camera.

James and Kathy Blaikie reckoned 1974 was going to be a very good new year.

Chapter 2

BOSTON 1974

The older sections of the city lay on a peninsula two miles long and half as wide. From the air the jut of land resembled the bow of a ship, with the Charles River on the left as it plowed northeast into Boston Harbor. Near its center was Beacon Hill, the last vestige of the *Trimountain* encountered by the first English settler in 1625.

By the mid-nineteenth century, the three hills had been leveled and shaped into one, a remarkable engineering achievement in its time and place. The excavated stony soil was used to even off several bays and coves of the original town, and in the latter half of the century, the prowlike outline was completed when the Back Bay of the Charles was filled in.

The modern-day peninsula had twice the land area of the original and held some of the most expensive real estate in the country.

Skyscrapers rose above the antique silhouette of slender steeples and conical turrets. Along the notoriously narrow and often winding streets were cobblestoned squares, brick walks, gaslights, and white-columned porticoes of earlier centuries. Yet around almost any quaint corner a glassy tower dwarfed its older neighbors.

Approaching its 350th anniversary, Boston was preparing for the nation's bicentennial as earnestly as any younger town in the country. The self-proclaimed Athens of America or Hub of the Universe—Beantown to tourists—had plenty to attract history-hungry visitors from around the world and intended to showcase its treasures in 1976 as never before.

The revolutionary paths of Paul Revere and George Washington were being carefully laid out on streets and in brochures. In greater Boston the birthplaces of three Massachusetts presidents, including John F. Kennedy, were receiving similar attention.

A less glorious past was being ignored. After the American Revolution, Massachusetts did become the first state to abolish slavery, but the practice had existed there for more than a century. Among America's earliest drug traffickers were respectable Bostonians. Like their British cousins, they ran opium from India to China. Proceeds from the nineteenth-century narcotics trade helped finance the development of the patrician Back Bay district and other local opulence.

Visiting in 1868, Charles Dickens eagerly toured the original Harvard Medical College, scene of a notorious murder in blue blood two decades before. There, near the Massachusetts General Hospital at the northern foot of Beacon Hill, a Harvard professor repaid his debt to Dr. Parkman, a wealthy benefactor, by murdering and dismembering him. After Dr. Parkman's remains were found in the depths of the medical school, a Professor Webster was hanged by the neck until dead. The gallows no longer stood near the site of the present-day Boston Garden, home of the Celtics basketball team and the hockey Bruins.

An earlier tale of the macabre had it that the alluring young wife of an older Bostonian had been missing for several years by 1800. After her husband died, his imposing house on the harbor was being razed for the latest phase of waterfront expansion. Laborers made a shocking discovery in the depths of the mansion. After forcing open a rusty iron gate, they found two skeletons locked in eerie embrace on the stone floor. Shreds of clothing told the story of a wife and her sailor trapped in their love nest by a vengeful husband.

According to lore, Boston-born Edgar Allan Poe was

inspired by the ghastly tale to write "The Fall of the House of Usher," in which lunacy similarly sealed a young woman's fate.

July 29

Not far from the purported Usher site, Commercial Wharf jutted eastward into Boston Harbor as it had for more than a century. Its five-story granite warehouse, wide as a football field and nearly twice as long, gave the impression of a massive promontory overlooking the water. Converted from storage space into fashionable upper-story apartments and first-floor businesses, it was the location of the Edwin C. Bacon Insurance Agency. On a warm and humid evening, the founder and head of the company at 49 Commercial Wharf was working late, as he often did.

Two months short of his forty-fifth birthday, the tall and husky Edwin Conant Bacon was in the back office of the three-room agency. The Harvard graduate kept his office as shipshape as might be expected of a former naval officer who had seen action on a destroyer in the Korean War. To the disbelief of Ed's former secretary, she had once returned from lunch to find him unabashedly tidying up her desk, paper clips and all.

Yet there was nothing in his manner or bearing consistent with obsessive attention to detail. The droll Edwin Bacon was given to leisurely movements, and his rugged features were softened by sensitive brown eyes and a ready grin. Although he religiously bought his clothes from Brooks Brothers, he wore them irreverently. That evening, he'd shed his navy blue blazer and was working in a narrow-striped, button-down Oxford-cloth shirt with the sleeves rolled up.

Officially, his reason for keeping late hours was a preference for working alone and more efficiently. However, more than one colleague who knew him well came to understand it was procrastination toward a business that did not much interest him. They saw in him a Renaissance man of incredibly diverse and keen interests, and insurance was not one of them.

Shortly after sunset he got his regular telephone call from thirteen-year-old Hilary, the younger of his two daughters. In the fall she would enter the third form at the exclusive Winsor School in Boston, but she sounded more mature than a girl about to start her high school studies. She reported that the light in his office at the family's Back Bay townhouse had burned out.

"Could you bring some light bulbs with you?" she asked, and once more her earnest concern suggested someone older dwelled in the wisp of a strawberry blonde.

"Sure," her father promised. It was remarkable to him and others that while Hilary resembled her fair-haired and blue-eyed mother, she shared her father's vulnerability. Meanwhile sixteen-year-old Brooks had his brown eyes and amiable features but displayed her mother's resiliency.

After the crisis of the light bulbs was resolved, Ed Bacon heard his daughter sign off with her usual, "Love you, bye-bye."

He jotted notes to his young secretary, paper-clipped them to various insurance documents, and walked the material to her desk in the empty front office, the reception area. Patricia Haskell had not been in that day, a Monday, for she was tacking vacation days onto summer weekends instead of using them all at once. She was expected in the following morning.

So was Rick Adams—James Richardson Adams III—Bacon's sales associate of several months. He had also been off that day, extending a weekend visit to his ailing mother in Philadelphia.

James Blaikie, the former McGovern campaigner in his fourth year with the Bacon agency, had been in that day and had left early in the evening.

Blaikie was very much on Ed Bacon's mind these days. He could not understand how Jim had been able to afford his major purchases, which recently included a second new car and an expensive house in a pricey section of Brookline. Blaikie already owned a boat, and lately he seemed ever more bent on leading the life of a Kennedy, without the inherited wealth.

Blaikie certainly hadn't been receiving his income from the office. Complaining to family and friends that Blaikie was not producing, Bacon had not shared commissions with him for more than a year. As Bacon had told his wife and younger brother, he was ready to reorganize the agency and leave Blaikie out of it.

Like Jim, Ed Bacon had also lost his mother the previous summer. The former Pauline Conant, descendant of the seventeenth-century founder of Salem, died in the company of her maid at her Back Bay home at the age of seventy-seven. She had been a widow for fifteen years, since her husband's death at the age of eighty-four.

For more than half a century, Charles Edward Bacon had been a driving force in the Allyn & Bacon textbook publishing company, founded in Boston by his father. He and another publisher, the founder of Time magazine, had a common ancestor in the first Henry Luce to reach America in the seventeenth century. The Bacon lineage went back to a Mayflower voyager, as did Pauline's, and Charles Bacon, a tall quintessential Yankee with chiseled good looks and succinct charm, indulged his radiant wife's delight in society. From the time of their marriage in 1918, the Bacons were major players in the city's particularly exclusive brand of high society.

They entertained often in their Back Bay mansion on Commonwealth Avenue, a Parisian-style boulevard around the corner from the Ritz-Carlton Hotel. The reigning royalty of stage, opera, and literature and the exiled Princess Ileana of Romania, cousin of then-Princess Elizabeth of England, were among their guests.

Growing up in the 1940s, Edwin Bacon and his brother Frank, younger by five years, took part in the dazzling activity without complaint. One of the fringe benefits was a steady stream of debutante company. For Francis Lyman Bacon, the handsome image of his father, it also meant a brief, storybook romance with an English ballerina. A guest at a Bacon family reception, the British beauty and the Harvard sophomore found enough to talk about to resume their conversation later. The idyll took Frank all the way to Chicago, where the ballerina danced with her touring company, but Harvard tugged at him, and they went their separate ways.

Ed, with the craggy looks of a Conant, had been content with local charm and was a regular at the coming-out parties of socially registered women.

Frank, who had little interest in the social swim, married first and moved into a sylvan redoubt miles from the city. Ed stayed in Boston and, like his father before him, followed the lead of a socially active wife. She was a vivacious blonde with an improbable nickname for a Bacon: Smoki. Some said the sobriquet, which predated her meeting Ed, described the trail she blazed across the Boston social scene. Not all said so flatteringly.

The brothers remained close at heart, but grew apart economically as well as socially. Frank made his first million as a computer systems entrepreneur in his early thirties, at a time when Ed was trying to find his way in the insurance business. When their mother attended to her will in the summer of 1973, Frank had a suggestion. Wealthy in his own right, he urged her to leave her money entirely to Ed. Frank wanted only the family's antique possessions. He had seen a family torn apart by clashes over heirlooms and wanted nothing of the sort coming between him and Ed.

Frank's instincts proved correct and after Pauline Bacon's death in September 1973, her will presented no problems.

In his office on Commercial Wharf the following July, Ed Bacon was counting on his inheritance and new business to save his agency. It was making little headway. Worse, it was nearly on the rocks.

Sometime before ten o'clock, he received a telephone call he had been expecting from a contractor in nearby Somerville. Al Powers had done house repairs and decorating for Bacon and his parents before him.

"I just got home and saw your message," said Powers.

"Thanks for calling back," Bacon replied. "We had quite a bit of rain leak in from the skylight at the house and it stained some walls. I'd appreciate it if you could come around and give me an estimate on repair work."

Powers said he certainly would and they agreed to meet at the Bacon house the following evening at six-thirty.

Their brief and unremarkable conversation ended.

Then began the mystery of Edwin Conant Bacon.

Chapter 3

BOSTON
July 30, 1974
6:30 A.M.

Despite the warmth of the day, Smoki Bacon awakened with the feeling she had slept in some cold and damp netherworld, like the morbid setting of her awful dream. Sitting up, she saw what she had sensed uneasily through a night of mostly fitful sleep—her husband was not beside her. Ed had not come home at all after she had fallen asleep around ten o'clock the previous night. Extraordinary as his overnight absence was, it distressed her largely because of her seemingly palpable dream, which had plunged her into clammy, shivering terror. Upon awakening, her sense of relief was cut short by the discovery she was alone in bed.

Smoki recalled the nightmare with a shudder. In it an old Boston streetcar was receding from a gaslit street corner into the darkness. There were two people in the rear window looking out and sadly waving to her. The distinguished elderly woman was her late mother-in-law, Pauline, every dignified inch the descendant of a Mayflower Compact signatory. When Smoki recognized the man next to Pauline Bacon, she recoiled in her dream, for he was her own husband. Soon Ed and his mother were disappearing in the swirling haze, leaving a thunderstruck wife to grasp for reality.

Smoki pulled a robe over her nightgown, strode to

the bay window, and whipped open the curtains. Nowhere along narrow and lifeless Fairfield Street, two stories below, could she see Ed's car. Her artist's eye lingered a moment on the slate mansard rooftops of the tall brick houses across the way. Against the dawning light, somehow menacing in its silent fury, the Victorian skyline appeared on fire. It promised to be another sweltering day.

She recalled another time in their seventeen years of marriage that she and Ed had unexpectedly spent a night apart. Following a colossal argument, he had sought overnight refuge at the Parker House Hotel in downtown Boston. However, his failure to return home last night could hardly be a repeat performance, for they had parted without incident the previous morning. Ed did frequently work late at his insurance brokerage on Commercial Wharf, and Smoki assured herself he simply must have fallen asleep and stayed the night there. She went to the telephone beside their bed.

She dialed his office at about 6:35 A.M. and waited for an answer.

Nothing could have happened, she thought. He was good and safe there with his prized sled dog, Kayak, ever at his feet at the office. Always under foot, as far as Smoki was concerned, when the shedding machine returned home. How could a man as fastidious as Ed allow it?

Was he already making the ten-minute drive back home from Boston Harbor? Anxiety flared into anger the longer her call went unanswered. Ed's secretary would not be showing up at the office for another two hours. How inconsiderate of him to leave her mystified and anxious like this! Brooks and Hilary would be waking up before long and, if he had not returned by then, they would be wondering where on earth their father and Kayak were. After nearly a minute of futile ringing, Smoki tossed the phone on the bed and let it continue purring away. Let Ed answer it and have a *mystery* morning of his own! She marched to her shower.

At her vanity fifteen minutes later, turning a brush under her blonde hair in a pageboy cut, she could still hear the telephone ringing on the bed and let it continue. She tried to concentrate on the day's events. She was to meet with her friend Marilyn Carrington, a black educator also of the Back Bay, at nine o'clock. As members of a local affirmative-action group, they were scheduled to monitor a court hearing on the quality of teaching facilities at a city trade school with a predominantly black enrollment. The Boston school desegregation crisis was an international focal point.

Smoki considered wearing a blue pantsuit as a power outfit but did not want to give anyone the ammunition to peg her as a strident civil rights advocate, a popular charge during the city's traumatic school desegregation period. This was 1974 in the land of abolitionist William Lloyd Garrison, but plenty of people were still thinking as though it were 1874 in the land of cotton.

She decided at last on an unimpeachable frock, but even as she was viewing her mirror image in the white-and-blue-flowered print dress, the glacial eyes staring back at her knew she would not keeping her appointment that morning.

Shortly before seven, she telephoned Marilyn Carrington and immediately launched into a breathless announcement: "Something *terrible* has happened."

A brief silence on the other end was followed by Marilyn's concerned voice. "My goodness, Smoki, *what?*"

"I don't know," Smoki blurted, "but something has happened to Ed, I'm sure of it. He hasn't been home and I can't reach him at his office. I'm going there right now."

She declined Marilyn's offer to meet her on the waterfront and promised to attend the civil rights hearing if she possibly could.

Gratefully, she heard no sound from Brooks or Hilary in their rooms above, and she scrawled a note for them: "I've gone to the pharmacy and will be right back." She stuck the white lie in the molding of the mirror on the second-floor landing and descended the dark wooden staircase to the first floor. There she was disappointed but not surprised to see the foyer and adjacent living room empty. As ever, the portrait of an early nineteenth-century ancestor whom Ed strongly resembled sent his solemn gaze out over an expanse of maroon oriental carpet. In the dining room a shining, long mahogany table with its centerpiece of flowers seemed eerily to be awaiting formal guests. In a macabre flash, she wondered if they might already be there, invisible in their white ties and evening gowns.

She did not stop to make coffee either in the serving station off the dining room or in the deserted basement kitchen proper, where scullery maids had been kept in their proper place at the raised hearth a century before.

What really had Smoki's adrenaline going was that awful nightmare. Seeing your husband join his deceased mother in a museum piece of a streetcar and fade with her into the mist was not guaranteed to get a wife's day off to a great start. Especially when the wife awoke without him.

She did not believe in premonitions, but earlier seemingly clairvoyant experiences, combined with her dream, had left her predisposed to morbid thoughts.

After all, years before she had dreamed of an automobile accident the night her younger brother had nearly died in one.

Then there had been the incident after a charitable benefit at the Sheraton Boston Hotel years back when she had gathered an armful of flowers from tables, bouquets that would take on ghastly significance. Leaving the ballroom, she and Ed had run into Lieutenant Governor Elliot Richardson and his wife, whom the Bacons had known for years from the Harvard Club as well as through political circles. Richardson was to be lionized for his Watergate stand against Richard Nixon in 1973.

A bemused Anne "Hap" Hazard Richardson asked, "Smoki, what on earth are you going to do with all those flowers?"

"I'm taking them to a funeral," Smoki airily responded.

Hap and Elliot reacted to her flippancy with mild amusement. Ed's smile was even fainter than theirs.

"How would you feel if something terrible happened after a wisecrack like that," he fumed as they left the Back Bay hotel.

To this day, Smoki had no idea where her incongruous remark had come from but she would never forget it; hours after uttering it Ed got the news by telephone that her father had died in a Boston & Maine train accident.

Smoki Bacon did not consider herself superstitious, but her history of fateful glimmerings did not leave her feeling terribly rational this morning. Back on the first floor where she nervously checked her appearance in the foyer mirror, she realized her father's death, her brother's nearly fatal accident, and the dream about Ed and his mother had all involved vehicles.

She pulled open the weighty oak and glass door into the vestibule and then a similar but heavier outside door and descended the several stone steps to Fairfield Street. Walking toward her car shortly after seven o'clock, she saw the imagery of the dream more clearly. The gaslight had been a funereal sort of candle and the streetcar taking away her husband and his mother had been a symbolic hearse.

Stop being so damned morbid, she imagined Ed telling her.

In 1974, there were no old trolleys in Boston. But functioning gaslights still distinguished straight and narrow Back Bay streets. Tall brownstone, brick, and granite houses stood in tight rows like rare books. East on Marlborough Street and north on Berkeley, Smoki Bacon drove toward Boston Harbor. She listened with satisfaction to Watergate reports on the radio. The previous day the House Judiciary Committee had passed the second article of impeachment, charging Nixon with failure to carry out his constitutional oath. The last of three articles was expected to come to a vote that day.

Like much of the country, she had joyfully been following the mess on television. A Kennedy–McGovern Democrat, it did her heart good to see Tricky Dick getting his comeuppance at last.

As a graphic artist at the Cambridge technological firm of Bolt Beranek and Newman, she had taken a minor but essential part in the Watergate hearings. She had created the oversized illustrations used by BBN scientists to explain their acoustical analysis of an infamous gap in a White House tape recording. The conclusion was that someone had attempted to erase eighteen and a half minutes from a Nixon conversation about the Watergate break-in. There was widespread belief that Nixon himself had made the clumsy effort.

As she drove northeast on Storrow Drive, sailboats glided on the Charles River to her left. To the right, the brick and slate-roof jumble of Beacon Hill stepped up eastward to the eighteenth-century Massachusetts State House with its golden dome.

She searched in vain for a sight of Ed's car heading home in the southwest lane, and then a tree-lined median blocked her view of oncoming traffic. Ed had better have a damn good reason for upsetting her like this when she reached his office!

7:15 A.M.

The sunrise over Boston Harbor enflamed the dormered roof of the old Commercial Wharf warehouse and cast its south wall of rough-hewn granite blocks in violet. The multipaned bowfronts of first-floor shops and offices in the nineteenth-century structure looked like so many windows on an enormous oven.

Smoki drove onto the wharf and turned right into a parking space at dockside across from her husband's office at Number 49. A tall, shapely blonde, she appeared a decade younger than her forty-six years in a sleeveless cotton print dress with a scooped neckline.

The silver barrettes holding back her hair at either side enhanced the impression of fewer years.

She got out of the car and saw no one in the morning serenity. The only sounds were the halyards rhythmically slapping at the masts of sailing yachts at their slips and the melancholy cries of seagulls. *How terribly peaceful,* she thought, hurrying across the lane toward the Bacon agency.

So intent was she on getting there, she did not look for Ed's car among the parked vehicles. The heavy curtains in the bowfront of the agency were parted, but she did not peer inside as she approached the entranceway. It was locked and she did not have a key for it or for the agency door inside.

There still was not a soul to be seen. She returned to her car and drove back to Atlantic Avenue, the broad access road to the waterfront. At a nearby service station on the edge of the North End, a warren of twisting one-lane streets, she telephoned the owner of Commercial Wharf at his residence. He heard out her concern and advised her to look for the building superintendent at his office in the building.

Minutes later she was back on the wharf and anxiously following Frank Doherty to the Bacon agency. The super had never met her before but knew of her as the wife of the insurance executive at Number 49. The two men had frequently walked their sled dogs together along the wharf and Doherty had gotten the distinct impression Ed did not share his wife's enthusiasm for the social whirl.

At Number 49 Doherty unlocked the outer door and preceded Smoki into the hallway. Immediately on the right was the solid wooden door to the Bacon agency. It was locked.

He consulted his ring of keys and unlocked it. Pushing the door inward clockwise, he was able to open it only a few inches. Something was blocking it. Doherty squeezed a look inside and saw what was on the floor obstructing the door.

"Good God," he said.

7:20 A.M.

"What is it?" Smoki cried. When Doherty did not answer, she brushed past him and was able to peer inside and get a glimpse of her husband lying face down on the floor. Lowering to her knees, she reached inside and touched his neck.

It was cold and stiff.

"*O my god o migod omigod* . . ." The longer her chant continued the faster it came and then a shriek filled the stone-encased hallway. "My god," she sobbed, "he's *dead*."

Doherty again prevented her from going into the office and locked the door. Smoki screamed objections, but Doherty said he was going back to his office to telephone the police. She followed him outside into the rising heat of the day.

7:25 A.M.

A panting Siberian husky was eyeing their movements in Doherty's office as Smoki paced, wringing her hands, and the grim-faced superintendent telephoned the police. Doherty left to await the arrival of a cruiser several doors down at the Bacon agency.

Smoki telephoned longstanding friends Louis and Katharine Kane at their Beacon Hill townhouse. Kathy, a deputy mayor of Boston, answered and Smoki's words came tumbling out.

"Kathy, something terrible has happened. Ed has died. I just found him in his office."

"Oh, *no!*" Kathy exclaimed. "Smoki! How did it happen?"

"I don't know. I assume it was a heart attack. We're waiting for the police. Is Lou there?"

"He's on his way out of town, but I'll try to reach him at his office before he leaves."

"O, I'd appreciate it if you could, Kathy. I'd like someone reliable here. Lou is Ed's best friend. I've got to get back to the girls. This is so . . ." Her voice trailed off.

Kathy comforted her and assured her either she or Lou would get to the waterfront immediately.

Smoki next telephoned her widowed mother in south suburban Weymouth, broke the news, and asked her to come immediately by cab to the Bacon house in the Back Bay. Someone had to be there when Brooks and Hilary awakened.

There was no answer at the home of Ed's brother in Dover, a sylvan preserve fifteen miles southwest of Boston. Frank Bacon, thirty-nine, was now the lone survivor of the Charles Edward Bacon family. Smoki called Frank's summer home in Wolfboro, New Hampshire and spoke with his wife. A disbelieving sister-in-law tried to console Smoki and promised to locate Frank.

Smoki's last call was to Gary Brennan, her boss at Bolt Beranek and Newman. He told her not to worry about the project she had due that morning and to do what she had to do there, knowing her colleagues would be pulling for her and her daughters.

She left Doherty's office and made her way back along the wharf to Number 49, where Doherty somberly awaited the police.

7:40 A.M.

Louis Isaac Kane, a friend of Ed's since Harvard, parked at dockside and the raw-boned six-footer strode across the lane toward the Bacon agency. A look of concern creased his leathery face. The retired Marine Corps captain approached the wife of his college clubmate and she greeted him with a forlorn gaze.

"Smoki," he said, taking her by the shoulders and looking down into her brimming eyes.

"O, Lou, I'm so glad Kathy reached you. Ed . . ."

The forty-three-year-old Kane closed his eyes a moment and then stared at the window of the agency. "I am so sorry," he said gently. *"So* sorry."

Looking down at her clasped hands, she told of finding Ed's body. The superintendent had locked the office door and police should be coming along.

"He seemed so well when I saw him a few days ago," Kane said, shaking his head. "It's *hard* to believe, Smoki."

"I know, Lou. There were absolutely *no* warning signs that I could see."

Kane walked up to the bowfront window. Through the panes he could dimly see to his left the clothed body lying on the floor of the reception room. It appeared as though Ed had toppled forward or crawled toward the door. Lou Kane returned slowly to Smoki with downcast eyes.

From Atlantic Avenue a police cruiser pulled onto the wharf and came to a halt in front of the agency. Two patrolmen ambled to the outer doorway and Frank Doherty showed them into the hallway. One of the officers closed the door behind them. The cruiser, with its shortwave radio occasionally squawking like a mechanical fowl, began to attract passersby.

The Bacon agency, like other offices and shops at Commercial Wharf, was a wood and plasterboard enclosure constructed in one-time warehouse space. Superintendent Doherty pointed out the front entrance to the agency and told of the body blocking it. He mentioned a door in the back as the only other way in. One of the patrolmen strode down the hallway alongside the thirty-foot length of the agency and turned a corner to the right. Behind the sixteen-foot-long rear wall of the agency was a utility room of trash containers and storage boxes. The door was locked and had no external latch.

Doherty explained it was secured from the inside by a slide bolt and could not be opened from the outside. He unlocked the front door and a patrolman squeezed inside, pushing the body back several inches in the process.

With his head of short-cropped dark hair less than a foot from the door, Bacon's body stretched back almost at a ninety-degrees angle to the doorway. The face pressed straight down on the carpeting. His legs were slightly splayed and his arms were folded under his upper torso with his elbows extended as though he had been clutching at his chest.

The patrolman sought the carotid artery and felt only cold, hard flesh.

Shortly after eight o'clock a second cruiser arrived and two patrolmen replaced the responding officers whose duty had ended on the hour.

At approximately eight-fifteen, a patrolman came out of the building and seemed to be looking for someone. He walked up to Smoki, confirmed she was Bacon's wife, and offered his condolences. When she was able to speak, she answered his questions about her husband's failure to return home the previous night and her discovery of his body that morning.

The officer said that was all the information he needed at the time, thanked her, and explained that a medical examiner was on the way to make the official pronouncement of death.

The officer returned to the agency, and Smoki asked Lou Kane if he would be able to stay and deal with any further questions. "I *have* to get back to the girls," she said.

Kane said he would. He and his wife had two daughters close in age to the Bacon girls and he could only imagine how difficult the news would be for Brooks and Hilary to take. Seeing her to her car, he assured her that he and his wife would join her at the Bacon house later in the day.

As dapper James Francis Blaikie, Jr. left his large secluded colonial house in the dignified Fisher Hills section of Brookline that morning, he was the picture of a young man on the way up. He approached his Ford LTD with its "JB" vanity plates in the driveway with his usual hustling gait and preoccupied look.

There was evidence of accomplishment in his two-and-a-half story stucco dwelling on treed and rolling grounds in the old established suburb immediately west of Boston. In April, eight months after the death of his mother and a month after his father's death, Blaikie paid $74,500 for an estate that would command ten times that much in the Reagan era.

Their panoply of affluence also contained the grand piano for exotically beautiful Kathy, the new car for Kathy, and the fashionable clothes for Kathy. Yet in a rock-solid neighborhood of bankers, attorneys, and doctors, there was nothing extraordinary about their trappings of success.

Most intriguing was the pair themselves, a study in fascinating contrasts. Five feet, seven inches tall and weighing more than two hundred pounds, twenty-eight-year-old Blaikie and his hair-trigger smile might have gone unnoticed in a crowd. Not so his petite, raven-haired wife. A year younger than Jim, Kathy had met him while they were students at Northeastern University in Boston, where he had studied business administration. Childless after six years of marriage, they personified upward mobility, dining almost nightly at expensive restaurants, moving in young and hip circles.

However, as Jim Blaikie climbed into his car, appearances were deceptive. He was nearly $100,000 in debt. His checking accounts at his Boston bank were repeatedly overdrawn and he was nearing the limit of a revolving credit account. Although such financial binds were not remarkable in the fast lane, the couple's earnings were. Kathy worked on and off at part-time jobs and Jim had barely made $1,000 at the Bacon agency so far that year.

The previous March he had sold the thirty-foot sailboat to an area doctor, who did not know the sloop was not Blaikie's to sell. Jim still owed nearly $15,000 on it to a credit company—the amount the unsuspecting physician paid him for it. Blaikie had pocketed the doctor's money and was making $200 monthly payments on the craft. Neither the doctor nor the credit company was yet any the wiser.

Jim eased his car out the driveway through an open-

ing in the tall shrubbery that screened his estate from
Fisher Avenue.

Ed Bacon had told a friend he thought James Blaikie
was a genius. Jim had been called ruthless to his face
by a longtime friend.

Whatever he was as he headed for Boston's waterfront half an hour away, it was an extremely impressive
house of cards he left behind.

8:35 A.M.

Minutes after Smoki Bacon's departure, a state medical examiner for Suffolk County and additional Boston
police officers arrived at 49 Commercial Wharf.

Matthew Lappin, M.D. and a police sergeant were
met by the patrolman at the front door. He directed
them down the hall to the rear entrance of the Bacon
agency.

Inside the windowless back office, they saw to their
left a fretting black and white sled dog leashed to the
leg of a desk along a side wall. The animal seemed
more curious than alarmed by their presence. The
desktop was orderly, as was the surface of a conference table along the opposite wall.

Dr. Lappin and the officer crossed the twelve-foot
carpeted office to an opening between the partition
walls and entered the smaller, middle section of the
agency. A desk on their right and another on their left
showed no sign of disturbance. Beyond the opening
between the partitions ahead was the front office. Pale
gold sunlight was streaming in through the bowfront
window.

Entering the front office, Dr. Lappin greeted a patrolman and saw a standard-sized metal desk on his
left and, on his right, a smaller metal desk. In front
of this lay the body, almost perpendicular to the front
door.

Crouching beside the body, the medical examiner
found neither wounds nor any other marks of violence.

At 8:40 A.M. he pronounced Edwin Conant Bacon dead.

There were no indications of forced entry into the agency or a struggle inside. In the absence of any signs of foul play, it was looking like a routine case of sudden death by natural causes.

A police photographer took pictures of the body and a county mortuary vehicle arrived. To make way for a gurney stretcher, Dr. Lappin and a police officer carefully rolled the body over on its back and away from the door.

The face was contorted in a grimace of pain and there were blue-red patches on the throat, evidence of convulsion.

More pertinent than the body at the moment was a sheet of note-sized paper that had been lying under it.

Dr. Lappin picked up the barely wrinkled piece of plain white paper. Written with a felt pen in capital letters a few inches from the top was the statement:

I CAN'T STAND IT ANYMORE

The note was unsigned.

The case of Edwin Conant Bacon was no longer one of a simple sudden death but a possible suicide. Murder seemed unlikely to the investigators. Only a killer five or six inches thick could have slid out the obstructed front door. The rear door had been locked from the inside. All the bowfront windows were sealed and no one larger than a small monkey could get through one of the panes anyway.

Still, the note was evidence and could not be revealed at the time. Wary of disturbing the scene, police did not look for anyone with the agency to explain the layout of the place.

As an unfortunate result of the necessary secrecy, they were operating in an informational vacuum.

Police searched the front office, where the body had been found. No bottle, jar, or other container associated with a possibly toxic substance turned up on or in the desks. Nothing suspicious was found on shelves or the magazine table between two metal-framed captain's chairs in the bowfront.

Focus centered on the room because it was assumed to be Ed's office. But it was not. It was the reception room.

Police spoke of the back office, where Kayak was leashed, as the "rear room." It was indeed the last and innermost of the three offices in a row that comprised the Bacon agency. But, more importantly, it was Bacon's office.

The sled dog, who normally had the run of the agency, was tethered in Bacon's office. Yet it was that office that received the least thorough inspection.

There were further consequences of tight-lipped policy. Ed's friend Lou Kane, standing outside the Bacon agency, was not even told of the note's existence.

Without the benefit of his or anyone else's knowledge of Ed Bacon or the agency, authorities were seeing the case as a suicide within ninety minutes of the body's discovery.

8:50 A.M.

The originally crimson brick common to most of the Back Bay had been darkened by a century of salt air and smog into facades of deep maroon. As Smoki approached the two-and-a-half–story Bacon townhouse built in 1872, it seemed to be the color of dry blood.

Inside the cool dimness of the house, she left her sunglasses on. Off the foyer and across the expanse of oriental carpet in the livingroom, her seventy-six-year-old mother sat hunched over her cane in an armchair near a cold and black hearth.

"Thank you for coming," Smoki said, entering the room. After giving her mother a hovering embrace, she briefly reported the circumstances of Ed's death.

"It is so terrible," Ruth weakly trilled.

"Yes, Mother, it is," Smoki said, appearing to hold back her tears. "I must get the girls." She excused herself, left the room, and climbed the heavy mahogany-railed staircase.

The older Brooks was in the shower. Hilary was dressing when her mother entered the room. The sunglasses were a tip-off to the alert thirteen-year-old that something was wrong. Smoki never wore them indoors.

"Please come downstairs," Smoki said in the tone of a kindly commanding officer. "I have something to tell you."

Hilary nodded warily.

When Smoki repeated the request at the bathroom door, Brooks snapped, "I'll come when I'm finished, Mother."

Smoki did not react to the backtalk and retreated down the staircase.

Brooks made much in her mind of the leniency. It meant Smoki was cutting her a break because her father was dead. Brooks reasoned that as long as she stayed in the shower, she would not have to hear confirmation of his death.

Smoki did not know that Brooks had awakened shortly after seven-thirty and gone down to her parents' second-floor bedroom. She did not expect to find her mother there, for Smoki was usually enroute to her office by then, but she was surprised to see her father's side of the connected twin beds empty. Usually, after coming home late from his office, he would sleep in past Smoki's departure. His absence was most alarming.

Brooks's puzzlement turned to shock half an hour later. Unbeknownst to Smoki, who was on Commercial Wharf, someone from the graphics department of Bolt Beranek and Newman called the house shortly after eight o'clock. Brooks answered the phone and Smoki's colleague said he was sorry to hear about her father. He did not mention Smoki had just called with news of his death.

"What are you talking about?" the already anxious sixteen-year-old asked with a touch of panic in her voice.

The caller awkwardly apologized, thinking it must be one of the terrible practical jokes people had a habit of playing at their department. He rang off, leaving Brooks Bacon even more suspicious about her father's absence.

Now all Brooks could do to delay the inevitable was to take her sweet time showering.

Smoki paced the living room, where her mother sat in silence. Over the fireplace with its fluted side columns, the painting of a Conant precursor again caught Smoki's eye. She did not focus so much on his likeness to her husband as on the withered look of the hand across his breast. It was a fixture of early American portraits that she could not abide.

Brooks and Hilary filed stoically into the living room like schoolgirls prepared for a reprimand. Brooks, her brown hair still damp from the shower, and the younger reddish-blonde Hilary sank in a long sofa of white quilted silk. Their mother sat down between them. Both girls were still very tender from the death of Grandmother Polly ten months before, and they faced their Grandmother Ruth, who was obviously struggling to keep her emotions under control.

As Smoki spoke, she thought someone else was delivering her words and she heard only a few of them: "... very sad ... father ... died ..."

Then the announcement sank in. "I have something very, very sad to tell you ... Your father has died."

After regaining her breath, Hilary raged, "You're lying! He is *not* dead." Her slender frame was convulsing in sobs.

"No, my dear," Smoki whispered, "I'm afraid I am telling you the truth." She pressed her daughters to her.

Brooks had retreated to a time before the words had been spoken, and she intended to stay there. She would not weep, for to do so would mean her father was dead, and he was not dead.

Grandmother Ruth's nodding and her glistening eyes told Smoki there was no kind way to break the unkindest news and she was doing as well by her daughters as a mother could.

Moments later Brooks told Smoki of something Ed had not mentioned to her. He had purchased several sled dogs the previous winter to team up with Kayak. They were kenneled in New Hampshire. What, the girls frantically worried, would happen to the dogs, including Kayak at their father's office?

"Don't worry, my dears," Smoki reassured them with hollow bravado. "They will be taken care of. *Everything* will be taken care of."

Brooks in the seclusion of her fantasy world and Hilary in her inescapable misery did not focus on the fear gleaming in their mother's eyes.

For all the aristocratic trappings, the Bacons of Fairfield Street had less than a hundred dollars to their name.

9:05 A.M.

Ed's younger brother was ten miles west of Boston, arriving by car from baronial Dover at the house of a colleague in plush suburban Wellesley. Francis Lyman Bacon, founder of a highly successful computer systems firm bearing his name, had come to pick up Jim Sullivan, who was having car trouble. Frank parked in the Sullivan driveway and when he got out of his car, he saw Jim coming down the back steps of his house with a troubled expression.

"Hi, Jim," Frank called suspiciously.

Sullivan, a fellow Groton alumnus of the Bacon brothers, did not crack a grin when he returned the greeting. Standing squarely before Frank, he said, "Your wife and the kids are all right, Frank, but I have some terrible news."

"Oh, what's that, Jim?" Frank's boyishly handsome face suddenly showed its thirty-nine years. *Terrible* did not mean the cat had disappeared at Wolfboro; it meant death.

Looking Frank in the eye, Sullivan told it straight. "Your brother has died."

Frank Bacon winced as though he had been blind-sided on a football field or hockey rink as a varsity star at Groton. With the look and manner of his late father, he raised up his six-foot height and lifted his strong chin. Tears welled and his pale green eyes seemed to be searching out something in the billowing summer trees.

Sullivan quietly explained that Frank's wife had telephoned from their summer house in New Hampshire, relaying Smoki's message that she had found Ed's body in his office.

Frank Bacon's expression of sorrow instantly hardened into a frown of intense concentration. His jaw clenched and he appeared to be contemplating a terrible knowledge.

9:20 A.M.

Ed Bacon's attorney received a telephone call at his State Street office from Smoki. In a breaking voice she told Zalman O. Davlin of Ed's death. Zal listened, comforting her at intervals, and said he would come around to see her that afternoon.

When he put down the receiver, he shook his head in disbelief. A longtime friend of the Bacons and co-trustee of Ed's estate with Smoki for the past year, he knew Ed was carrying extra weight and smoked too much, but his death still came as a shock. The man played tennis frequently in the summer and raced dog-sleds in the winter. But then, athletes in peak condition, including professionals, were known to keel over without warning from unknown heart defects.

Ed had seemed his usual congenial self and appeared in fine spirits the previous month when they had gone over his will and insurance coverage. Fortunately, Zal thought, they had gotten all that in order.

Including the inheritance from his mother, there would be about half a million dollars insurance and stocks going to Smoki and the girls. Then there were also the Bacon Insurance Agency, the couple's town-house in the Back Bay, and Ed's stake in a considerable real estate venture with his brother Frank and others.

But, first things first. Zal decided some Jewish mothering would not hurt Smoki and the girls at such an awful time. He telephoned his wife to ask if she would like to pay them a visit. Crushed by the news of Ed's death, Helen Davlin instantly agreed that the bereaved Bacons could certainly do with some friends at this terrible time. She would pick up some food and get over to the Bacon house as soon as possible.

Zal was not too surprised to hear about the involve-ment of the medical examiner's office in Ed's death. Ed *was* a relatively young man. If he had dropped dead at ninety, the police might instead have called a public health department doctor to pronounce death at the scene. But a cop was more likely to call in a medical examiner in the case of a forty-four-year-old man who had presumably died alone in his office.

Along with the Bacons, Zal was unaware of the ap-parent suicide note. Ed had been pronounced dead nearly an hour earlier, and the authorities had not communicated with his family.

9:25 A.M.

Fury threatened to ignite within Frank Bacon's sor-row. Preferring to be alone after getting the news of Ed's death from Jim Sullivan in Wellesley, he headed back home to Dover. Driving along country roads, he could not escape an awful irony. After years of strug-gle, Ed had finally been coming into his own and now he was dead.

Frank anguished over the memory of the amiable brother who had preceded him to Groton and Harvard, without the air of superiority common to some older brothers. More than anything else, they had been close friends. Now, everything—the reorganization of his business and his inheritance—had been nipped in the bud. The stocks from Pauline Bacon would now go to his daughters, but they had lost a father.

Then there was Smoki, the darling of the Boston social scene. More often than he liked, Frank had heard Ed's complaints that one cultural or civic crusade of hers or another, usually more than one at a time, got more of her attention than he did.

Yet Ed was also fond of posting newspaper clippings of his family on a bulletin board at his office. He proudly displayed pictures and stories of Smoki heading a charitable drive; Smoki in the Public Garden with Brooks and Hilary; Ed handsome in white tie and tails dancing with a radiantly gowned Smoki at Waltz Evening, a militantly exclusive Boston institution.

Then there was James Blaikie. Jim was claiming he had pumped considerable amounts of money into the company. If he was to be believed, he had put more dollars into the agency over the past two years than he had been getting out of it, by far.

It troubled Frank to think of him heading up the agency by default. Ed had once held out the possibility of a partnership for Blaikie, but no such relationship had ever materialized.

Apart from the Blaikie problem, Ed had been making strides in recent months and even weeks. His large, established clients were doing well by him. He'd had a very good shot at selling a pension plan of his own design to the Raytheon Company, which would give the high-tech giant more bang for its insurance buck. For Ed it could have meant huge commissions on a multi-million-dollar program.

With Ed gone, Frank considered it unlikely the Bacon agency could survive. Ed's charm and analytical expertise had kept the business, such as it had been, going.

These bitter thoughts seared Frank Bacon's mind, but one in particular threatened to blind him with rage. Ed's sudden death in his office reminded Frank of a rumor he had heard the previous year about the death of James Blaikie's mother. If it was true, the implications were sinister. They were so bizarre he almost did not want to consider them.

9:50 A.M.

On Commercial Wharf Lou Kane stood near the open rear doors of a mortuary van as attendants wheeled Bacon's covered body out of the building. They asked for help to get the stretcher into the vehicle and a patrolman begged off. He had a bad back to think of. Lou volunteered to take his place and lent a hand.

The doors slammed shut and he watched the van pull away. Lou Kane could not believe the scene. It seemed impossible that the congenial young man he had befriended at Harvard twenty-four years before had come to this early end.

After the van had disappeared on Atlantic Avenue, Lou saw James Blaikie step out of an office next to the Bacon agency. Kane assumed neighbors must be providing a haven for arriving Bacon staff. Carrying a paper coffee cup, Blaikie caught sight of Kane, looked surprised to see him, and nodded morosely. Lou returned the mute greeting with a cool stare.

He knew Blaikie very well from the McGovern campaign two years before. Kane, a former Marine commando who opposed U.S. involvement in Vietnam, had served as a finance cochairman of the Democrat's Massachusetts committee in 1972. As treasurer, Blaikie processed cash contributions and wrote checks for campaign operating expenses. Following McGovern's loss to Richard Nixon, Kane was shocked to learn bills had gone unpaid and the committee's account at a Boston bank was overdrawn by more than $17,000. When a furious Kane questioned him about the deficit, Blaikie's explanation was simply that funds had run out. Because of the cash involved, no complete audit of the Massachusetts operation was possible. Blaikie was never charged with irregularities.

Since Massachusetts had poured more than three million dollars into McGovern's campaign, more than any other state, the national finance chairman readily covered the overdraft.

Two years later on Commercial Wharf, Blaikie with his cup of coffee did not strike Kane as a mourner but as an observer of the terrible scene. He appeared exactly as he had when Lou confronted him with the financial mess of the McGovern campaign. Nonchalant.

Lou Kane felt strangely troubled as he crossed the lane toward his car at dockside.

Around ten o'clock another of the Bacon agency's three full-time staff members arrived at Commercial Wharf and found several police cruisers outside. Patricia Haskell, twenty-six, had been Ed's secretary for seven months. A pretty and perky blonde, she did not reach the front door of the agency, where a patrolman was standing guard. People from the adjacent firm intercepted her and gently explained what had happened. Appearing incredulous and shaken by the news, she did not resist their invitation to their office. There she tearfully collapsed in a chair.

Pat was joined by tall, slender James Richardson Adams III, a salesman for Bacon since the previous autumn. Rick, who had known the Bacons socially for several years, looked extremely upset as he expressed disbelief that someone the age of forty-four could die so unexpectedly. A decade Ed's junior, he nervously said he had just returned to Boston from a three-day trip to Philadelphia.

Gathering in the office with Pat and Rick, Jim Blaikie joined in their expressions of grief.

Learning that the Bacon agency would be sealed off by police order for the next twenty-four hours, they spoke vaguely of seeing one another the next day. No one observed aloud that the official closing of the office was not consistent with a case of death by natural causes.

In a later conversation with police that morning, Jim discussed the problem of Kayak tied up in the Bacon agency. Jim politely offered to take care of Kayak at home until Mrs. Bacon should decide what to do about the sled dog. The police appreciated his help.

11:30 A.M.

Helen Davlin, wife of the Bacon attorney, arrived at the family's townhouse wearing a courageous look and bearing an enormous smoked ham.

Since the Davlins were Jewish, the gift brought an inscrutable question from Smoki's seventy-six-year-old mother. "Is it kosher?"

Helen's rollicking laughter brought looks of puzzlement from the elderly lady and forebearance from Smoki.

Evidence of the variety and number of Ed and Smoki Bacon's social circle, sympathetic visitors began arriving by noon. A call from Smoki to one friend had gotten the grapevine humming to all.

Peter Fuller, racehorse breeder and son of a former Massachusetts governor, sent his chauffeur around with a stuffed turkey. The Irish owner of a Jewish-style delicatessen also helped overload the dining room table.

Ed's affiliations—among them the Harvard Club and *The* Country Club, the nation's first, in Brookline—helped account for many arrivals. So did Smoki's work with the Ward 5 Democratic Committee, the Boston Ballet Society, and the Institute of Contemporary Art. The first-floor rooms with their twelve-foot-high ceilings were filled with hushed exchanges of disbelief at the sudden death of Edwin Bacon.

Cafe and high society mingled amiably. Even in mourning, the Bacon house was living up to its reputation for an open-door policy toward every ethnic background, political persuasion, and religious belief that Boston had to offer. There were many.

Smoki reacted passively to the breathtaking show of goodwill around her. There was no recognition in her eyes when she faced longtime friends. She and they might have been in different dimensions.

Brooks and Hilary were looking slightly overwhelmed by sympathy. Every time Hilary got her tears under control, the condolences of yet another well-intending adult got them going again. Brooks did not have to cry, for her father was not dead.

Bacon attorney Zalman Davlin arrived, and Smoki confided to him that she was astonished and even a little embarrassed by the outpouring of kindness and moral support. "Smoki," Zal said in his reassuring manner, "you've done a lot for these people over the years. It's their way of showing how much they appreciate it. Plus, you know how terrible they feel. This is where we want to be, with you. Relax."

Fortified by Zal's sensibility, Smoki drifted further on automatic pilot through a combination Irish wake and Yankee memorial service, with benefit of kosher.

Looking no happier than he had appeared on Commercial Wharf hours before, Lou Kane was there with his attractive wife, Kathy, who had postponed her appointments at city hall. Her shock was as obvious as her husband's. Their friendship with the Bacons had been a close one, as the lives of the two families had been remarkably parallel. Ed and Lou had served in the Korean War. The couples had married within four months of each other. Kathy had given birth to the Kanes' first daughter shortly after Brooks was born to Smoki and Ed in 1958. The second Kane girl arrived six months before Hilary in 1960. Their marriages and their children had grown together.

Lou told friends of seeing Ed twice in the previous two weeks. He had never seemed more hopeful and confident about his business.

Frank had telephoned from Dover late in the morning and promised to come right into town to see her and the girls. Smoki had more mixed emotions than usual about her youthfully handsome brother-in-law. On one hand, his largesse toward Ed could not have been greater. On the other, his dismissive attitude toward her and her lifestyle troubled her. Today she needed his family loyalty and feared his disregard more than ever. The girls were simply eager to see their dashing Uncle Frank.

When Francis Lyman Bacon did arrive early in the afternoon, Smoki was more than anything else pained by his appearance. Frank, whose abrupt charm epitomized Scott Fitzgerald's definition of aristocracy, appeared carved in stone. His expression was not flickering on the verge of his next ironic remark as it usually was.

He and Smoki primly and briefly embraced in the foyer and she gratefully saw no glimmer of accusation in his eyes. She felt herself in the presence of his father, the ever-dignified Charles Edward Bacon.

"I'm so glad to see you, Frank," she murmured. "The girls . . . we needed to see you. Poor Ed . . ."

"Yeah," he said, nodding. "It should not have happened." His choice of words reflected his suspicions. *Should* was not a verb to be associated with an unexpected heart attack. Smoki did not pick up on it. She seemed at the snapping point.

He followed her through the parting crowd in the living room, where Brooks and Hilary spotted him. They made their way past guests to reach him and his arms went around their shoulders. Their hugs felt as comforting to him as he hoped his did to them.

"You two are doing all right, aren't you?" he said, smiling gamely down at them, and they nodded bravely. "It's not easy," he continued, "but we're all going to have to be strong about it, aren't we?"

Smoki was nodding in vague agreement from her private universe. She asked the girls if they would help Grandmother Ruth and Helen Davlin, and after they had disappeared in the direction of the dining room, she told Frank how she had found Ed.

The idea of his brother lying dead for untold hours on his office floor stirred a silent anger in Frank.

"Have you gotten any word from the medical examiner?" he asked.

"No, not yet," Smoki replied.

The lack of information deepened his foul mood. He had to find out how Ed had died, but he did not want to bring up the subject with Smoki in her precarious state.

Lou Kane suddenly appeared at Frank's side. "What an awful day this is," he said, gripping his friend's shoulder.

"Yes, it is, Lou."

When Smoki left them, Lou Kane said, "Frank, I don't like the confusion about Ed's death. The police have sealed off the office. Nobody there would tell me a thing about what they found inside."

"I'm with you, Lou," Frank said. "Obviously they're not convinced it was a natural death."

Lou Kane nodded with a look of concern. "Which means suicide or foul play are possibilities."

Attorney Zalman Davlin introduced himself as executor of Ed's estate and gave Frank his card. "You let me know if there is anything I can do," he said firmly, peering through his owlish glasses. "I'm taking this like it's family."

"I appreciate that, Zal."

"For openers, I think we should look in on Ed's office tomorrow and go over his papers," Zal said. "The twenty-four-hour quarantine will be up around nine o'clock."

Frank agreed and settled on an eleven o'clock meeting at the Bacon agency. Zal wished him well and said he was returning to his downtown office, where he could be reached that afternoon.

"Zal, can I talk to you outside a minute?" Frank asked.

"Sure," the attorney said.

In the warmth on the sidewalk of the narrow, lightly trafficked Fairfield Street, the two men walked north toward Marlborough Street and the Charles River, in the direction of Zal's car.

Frank came right to the point. "Zal, you never met me before in your life. I am going to make you think I am insane, but I have to tell you I am sure my brother did not die of natural causes. In fact, I believe he was murdered."

As anticipated, Davlin glanced at Frank as though he were mad indeed. "What on earth makes you think that?"

"I have my suspicions," Frank said.

"Do you mean you suspect a particular person?"

"Yes, I do. I just don't want to go off half-cocked. We don't even know the cause of death."

Zal Davlin nodded. "If there was foul play, you should be hearing something very soon. Let's stay in touch on this."

At home later in the afternoon Frank learned something that only raised his doubts. On the telephone with a Boston funeral home, he was making an appointment to meet there with Smoki the following morning and arrange Ed's burial. In the course of the conversation he was told that the body had not yet been transported from the Suffolk County mortuary. The medical examiner had decided to perform an autopsy.

In possession of the apparent suicide note found under Bacon's body, the chief state medical examiner for Suffolk County conducted the postmortem on Edwin Bacon at the Suffolk County morgue that afternoon. Dr. Michael A. Luongo detected purple blotches on the skin of the throat, upper chest, and abdomen. He concluded they were signs of burst capillaries caused by severe convulsions.

The medical examiner drew a blood sample and collected a portion of stomach contents for toxological analysis by the state police chemical laboratory.

Weighing the internal organs, Dr. Luongo found them nearly twice as heavy as normal, a condition attributed to congestion with bodily fluid.

In keeping with policy, he did not officially speculate in his notes how Edwin Bacon had died.

From his findings, an assistant typed up a death certificate that indicated that an autopsy had been performed. However, following standard procedures for cases of mysterious death, two sections of the certificate were left blank: "cause and manner" of death and "accident, suicide, or homicide." These sections would be filled in some days later after the laboratory report came in.

The preliminary death certificate was needed in order to release the body to the funeral home later in the day.

The autopsy was part of an official investigation into a possible death by suicide or homicide. However, the medical examiner's office did not convey any information about it to the Bacon family.

6:30 P.M.

Evening brought a new wave of friends and neighbors to the Bacon house, and yet another ring of the front doorbell did not surprise Smoki. But she was puzzled when she went into the vestibule and peered through the curtains of the front door. A man was standing outside, lined by the reflection of sunset on the brick houses across the street. He was wearing work clothes and Smoki realized it was Al Powers, a contractor from nearby Somerville.

She let him in and he seemed ill at ease standing in the foyer, glancing at the subdued gathering in the living room. Smoki had not expected him and showed it.

"What can I do for you, Al?" she asked distractedly.

"Why, I came for the appointment I made with Mr. Bacon," he said, frowning and checking his watch.

The connection between her husband and an earthly appointment startled Smoki. Then she remembered her conversation with Ed the previous day about arranging for the repair of rain damage upstairs.

"Oh," she said, flustered. "Then Ed got in touch with you."

"He did," Al said, looking mystified by her surprise.

"Al, I'm sorry," Smoki said. "I'm not myself. You see, Ed has passed away."

Her words sank in and his color rose. "I'm sorry, Mrs. Bacon. I didn't know."

Smoki said he need not apologize and explained Ed

had died alone at his office late the previous night or early that morning.

Shaking his head, Al said, "He sounded just fine when I talked to him last night."

"What time was that, Al?"

He thought a moment. "It must have been sometime between nine and ten."

Powers paid his respects and said he certainly did not want to bother her at a time like this.

"You've come all this way, Al," Smoki said. "You might as well have a look upstairs."

Powers dutifully trudged up the staircase.

Smoki broke away from guests when Powers came back down to the foyer looking indignant. Seeing him out, she suggested they talk at some later date about the project. On the doorstep he nodded over his shoulder and she caught a glimpse of a disapproving frown.

Try to be considerate, she bitterly mused while closing and locking the door, and yet one more person thinks what a cold-blooded bitch Smoki Bacon is. Her husband has just died, and she's worried about interior decorating. On the other hand, if I had turned him away, he might have resented the waste of his time coming here. Another no-win situation. *Smoki,* she lectured herself, *you are getting paranoid.*

Powers was now the last known person outside the family to have spoken with her husband, as late as ten o'clock the previous night, nine and a half hours before Smoki had got Frank Doherty to open Ed's office.

Smoki left her guests to the care of her mother and daughters and dragged herself upstairs. Bed was uninviting and although she was exhausted, she knew she would not sleep that night. Television carried reports of the day's Watergate proceedings. The House Judiciary Committee had passed the third and last article of impeachment against President Nixon by a vote of twenty-seven to ten. It accused Nixon of defying committee subpoenas. But the once-riveting political drama seemed to be taking place on another planet.

A neighbor had given her a sleeping pill, but she did not want to take one for the first time in her life.

The grotesque day contrasted in her memory with the glorious previous weekend on Cape Ann, northeast of Boston. Brooks had remained in the city where she was nursing her acting bug that summer as an usher at the Charles Playhouse. Smoki, Ed, and Hilary had stayed with friends at their spacious Victorian house in Beverly Farms, bastion of Cabots and Lodges.

Ed had driven up the coast of granite heights and sandy beaches to Manchester-by-the-Sea, where he and his family had summered. Smoki had a society page clipping somewhere of dark-eyed Master Edwin, eight, with his chipmunk grin, and three-year-old Master Francis, a towhead with a sunny smile. Wearing short pants, they were leaning against a pillar at the Charles Edward Bacon summer house. She would have to find it.

Ed, Smoki, and Hilary arrived back in Boston from Beverly Farms on Sunday night. Monday morning, Smoki awakened around six-thirty as usual. Ed was half asleep when she left for her Cambridge office.

She did not see him again for twenty-five hours, and when she did, it was too late to say the things that were now rapidly flooding her mind.

Chapter 4

July 31

The morning after the discovery of Edwin Bacon's body, Frank drove into Boston from Dover and picked up Smoki for their nine o'clock appointment at the Kenmore Square funeral home on the western edge of the Back Bay. In the gothic stillness of an office at J. S. Waterman & Sons, an assistant listened with professional deference to the brother-in-law and widow. However, he began fidgeting when Smoki informed him she wished to have Ed cremated in keeping with his wishes.

Staring into the middle distance, he said cremation would not be permissible. In cases of death that were not obviously natural or accidental the decedent's remains could not be destroyed. Exhumation at some later date might be necessary.

He did not say so, but for all he knew, a possible murder suspect was looking at him across his desk, asking that her husband, perhaps a victim of foul play, be rendered into ashes.

Smoki was unaware that an autopsy had been performed on her husband's body and did not pursue the subject.

Frank said nothing. He had not expected cremation and exhumation to be topics of the day.

Smoki decided the casket would be closed. She was to meet that afternoon with a priest from the Episcopal Church of the Advent on Beacon Hill and expected the funeral service would be held there two days later. Ed was to be buried in the Bacon family plot at Mount Auburn Cemetery in Cambridge.

She and Frank emerged from the funeral home into another day of Boston's annual heat wave. At the edge of bustling Kenmore Square, a Boston University student haunt and subway station for Fenway Park, he told Smoki he was going to meet later in the morning at Ed's office with attorney Zal Davlin.

"I need your help, Frank," she said with a ring of fear in her voice as they were walking to his car. "I don't know what to do about the agency, and I just do not trust Jim Blaikie." She looked up at Frank, who nodded with understanding. "You know Ed had been wanting to get rid of him."

"I know, Smoke," he said, calling her by his one-syllable version of her nickname. "Zal and I will do all we can to protect your interests." He looked less hopeful than he sounded.

As they drove east alongside the tree-lined mall of Commonwealth Avenue toward Fairfield Street, she was again reminded of Charles Edward Bacon. After meeting Ed on a Harvard–Dartmouth football weekend in 1956, she had come to know the Bacon patriarch as the quintessential American aristocrat, the type who met the social responsibility that went with his status. When America entered World War I, the man was in his forties but enlisted in the American Expeditionary Forces. And what did the publisher do on the troop transport heading for Europe but conduct French lessons for the young soldiers aboard ship with him. Following her marriage to Ed in 1957, Smoki had become even more impressed by the depth of Charles Bacon's humanity. His death a year later, six days before the birth of Brooks, had saddened her deeply.

At least he had lived to see two of the three grandchildren born by then to Frank and his wife.

Frank stopped the car in front of her house and continued looking straight ahead. "How are the kids holding up?" he asked gently.

"Not great," she said. "They're being brave, but

they're at such a vulnerable age. Teenagers and fathers, girls especially . . .'' Her voice cracked and, saying goodbye, she left the car.

Smoki climbed the front steps to the house. Inside the blessed coolness of the foyer she caught sight of her haggard features in a mirror and felt a jolt of panic. *Socialite* Smoki Bacon, she thought bitterly, had next to no cash. It would be two days before she got her next twice-monthly paycheck of $210 for her part-time job. She had no idea what major outstanding bills there were, for they were Ed's department. Days before his death Ed had made two overdue mortgage payments on the house, narrowly averting the latest threat of foreclosure. There would be tuition for her daughters coming up soon.

Insurance money would be coming, and Ed's trust from his late mother would revert to the girls. But how much time would all of that take?

James Blaikie picked up Patricia Haskell at her apartment in a South End rowhouse that morning and drove her to the Bacon agency. It was the first time he had done so even though she did not live that far off the route into town from Brookline. She assumed he was being considerate because of her distress the previous morning.

There were no police at the agency. Twenty-four hours had passed since the discovery of the body and they figured it must be all right to go inside. Jim had keys and led Pat into the agency.

Neither seemed happy to be back, and they had a subdued talk about what might have happened to Ed. A heart attack seemed most plausible, they agreed, but then why had police sealed off the agency for a day?

Rick Adams came along and the trio commiserated for several minutes. Pat, the youngest, appeared most upset of all.

Except for the surreal atmosphere of an office where her boss's body had been found, there was nothing out of the ordinary about the place.

Jim went to his middle office and Pat looked in on Ed's rear office, which seemed in usual good order. The desk and conference table were as neat as ever.

She automatically set about tidying up as she customarily did first thing in the morning. On his desk was the Playboy Club coffee mug from which he would endlessly drink coffee, letting it cool and then gulping it down. It was not boorishness, he'd once jovially explained, but a habit dating back to his Navy days. On a destroyer on the high seas, it was impossible to sip beverages politely with pinky extended.

However, the mug, two-thirds full, was not on the right hand side of the desk where she would ordinarily find it. Instead it was on the left rear corner. Ed, a right-hander, would have had to stretch awkwardly for it while seated at the desk. The contents looked scummy and wretched, exactly as she'd have expected of coffee, cream substitute, and sugar that had been sitting there for at least twenty-four hours.

Pat picked up the mug and found the rear door of Ed's office locked from the inside as usual. She slid back the bolt and opened the door. Across the utility room behind the agency and to her left was the restroom. There she emptied the unappetizing contents of the mug into the sink. In her nervous haste to rinse it out, the mug struck the sink and broke in two. She tossed the fragments into the trash bin, rinsed the sink, and shakily returned to the agency.

Her queasiness was made worse by a discovery in the reception room, her office, where Ed's body had been found. In a black ceramic ashtray on the low table in the bowfront was a crumpled man's handkerchief. She picked it up and gasped, for there were specks of blood on it. Poor Ed, she thought. With his smoker's cough he frequently hacked into his handkerchief, but the blood struck her as unusual. Yet she assumed the police had finished with the place and she dropped the sorry handkerchief in a wastebasket.

Finding the kind of paperwork Bacon usually left on her desk, insurance forms and documents at various stages of processing, Pat decided work was the best antidote to her anxiety, and she plunged into it. Bacon's brief notes attached to the papers (''Pat, please'' do this, take care of that) were eerie to behold. Everything was so normal she could not get over the feeling that Ed would lumber into the office with his usual pleasant greeting, and she would faint dead away.

Rick found a ring of keys in the middle drawer of Ed's desk, where he knew Ed had kept them. Included were keys to the bank of file cabinets against the back wall. However, the cabinets were unlocked. It was not unusual. Some of the drawers contained information and material needed at times by everyone at the agency. Glancing into each of the drawers, he saw Ed's checkbook and bank statements in one of them. He locked the cabinets by pressing in the cylindrical bolts near the top and hung onto the keys for Ed's brother and attorney.

Around eleven o'clock Frank Bacon and Zal Davlin arrived separately, looking no more cheerful than Ed's staff. Frank, who barely knew them from his visits to the agency, stoically accepted condolences. He explained that he and Davlin were there to gather Ed's personal papers and get started sorting out agency affairs. He assured them the company would continue to operate as long as he and Smoki had anything to say about it.

The brief conference broke up, and Frank and Zal proceeded through the agency to Ed's back office. Jim Blaikie busied himself at his desk in the middle office while Rick handed the attorney the keys he had retrieved from Ed's desk and offered to help locate things. Zal was especially eager to find Ed's personal insurance policies, particularly life coverage, as he wanted to begin the claims procedure.

While Zal and Rick were searching the filing cabinets, Frank found the life insurance policies in the bottom drawer on the right side of Ed's desk. In a blue plastic folder, each policy was contained in an individual clear plastic pocket. Frank consulted the folder as Zal stood nearby and read off life insurance policy numbers from a list Ed had provided a few weeks before his death. Altogether they were worth $250,000.

The first two policies Davlin asked for, each with a value of $100,000, were in the folder.

Then Davlin recited, "A Federal Kemper Life Assurance policy, number 613600, for $50,000."

Frank Bacon was casting a cold stare down at the folder. "The Kemper policy isn't here, Zal," he said, betraying no emotion.

James Blaikie came in from the adjacent office. Like Rick Adams, he expressed surprise at a missing policy. Ed was so fastidious about his papers. Jim optimistically urged Frank and the attorney not to worry. The policy was probably around somewhere in the office and would turn up.

The firm set of Frank's jaw and his distant gaze suggested a man keeping thoughts to himself.

Frank and Zal turned their attention toward agency books in Pat Haskell's office and with her help, they got an overview of the financial picture. It was not a pretty sight.

Gross revenues the previous year had been a pathetic $19,000 and change. Seven months into 1974, company income was running behind the previous year's total. There were several business checking accounts. One was in the name of Edwin C. Bacon and another was a Bacon–Blaikie joint account. Altogether the agency had barely enough cash flow to meet payroll and the office rent was several months in arrears.

Income from a major account in the next few months might just keep the agency afloat, but its chances of surviving the year were slim.

It was amazing to Frank that the company had not folded long ago.

Ed's chronic financial difficulties had been costly to his loyal kid brother over the previous decade. Frank invested $125,000 in a professional personnel service started up by Ed. The operation swiftly went belly-up. At the time of his death, Ed owed Frank about $50,000 for personal loans. Worse, Frank had backed a $14,000 bank loan for Ed the previous January to cover as much as possible in overdue bills, including tabs at the Harvard Club and The Country Club. Ed promised to repay the loan after his inheritance had cleared probate. It did in May, but Ed never got around to retiring the debt. Frank had always found it impossible to be stern with him.

Ed had formally assigned the company's assets to Frank as collateral for the personal loans, and as a result Frank was technically in charge of the agency. *In charge of a sinking ship,* he thought to himself.

Outside on Commercial Wharf, Zal told Frank he would begin making claims on all of Ed's life insurance policies that afternoon. He was not terribly concerned about the Kemper policy, for he had its identification number from Ed.

"Besides," he said, "the only people the policy can do any good are Smoki and the girls. Ed made that clear to me just last month as we were going over his estate. He emphasized that his wife and daughters were the designated beneficiaries of all his policies."

"I hear what you're saying, Zal," Frank said, softening his frown with a grin, "but you saw Ed's office. An admiral could run an inspection and Ed would get a promotion. My brother did not misplace things."

Zal nodded, kindly.

"There's more, Zal," Frank said, glowering. "Since we talked yesterday, I found out the medical examiner did an autopsy on Ed. I found that out from the *undertaker!* We've got police, medical examiners, DAs crawling all over this town, and I have to hear from an *undertaker* that my brother's death is under investigation."

The attorney's comforting smile dissolved. He left with a promise to call the medical examiner and find out what he could.

Following her return from the funeral home, Smoki was grateful for an early-afternoon visit from black community leader Marilyn Carrington. The first person Smoki had spoken with by telephone after awakening alone Monday morning, Marilyn had long been one of Smoki's closest friends.

At least as much as Watergate, the federal court-ordered desegregation of Boston schools was preoccupying Boston that summer. Smoki had proved a Back Bay socialite could gather friends to hear black leaders speak on the city's racial crisis as well as she could engineer a white tie soiree.

Charges from titular friends that she was merely engaging in radical chic fazed her no more than jibes about her social addiction.

Marilyn stayed for the visit of an Episcopal priest from the Church of the Advent. While the trio were thinking aloud about Ed's funeral service, James Blaikie arrived unexpectedly and solemnly offered Smoki his condolences.

In a modish suit that contrasted sharply with the sedate trappings of the room, Jim respectfully followed the discussion. Given Ed's love of classical music, Smoki suggested Bach and Brahms and asked if the Navy Hymn could also be performed by the organist. The priest nodded assuringly and made a note of it. For readings he suggested lines from the Book of Common Prayer and several from Psalms, including "God is our refuge and strength" and "The Lord shall preserve thee from all evil."

Jim had been minding Kayak and to Smoki's relief he offered to continue caring for the malamute until after the funeral. But as he was leaving, he also had unwelcome news. He asked if she knew Ed had recently ordered another sled dog, which was about to be transported to Boston from Colorado.

"No, Jim," she said evenly, dreading an addition to Kayak and the dogs already in a New Hampshire kennel. "Is there any way you can stop the shipment?"

With a hint of his confident grin, he assured her he would call off the dog. Sadness returned to his face as he said goodbye.

Neither Smoki nor anyone in the family was aware police had found Kayak leashed to Ed's desk. Had she known, she would have thought it strange, for the dog had the run of the offices while Ed was there alone. Ed only tied him up to keep him from affectionately pawing others.

Drifting deeper back into the fog that had enveloped her most of the past thirty hours, Smoki rejoined the discussion of her husband's funeral.

But James Blaikie, the person in charge of the agency, slipped in and out of her thoughts. She did not know what to make of him. She had not seen much of him while Ed was alive and hardly knew him or his attractive wife. He and Kathy had gone with Smoki and Ed to a gala campaign appearance of George McGovern and actress Shirley MacLaine at a private estate on the North Shore in 1972. Kathy had been reticent, Jim the effervescent political operative, basking in the glory of his candidate. Other than that, she knew of him only as a person Ed had brought into his company and had lately been intent on removing.

Zalman Davlin telephoned the Suffolk County medical examiner's office that afternoon as he had promised Frank Bacon he would. In his twenty-second-floor law office with a view of Boston Harbor, the attorney asked an aide for a status report on the inquiry into Ed's death. Moments later he heard what Frank had learned from the funeral home—the medical examiner had performed an autopsy on Edwin Bacon the previous day. No conclusion on the cause and manner of death had been reached, Davlin was told, and the aide said nothing of an apparent suicide note.

"As soon as we have the state police lab report on the autopsy specimens, we'll let you know," the aide said and added it could be days or weeks in coming.

Zal Davlin was perplexed as he depressed the cradle button on the telephone. Lab tests meant a chemical substance was suspected as the cause of death.

He immediately called Frank Bacon, who was also concerned by the news.

"So it could be suicide," Frank thought aloud, "or murder."

"It looks that way," Zal responded.

"Well, I know my brother didn't kill himself, Zal. He had too much going for him, despite the business problems."

With an agreement they would have to wait for the lab reports, they rang off and Frank Bacon had the sensation of falling into the deep end of the pool. And, for all his athleticism, he had never taken to swimming.

The story of Alma Blaikie again came to mind. A friend and former McGovern campaign aide had called the previous summer to tell him that Jim's mother had died of a gunshot wound. Word had it her death had been ruled a suicide and Jim, her only child, inherited the family house. When Frank asked Ed about Mrs. Blaikie, his brother replied he understood she had died of a heart attack. Frank responded that was not what he had heard but Ed did not pursue the matter. His lack of curiosity suggested to Frank that he already knew and discounted the rumor. Not someone to traffic in unsubstantiated stories, Frank said nothing more on the subject.

The matter had not occurred to him again until the previous morning when Jim Sullivan had broken the news of Ed's death.

But the idea of someone murdering a parent, or anyone else, for financial gain was too weird for Frank to entertain. Those things happened in books or movies. Furthermore, he could not imagine what motive James Blaikie would have had for killing Ed Bacon.

If Ed had been murdered.

As Zal said, they would just have to wait for an official answer on that one.

Chapter 5

Thursday, August 1

The *Boston Globe* and the *Boston Herald* carried lengthy but innocuous obituaries on Edwin Conant Bacon. About his death they noted simply that he had died the previous Monday. If anyone in the press corps was aware of official questions in the case, no one had approached his family on the subject.

In the accompanying photo, Ed's chin was lifted above a white tie and winged collar. The slash of a smile suggested he might be looking down his narrow nose at a clumsy waiter. But, anyone familiar with Bacon knew he was more likely enduring his formal attire. Close friends knew he dressed to the nines at his wife's insistence, and reluctantly at that.

The papers reported his Groton and Harvard education and Korean War service as a lieutenant in the U.S. Navy from 1951 to 1953. Noted also was his stint teaching mathematics at the exclusive Middlesex School in Concord after the Korean War.

Newspaper readers that morning also saw that after teaching, Bacon went on to be a textbook salesman for Prentice-Hall publishers from 1954 to 1956.

Missing from the obituaries, though, was the family misfortune that had led to the hapless career move.

Ed's grandfather George Andrew Bacon and the head of the small John Allyn publishing company in Boston had formed Allyn & Bacon textbook publishers in 1888. A classical scholar and former educator, George

Bacon had a revolutionary publishing idea. Departing from the practice of producing elementary and secondary school textbooks written by college professors, he made authors of respected teachers. Typical of his innovative publications was a Latin textbook by the vaunted David Y. Comstock of the Phillips Academy in Andover. In Comstock's *First Latin Book* and a host of other Allyn & Bacon texts, public school youngsters across the country suddenly had access to the courses taught by prestigious boarding-school instructors.

The concept was an enormous success and the founder's son took it a giant step forward. Charles Edward Bacon added branch offices in New York, Atlanta, Dallas, and San Francisco to the Boston headquarters and Chicago office created by his father. He brought new authors to the Allyn & Bacon stable and the house became one of the country's leading publishers of primary and secondary school textbooks.

In the 1940s, Charles was grooming his sons Ed and Frank as the next Bacons to enter the firm. With the postwar baby boom swelling classrooms across the land, Allyn & Bacon was on the verge of realizing the most ambitious aspirations of its founder. In the fall of 1949, Ed was a junior at Harvard and Frank was in the fourth form, or sophomore high school year, at Groton. Approaching his seventy-sixth birthday, their father expected that within two years Ed would begin leading the company in its second half-century.

But calamity struck, shattering family dreams.

Charles Bacon's ailing brother and only partner was struck down by a hit-and-run driver in Wellesley. Following his death, his family exercised its option to take its half of Allyn & Bacon assets in cash. Charles Bacon anticipated no problem raising the share, more than a million dollars, at the First National Bank of Boston. But despite the impressive performance and excellent credit rating of Allyn & Bacon, the bank turned down his loan request. Unable to borrow the amount elsewhere, Charles Bacon was forced to sell the company to Prentice-Hall for considerably less than its value in 1950.

The event was both a psychological and a financial blow to Charles Bacon. Although his advanced age might have played a role in the bank's decision, he was left feeling betrayed. Made a titular chairman of the board, he did not realize the wealth that might otherwise have been his. Moreover, the Bacon publishing tradition ended, along with Edwin Bacon's hopes of continuing it.

As a result, when he went to work for Prentice-Hall in 1954, his job was not the entry-level sales position of a future publisher. It was a dead-end slot in his view and he left it two years later.

In 1956, twenty-seven-year-old Ed Bacon was adrift when he met Smokey. At the time Ed was involved in an unspectacular construction venture in New Hampshire. By early 1957 he and Smokey seemed altarbound and he took a management trainee job with the Ford Motor Company in Natick, Massachusetts. The couple was married in May, but not before his fiancee had modified the spelling of her nickname. She refused to be called by her natal first name, Adelaide, and calculated that *Smoki* was less undignified in connection with the Bacon surname. To some, it sounded even more theatrical.

The Ford job seemed to them the start of something big, as Ed was involved with an eagerly awaited new car model. Unfortunately, the Edsel, with its elliptical grill, inspired more gynecologist jokes than sales, and by 1958 Ed found himself selling insurance for a small agency.

His father died that year and Brooks was born.

Hilary came in 1960 and a year later Ed was starting up the Bacon Insurance Agency.

But for an untimely death a quarter-century before, he might instead have been the latest head of the family publishing dynasty.

August 2

National television viewers of the venerated July
Fourth concerts of the Boston Pops Orchestra and
Wagnerian fireworks have seen what little there is to
see of the Charles River Esplanade on Independence
Day. When it is not carpeted by a quarter-million
celebrants, it is a broad two-mile crescent of groves
and lagoons curving northeast from the Back Bay to
Beacon Hill, the city's most legendary neighborhoods.

At the western foot of Beacon Hill the Gothic tower
of the Church of the Advent rises from narrowly dignified Brimmer Street, as it has since 1883. Among its
notable parishioners at the turn of the century was Is-
abella Stewart Gardner, wife of pedigreed Bostonian
John Lowell Gardner. "Mrs. Jack," a New York merchant's daughter, had a fondness for beer, a pet lion
named Rex, and risque stories. For her excesses, it is
said she atoned at Lent by scrubbing the church steps
and sending black-bordered invitations to Holy Com-
munion.

The lady who bequeathed her Fenway villa as a museum also gave the church its Sturgis high altar. Less
flamboyant High Episcopalians worshiped before it
over the decades. Among them were the Back Bay Bacons. There Charles Bacon and Pauline Conant were
married upon his return from World War I. In 1954,
they attended Frank's wedding and three years later,
Ed and Smoki exchanged vows there.

In a letter to a friend, Pauline Bacon described
Smoki as "a charming girl, tall, willowy and blonde."

A memorable glitch occurred in the ceremony.
When the priest invited any naysayer in the throng to
oppose the union, a loud and resounding *bang* issued
from the back of the church. Ed and Smoki exchanged
nervous glances. She feared a shot had been fired by
a former female friend of his who had vaguely promised retribution for his exit from her life.

The couple was relieved at the reception in the Bacon house on Commonwealth Avenue when they

learned a folding chair had collapsed under someone in the choir loft. Judging by the volume of the crash, Ed figured it must have been a baritone.

Virtually everyone who attended Ed's funeral Mass had been at the Church of the Advent seventeen years earlier for his wedding. Smoki's mother was there as the only surviving family member of her generation. With Brooks and Hilary, the three children of their Uncle Frank and Dexter represented the new family generation.

Among all those familiar faces, as unalterably solemn as they had once been charmed there, Smoki experienced a hideously twisted *dèjà vu*. To be there without her daughters' hands to squeeze at her either side would have been unbearable.

As she had requested, the recessional was the Navy Hymn, and as the pallbearers guided the casket out of the church, Smoki wished she had not requested it. The bittersweet chords of the organ nearly pried loose her grip on her emotions.

From Beacon Hill the funeral procession motored west alongside the Esplanade on the southern, Boston bank of the Charles River. On the Cambridge side, the dome of the Massachusetts Institute of Technology glided by and soon was followed by the ivied walls and spired belfries of Harvard University.

Inside the stone and wrought-iron gateway of Mount Auburn Cemetery, the cortege followed meandering lanes across green and rolling terrain. Among the names on elaborate monuments heavy with moss and vines were those of Henry Wadsworth Longfellow, Oliver Wendell Holmes, Henry Cabot Lodge. Also buried there were mental health pioneer Dorothea Lynde Dix; Julia Ward Howe, suffragette and creator of "The Battle Hymn of the Republic"; and poet Amy Lowell.

In a wooded hollow, the mourners gathered about Bacon's casket, poised above an open grave near the granite headstones of his father and grandfather. His mother had been buried in the Conant family plot.

As the priest spoke Smoki felt the trembling of her

daughters' hands and her disbelief ebbed with his every word.

Standing beside his wife and their three children, Frank struggled inwardly to confine his thoughts to Eddie, who from their earliest years together had always had the time and a smile for his kid brother. But his gaze fell on James Blaikie, curiously there without his wife, and Frank did not buy the look of dejection on his fleshy face.

As the casket lowered, Frank promised his brother he was not going to forget.

Among the cheerless guests at the Bacon house that afternoon was Zal Davlin, who took Frank aside and quietly reported that the medical examiner's office still had not called about the cause of Ed's death.

"Christ, Zal," Frank said under his breath. "It's been four days. This thing is getting away from us, and if you ask me, we're being stonewalled. What do you think about getting a private detective?"

"That might not be a bad idea," the attorney replied. "I'll look into it."

"Good," Frank said, hoping his bitterness looked merely like sorrow to nearby mourners.

Chapter 6

Among the private thoughts behind James Blaikie's public face was a gnawing concern about mounting financial woes. He was on a tightrope walk without a net.

Money from the transaction on his heavily financed sailboat had helped pay overdue bills and tide him over. But that had been five months ago, and keeping up the boat loan, on top of other expenses, was not getting easier. If he stopped making the $200 monthly payments, the jig would be up. The credit company would soon come looking for their boat and eventually the doctor who thought he owned the thirty-foot sloop would come looking for Jim.

Blaikie's monthly expenses for the house, the cars, and other heavily financed acquisitions amounted to more than a thousand dollars, and then there were living expenses. He was getting zero income from the Bacon agency.

What he had going for him was that undeniable look of solid success—a beautiful wife from the Orient, a big house in Brookline, and position with a Yankee firm. Among those impressed by him was twenty-seven-year-old David DeWilde, Jim's friend for nearly a decade. Their wives had gone to college together with Blaikie.

While Jim was giving every appearance of making it big in politics and business in the early 1970s, David was parlaying his love of foreign cars into a thriving auto repair shop on the west side of Boston. David was known to lend money to people he liked and trusted.

James Blaikie thought David just might make him a short-term loan of a few thousand dollars. Surely he would understand Jim was temporarily strapped for cash in the wake of Ed's death. Once the dust had settled at the insurance agency, he would pay it back.

Jim thought he would try for a $5,000 loan from DeWilde, and he got it.

The weekend after the funeral, Smoki drove up to Wolfboro, New Hampshire, with Brooks and Hilary for a stay with the Francis Bacons. On Saturday evening, Frank suggested he and Smoki take a walk, and they left his wife with the five younger Bacons in the large Victorian house.

Strolling along the wooded shore of Lake Winnipesaukee, they agreed the serenity and dry air were welcome relief from the oppressive heat in congested Boston a hundred miles to the south. The subdued voices in the house faded behind them and distant motorboats purred in the dusk.

Frank spoke gently. "With everything you've had on your mind, Smoke, I haven't wanted to talk about Ed's death, but I think we have to."

"What's there to say, Frank? It happened. It's awful. It's not going to get better." Her every word sounded like an effort.

"I know," he said, "but there are still things up in the air."

She shot him a nervous glance.

"You know," he continued, "the funeral director was referring to an autopsy when we talked to him the other day."

She looked up as though recalling. "I assumed it was something of the sort, but I was too numb to ask him to be more specific. I thought it must be routine."

"No, it wasn't," he said carefully. "This is all going to come up, and I want you to be prepared for it.

An autopsy means the medical examiner suspects the death might not have been of natural causes.''

Her gaze narrowed. ''What are you *saying,* Frank? It must have been natural causes. How else could Ed have died?''

''It may very well be he died of a heart attack, but we have to be prepared for some other finding.''

''What, Frank? Suicide? Homicide? *Nobody* would kill Ed, you know that. Why *would* anyone? He was a pussycat. And as for suicide, that's impossible, too.''

''I agree he couldn't have taken his own life,'' Frank said. ''As for murder, remember Ed was trying to break away from Jim Blaikie.''

''Oh, Frank, I don't know. I don't think Jim Blaikie has whatever nerve it takes to do something like that. And why would he? You've seen what wretched shape the agency is in.''

''We just don't know, Smoki, and I think it would be a good idea to hire a private detective to find out what he can.''

She shook her head as though clearing it. ''Do you really think it's necessary?''

''I do, and Zal agrees, if we want him to go ahead and line someone up.''

''Frank, if you think and Zal thinks so, go ahead, but I can't imagine—''

''Take it easy, Smoki. I know this is rough on you, on all of us, but we've got to keep our heads together, for the sake of the kids and ourselves.''

The following week the Bacon agency continued to drift. Rick Adams, Pat Haskell, and Jim Blaikie appeared to be doing their level best to keep it off the rocks. There were sizable commissions due later in the summer and fall. In touch with Adams, Frank tried to keep morale up in the only way he could, by assuring them he and Smoki would keep the operation going as long as it was viable.

Jim returned Kayak to the Bacon house, where the dog continually searched for Ed.

Zal Davlin queried a number of private investigators and by Friday, August 9, had decided to recommend one to Frank. With much of the world that morning, the attorney watched live television coverage of a beleaguered Richard Nixon resigning from office under threat of impeachment.

That afternoon, ten days after Ed's death, Davlin telephoned the medical examiner's office again and finally got some information. To his relief, a clerk said that Ed Bacon had died of a heart attack after all.

Frank was both surprised and dubious. He agreed with Davlin that they should hold off on the private investigator but said he wanted to see the definitive death certificate. Zal expected it within a week.

Smoki Bacon's worst fears were put to rest. She was grateful that her family would not be further traumatized by the knowledge Ed had taken his life or had been murdered.

Brooks, with two and a half years on her sister, continued ushering at the Charles Playhouse in Boston's theater district. She had come to face the reality of her father's death.

At Wolfboro with the Francis Bacons for the summer, Hilary was a month away from her fourteenth birthday but secretly nowhere near believing he was dead.

The closed casket that Smoki had hoped would spare her daughters additional trauma had only convinced Hilary that their father was alive. Kayak was a comforting reminder of him, their sledding together, but also a constant challenge. It was all the girl could do to keep the powerful dog from her cousins' cats, and more than once Kayak had nearly got the better of her and one of the felines. Frank was arranging to sell the rest of Ed's dog team and he increasingly considered Kayak saleable if Smoki did not want the furry dynamo back in Boston. She did not.

A week after hearing Ed had died a natural death, Smoki was working at her drawing board in the graphics department of Bolt Beranek and Newman in Cambridge when she got another call from Zal Davlin. Perhaps, she thought, there is some progress at last on Ed's life insurance.

"Smoki," Zal said, "I'm afraid I've got bad news."

With imminent foreclosure on the house flashing in her mind, she paused before inviting word of yet another disaster. "What is it, Zal?"

"It seems the medical examiner's office gave me incorrect information last week," he said bitterly. "I just heard from them again, and I wanted you to hear it from me right away. The medical examiner has just received the results of lab tests and they indicate suicide. Smoki, they also found an apparent suicide note under Ed's body the morning you found him."

She listened carefully, but through the ringing in her ears she could barely comprehend Zal's words. The earlier benign report of a heart attack evaporated like a drowning sailor's pipe dream of land ahead.

Zal was saying something about a state police laboratory report and cyanide. She heard him say the note simply read, "I can't stand it anymore."

Then she was struck in rapid succession by two awful realizations. She would have to reopen her daughters' wounds and she must share responsibility for her husband's suicide.

The following day, August 16, Medical Examiner Michael A. Luongo looked over the state police laboratory report on specimens taken from Bacon's body. Chemists reported finding a cyanide concentration of 1.3 milligrams per 100 cubic centimeters of blood.

That meant an amount of the poison weighing little more than two ordinary aspirins, had dissolved in Bacon's bloodstream. It was enough to kill an adult male within one to ten agonizing minutes.

The report also said a substance "calculated as sodium cyanide" was found in Bacon's stomach contents. He had apparently swallowed more cyanide than was necessary to cause death.

Like any salt, sodium cyanide crystals dissolve unnoticeably in water. Its almond scent is neither obnoxious nor, in a sweet beverage such as coffee with sugar, readily detectable.

Ingested, however, the cyanide solution acts rapidly and lethally. Cyanide ions react instantly with stomach acid and the product is the volatile and deadly gas, hydrogen cyanide. That was what Nazis had diabolically released into "showers" filled with unsuspecting Jews.

The hydrogen cyanide painfully erodes and inflames the sensitive linings of the throat and lungs and, in cases of ingestion, the stomach. The gas is assimilated into the bloodstream where it prevents red cells from releasing oxygen. As a result the respiratory system shuts down, and the victim asphyxiates. No amount of deep breathing helps in the least and, according to rare survivors, the victim has a feeling of impending doom.

In fatal cases the oxygen-starved heart responds as though a coronary thrombosis is occurring and the victim experiences severe chest pains.

Internal organs fill with fluids, a feature that accounted for the excessive weight of Bacon's lungs and kidneys, as Dr. Luongo had noted in the autopsy. As the nervous system is deprived of oxygen, the victim becomes light-headed and dizzy, experiencing head pains and blurred vision. Convulsions follow, so severe that they damage the small blood vessels in the skin, as Dr. Luongo had also observed in his examination of Bacon's corpse. The victim then goes into a coma and dies.

Dr. Luongo had at his disposal his autopsy findings, the laboratory chemical analysis and the putative suicide note, "I CAN'T STAND IT ANYMORE." He also had a police report indicating no evidence of foul play at the Bacon agency.

Without suggesting a possible time of death, the medical examiner concluded in his report that

Bacon had died of sodium cyanide poisoning "on or about July 29, 1974," referring to the night or early morning hours before Smoki found her husband's body. Dr. Luongo formally ruled the death a suicide.

Chapter 7

Frank Bacon was furious when he received news of the medical examiner's ruling from Zal Davlin.

"Dammit, Zal," he said on the phone in Wolfboro. "They keep us in the dark for more than two weeks and then spring a ruling on us without a word of input from the family. From *anyone.*"

"Sadly, Frank, that is what has happened."

"Zal, no reflection on you. You've been doing everything you could to get to the bottom of this. The authorities won't talk to you one week. The next week they give you wrong information and a week later they hand over an official ruling—signed, sealed, and delivered."

Following a silence, Zal suggested that they go ahead with the private investigator. Frank agreed and asked him to hire one.

Hanging up, Frank smoldered at the spectacle of a law enforcement establishment that seemed bent on one objective—going through the motions and closing the case.

Lou Kane was also bitterly incredulous when Frank telephoned him.

"Lou, I've got to tell you I think James Blaikie poisoned Ed."

"You know, Frank, that doesn't surprise me."

"The only remaining question in my mind is *why?* It couldn't have been simply because Ed was getting rid of him. Blaikie had to know that as Ed's de facto successor at the agency, I'd be at least as tough on him. You know, a life insurance policy of Ed's is missing, but Zal says Smoki and the girls are the beneficiaries.''

''You're on the right track,'' Lou said. ''If Jim killed Ed, I'll wager the reason was profit. We just don't know what money was involved.''

Frank felt his molten rage of recent weeks cooling into resolve. ''I hate like hell to ask you this, Lou. I am not in the habit of asking favors. But we're getting nowhere on this thing. I've asked Zal to get a private eye, but do you think you or Kathy could also get the police to look into this again?''

''Frank, I couldn't agree more,'' Kane said firmly. ''You and Smoki haven't gotten the answers you deserve. We'll see what can be done about getting some.''

''I appreciate that,'' Frank said.

Despite the distress of the Bacons and their friends, city and county authorities had been under no legal obligation to call an inquest into Bacon's death. A little-known footnote to U.S. forensic history loomed large in the case of Edwin Conant Bacon, as it has in deaths around the country. In 1877, Massachusetts became the first state to abolish the age-old coroner system, inherited from England, and replace it with a medical examiner system.

The reason seemed enlightened at the time. Coroners were not physicians but political appointees without medical training, glorified constables in the view of the Massachusetts Medical Society. They had the power to authorize autopsies by doctors, coordinate medical and police investigations, and call for inquests.

As forensic historian Luke G. Tedeschi, MD writes, the Massachusetts legislature thought it all a boondoggle. Too many paid coroners were asking for too many costly inquests. Indeed, while London and New York each had four coroners, Chicago two and San Francisco one, Boston had forty-three at the time.

By substituting a few physicians for many coroners,

frugal Massachusetts did indeed reduce the number of inquests into mysterious deaths. The decision whether or not to call an inquest was shared by the medical examiner and the district attorney in a given county. Neither was obligated to do so. Many jurisdictions across the country adopted the Massachusetts model. Some, such as Allegheny County, Pennsylvania, did not. They recognized that without a single authority responsible for inquests, cases can fall through the cracks.

Journalists have long been aware of the consequences. More than one reporter investigating a mysterious death has been referred by a medical examiner to the district attorney, who promptly refers the reporter back to the medical examiner.

Such problems usually occur in economically depressed precincts. However, the Bacons of the Back Bay, who literally had friends in city hall, suddenly found themselves lost in the same bureaucratic thicket.

Contacting a major Boston area security company, Zal Davlin spoke by telephone with private investigator Thomas Cunningham, a retired Boston police sergeant detective. Cunningham listened to the account of a body found with an apparent suicide note and the autopsy finding of death by cyanide poisoning. He heard nothing out of line with the medical examiner's ruling of suicide.

However, Cunningham said he would go back over police reports and talk to the investigating officers on the case.

Davlin also telephoned news of the suicide ruling to the Bacon agency and it was received with expressions of shock by the staff. Patricia Haskell and Rick Adams could not believe it, but Jim Blaikie sadly recalled that Ed had been showing increasing signs of depression in recent months. Pat and Rick did not share Jim's perception.

Pat recalled aloud the seemingly innocent coffee mug with its scummy contents that she had found on Ed's desk the morning after the discovery of his body.

Had the foul-looking substance in the coffee been cyanide? Then there was the blood on the handkerchief in the reception room, she remembered. Had Ed coughed it up in the terrible throes of death by poisoning? She blanched at the recollection and wished she had not thrown the items away. The others reassured her that if they had been important, the police would have taken them as evidence the previous day.

As unconvinced as Frank by the official story, Smoki nevertheless accepted the suicide ruling. She resigned herself to the reality that she must not have known Ed at all, for he had never betrayed a glimmer of evidence that he could kill himself. Or had she missed the signs? From her volunteer work in suicide prevention she knew that people who failed at suicide were often those who were actually crying out for help, while those who gave no warning succeeded in destroying themselves. Still, Ed was too much the hedonist to inflict pain on himself, and, yet any explanation other than suicide was incredible to her or, rather, unthinkable.

In the living room at home her daughters received the new version of their father's death like shipwrecked survivors hit by another towering wave. Smoki was deeply concerned about Brooks and Hilary as they dissolved in her arms.

She struggled for the best consoling words she could find. "Whatever led your father to this, we may never completely know," she managed. "But you must not and should not feel any shame. Daddy loved you and you must not feel any guilt."

The smaller daughter was eventually able to get out a question. "Didn't he leave a note for me?" Hilary asked hopefully.

"No, darling," Smoki reported. "Now, we must all be prepared for the things people will say about such a death. Don't be surprised if you hear of people blaming me."

Brooks summoned the sophistication of her sixteen and a half years and consolingly said, "But Mommy, people always talk about you anyway."

They shared a tearful laugh at that.

Indeed, a barrage of rumors quickly began to get back to Smoki through scandalized friends. Gossip had Ed committing suicide because she was having an affair with Jim Blaikie. In another version, the two presumed adulterers had conspired to murder the cuckold. Yet another variation had Jim and *Ed* romantically linked. Ed's death by suicide or murder, depending on the source, had been the solution to their star-crossed homosexual love.

At the limestone Boston Police Headquarters in the Back Bay, a few blocks and as many worlds away from the fashionable shops of Newbury Street, private investigator Thomas Cunningham paid a visit to the homicide unit on the second floor. Nothing appeared to have changed, including the banks of cigar and cigarette smoke.

In shirtsleeves with a loosened tie, Sergeant Detective John W. Maillet looked up from his desk and his long face creased in a partial grin for his former colleague. "Tom, what brings you back," he said without the inflection of a question. "We don't have any royalty to protect around here."

Maillet was referring to Cunningham's primary work at the time, running security for visiting foreign dignitaries. Among them were two sons of Jordan's King Hussein at a private school in western Massachusetts.

"I'm here about a Boston Brahmin, John, as good as royalty," Cunningham said with a poker smile as he settled his tall frame into a chair beside Maillet's desk. "In this case, he happens to be dead. Gentleman from the Back Bay, name of Edwin Bacon. It hasn't come up here, has it?"

Maillet, approaching his quarter-century mark with the department, stroked his angular jaw. "No, it hasn't, Tom. Should it?"

"That's what I'm trying to find out," Cunningham said. "It looked like a suicide at the beginning."

"And?"

"The family doesn't buy it."

"Do they ever?" Maillet said, leaning back in his chair. "What about the ME?"

"Suicide. The family says he just inherited a lot of money. Very social. Would you believe his wife goes by the name of Smoki?"

"Smoki Bacon," Maillet said, consulting the ceiling. "I've run across that name in the papers. You mean it's for real?"

"Apparently," Cunningham said with a grin. "Bacon's brother is rich as a Kennedy. Everybody in the family went to Harvard but the Irish maids, and they went to Vassar."

"Jeez, Tom, Harvard doesn't teach you to kill *yourself.* How'd it happen?"

"Cyanide. In his office on Commercial Wharf. The responding patrolmen say the body was on the floor up against the front door. The only other door, in back, was locked from the inside. The ME found a note under the body."

He handed a photocopy to Maillet, who read it aloud: " 'I can't stand it anymore.' Man of few words." He handed it back to Cunningham. "Who do they suspect?"

"A quote—*business associate*—of Bacon's." Cunningham returned the note to his folder and stood up. "John, if anything comes this way on the case, will you let me know?"

"*Shoo-uh,*" Maillet replied in his native Bostonese.

As Cunningham departed, Sergeant Detective Maillet wondered what it would be like to go private and work bankers' hours. *Nah,* he thought, looking over his desk piled high with papers. *And give up all this?*

On an evening at Wolfboro that weekend, Smoki and Frank drifted away from their families and launched into a heated discussion along the lakefront.

"I can't understand how you could have kept so much information from me," she said angrily.

Frank's jutting jaw was a sure sign his patience was wearing thin. "Smoke, there was *no* information until the medical examiner made his ruling the other day.

That was the problem. Zal could get nothing out of them. What I did not bring up to you were rumors, speculations that Ed might have committed suicide. They were just that. When there's an autopsy, *obviously* the authorities are considering suicide. Or, what I think they should have been pursuing, the possibility of murder.''

The word shocked her into a calm. ''What are you saying, Frank? Ed was murdered?''

''I said I think murder is a consideration.''

''But Frank, who on earth would murder Ed? My god, that's worse to imagine than suicide. Someone hated Ed enough, or had something to gain by killing him? That's impossible. I know you suspect Blaikie, but I don't think he has the guts to do it. If *guts* is the right word.''

Frank adopted a soothing tone. ''Smoki, if you want to hear what I think, you are going to have to get control of yourself.''

She nodded vaguely.

''All right,'' he said. ''Do you know about the death of Jim's mother last summer?''

Smoki thought a moment. ''Only that she died, which I heard from Ed.''

''And how she died?''

''Just old age, natural causes, as I recall. Why?''

Frank spoke of the rumor that Blaikie's mother had supposedly shot herself to death.

''Oh my god, Frank. Suicide? And you're thinking—''

''I'm thinking the police should be checking how Mrs. Blaikie died and investigating Jim in connection with Ed's death. Zal Davlin agrees. I've asked Lou to speak with Kathy about asking the police commissioner to look into it.''

''And why wasn't I told?''

''I wanted to know how Ed died,'' Frank said patiently. ''This all came to a head Friday, with the medical examiner's ruling. Remember, a week ago we were told Ed died of a heart attack. If that finding had held up, we wouldn't be having this conversation.''

"Frank, I hear what you're saying, but this is something that happens in the movies, not to *us.*"

He nodded. "That's why I've been moving cautiously. But the cyanide means I've at least been half right all along."

"Meaning?"

"Ed did not die of natural causes."

The following week, Frank decided to do whatever he himself could to move the case along. Since Ed had died of cyanide poisoning, Frank asked himself, was there cyanide at the office? He also wondered why this perfectly logical question had not occurred to some law-enforcement official.

Frank asked Rick Adams to conduct a thorough search of the Bacon agency. On Wednesday, August 21, he and Patricia Haskell worked their way back from the reception room and turned their attention to Ed's office. Rick opened the bottom drawer of a file cabinet to the right of Ed's desk and was amazed to find a container he was certain had not been there the day after the discovery of Ed's body.

"Pat, look at *this,*" he said excitedly over his shoulder.

Startled, she walked up to Ed's desk, where Rick was placing a metal container the size and shape of a one-pound coffee can. According to the label, it contained potassium cyanide.

Jim Blaikie joined them. "Oh, that must be the stuff Ed bought to use as rat poison," he said.

Rick exchanged nervous glances with Pat. "That's funny," he said, "it wasn't here three weeks ago."

In the ensuing silence, Patricia Haskell felt horror turn into fear. She hurried back to her desk, found Zal Davlin's number, and quickly dialed it.

Concerned the magically appearing can of cyanide might just as magically disappear, Zal asked Rick Adams to bring it to his office at once. The attorney immediately telephoned Frank Bacon, who suggested it be kept there under lock and key. Zal agreed and said he would inform private detective Cunningham of the discovery.

At home in Dover, Frank returned the receiver to its cradle.

At last there was something tangible to deal with. There had been no cyanide in that cabinet and now there was. The murderer had planted evidence for the convenience of anyone looking for it. A man dies from cyanide in his office and the question occurs, or it should, What and where was its source? Its absence more than its presence would raise a potentially dangerous question: If the poison was not in the office, where was it?

The cause of death had been unknown for sixteen days after the discovery of Ed's body. That lapse of time must have been what the killer was playing for, Frank surmised. That was why he had not planted the cyanide *before* the discovery of the body but *afterwards*. If police had found it that morning with a dead man lying there, they might have been forced to go looking for the purchaser of the poison. If the buyer could not be identified as Ed Bacon, police would not have had a nice and neat suicide on their hands. They would then have had a dead man on the floor and a can of mysteriously purchased cyanide. Their investigation might have gone down a murder track as well as a suicide track.

Precious weeks had gone by. Frank's experience with crime detection was that of a reader, but he did not think one had to be a professional investigator to know a trail could get awfully cold in that time.

Whatever the killer's strategy, or sheer luck, it had served him well. He had not been linked with a crime, and, indeed, the police and medical examiner had never investigated the death as a murder. They had fallen for the suicide ploy from the beginning.

Had the police seen the suspicious brew in the coffee cup and the bloody handkerchief, as Patricia Haskell had a day later? If so, why hadn't they taken the articles as potential evidence? If they hadn't seen them, the oversight was inexcusable. Or had the murderer also planted them after police had left?

Frank telephoned the news to Lou Kane, who agreed the discovery of the cyanide was significant. He and Kathy had not yet gotten feedback from the Boston police commissioner, but Lou thought the development could well get some action. "We'll get word to him," he said.

Chapter 8

Outside Frank's house in New Hampshire, one of his family's cats loudly lost a race with Kayak late in the summer. The snarling Malamute crushed his prey to death between his jaws. It was the last quarry Kayak would hunt in that neck of the woods, as far as Frank Bacon was concerned. After confirming by telephone with Smoki that she had no desire to have the dog back in Boston, Frank agreed to arrange the sale of Ed's last sled dog. The incident was a blow to Hilary. She felt pity for Kayak and the guilt of a summer guest responsible for a disaster. Frank acquitted her of blame and reasoned Kayak would be happier romping with other dogs. Privately he knew Kayak's departure would be a relief to creatures great and small on the eastern shore of Lake Winnipesaukee.

The commotion did not augur well for the Labor Day weekend. Smoki and Brooks came up warily from Boston, joining a frazzled Hilary and the Francis Bacons, who tried to act as though a cat had not been killed. On a languorous Saturday afternoon, the widow and brother-in-law retreated to his study for an overdue talk about Ed's fiscal affairs. Neither looked forward to the discussion.

"What it is boiling down to is Ed and the agency are virtually bankrupt," Smoki said abjectly. "When all the bills are in, they'll probably exceed his assets by far."

"Except for his inheritance," Frank said across the desk. "As one of the trustees named by my mother, I can tell you that the money is discrete from the rest of Ed's estate and the agency. That's the way Mother set it up. Of course, you know, it now goes to Brooks and Hilary in accordance with her wishes.''

''Yes, I understand,'' Smoki said. ''But I believe there is a provision in Ed's will that I am entitled to something for . . . I think the term is 'reasonable comfort and support.' ''

''It doesn't come from his will, Smoki, but that is the term. It's from his *declaration of trust,* which he and Zal wrote in conjunction with Mother's bequest to him.''

''Which means?''

''Which means Ed's instructions reflect the way Mother wanted her money assigned. Her stipulation was that upon Ed's death it went to his children. At no time did she name you as a recipient of the trust fund in the event of Ed's death.''

Their gazes collided.

''Frank, I don't have to tell you I am struggling.''

''What about the quarter million dollars in Ed's life insurance benefits?'' He flipped through several pages of a legal-size document. ''In any event, here, in Ed's declaration, signed last summer: Money from the trust *'may'* be given to you by the trustees, Mother's attorney, and me. Not *shall* be given to you. Further, you, his wife,'' he resumed quoting, '' 'shall have no voice in determining whether any amount of principal shall be paid to or for her benefit.' ''

Smoki had numerous household expenses, including overdue utility bills, that required full and immediate payment. To cover them, Frank said he would advise his late mother's attorney to make emergency disbursements from Ed's inheritance. He did not think the attorney would balk at the idea since the well-being of Brooks and Hilary was involved. Ed's outstanding bank loan of $14,000 was to be repaid from the inheritance as arranged by Ed months before his death.

Smoki looked up grimly. ''Frank, you're telling me I am at the mercy of someone who has never approved of me?''

"Smoki, my approval or disapproval has nothing to do with the matter. I didn't write Ed's declaration. Zal Davlin did, and he's your attorney and Ed's. It merely incorporates Mother's stipulations."

"And she's your flesh and blood and I am an out-sider."

Frank looked surprised and angry. "Again, that has nothing to do with the matter, which is strictly legal. But aren't you aware I was adopted? Ed was adopted?"

Smoki's jaw slackened and her stare went blank. "What on earth are you talking about?"

"Do you mean Ed never told you?"

"That he was adopted? *No.*"

"Well, he was, and I was. Five years apart, presumably not from the same parents."

Smoki was shaking her head. "Excuse me, Frank, but this has taken me completely by surprise. Why on earth would Ed never have told me?"

"I don't know the answer to that one, Smoki."

Their discussion ended, and Smoki decided not to tell the girls of the revelation about their father that weekend. Frank had nothing more to say to her on a subject he kept largely to himself.

The Charles Bacons had never told their sons they had been adopted.

Both were grown before they found out. Ed learned in the worst possible way. Married and the father of two children in his late thirties, he answered the telephone in the dead of night at home and heard a voice announce, "You are adopted." The caller quickly hung up and if Ed knew who he was, he never said so. Although he kept the incident a secret at home, he did tell James Blaikie about it.

Frank had long assumed that he was adopted. But he did not seek confirmation until after the deaths of his parents and brother and then he got it from a cousin.

However, nothing was known about their natural parents. Ed had looked neither like Charles Bacon nor Pauline, who had been fifty-five and thirty-three, re-spectively, at his birth. Either his resemblance to his mother's ancestor in the portrait over the mantle was accidental, or she had selected it for him as a hint of his lineage. Some wondered if a young Conant had found herself or himself facing parenthood without enthusiasm and Pauline had come to the rescue.

There was also Frank's uncanny resemblance to Charles Bacon, from firm jaw and stiff upper lip to athletic bearing and ability. Frank was every inch the tall publisher who in his thirties had made a record-setting bobsled run down the treacherous Cresta Run in Switzerland. More than one relative or family friend wondered if Charles Bacon's legendary vigor had led to extramarital fatherhood in his early sixties, while his wife was in her late thirties.

It was obvious to those who knew the family well that Ed had been Polly's clear favorite and Charles had been openly partial to Frank.

Frank was convinced he was Charles Bacon's natural son. More than appearances and intuition persuaded him. He knew that shortly after his birth in January 1935, Charles and Pauline left for Europe with five-year-old Edwin and did not return to Boston until the fall. The timing suggested to Frank that his birth had been a blessed event for Charles Bacon but not for Pauline.

At home in Boston, Brooks and Hilary took the latest bolt out of the blue in good stride. By now they were veterans of unexpected jolts concerning their late father.

Brooks thought the mystery of his genealogy exciting. Hilary sensibly reminded her mother and sister that "Grandmother Polly always had such *good* taste."

Smoki was staggered by Ed's decision not to tell her about his birth. The vivacious blonde with blue-blood looks made no secret of the fact she had grown up on "the Farm," which was not a country estate. During the Great Depression it was a tenement district in Brookline and she had lived there in severe poverty.

In 1928, Smoki was born Adelaide Ruth Ginepra to first-generation Americans. Her mother's background was Scotch-Irish and her father's Italian. Alfred Leon Ginepra was a railroad engineer. He died, as Ed Bacon learned in a late-night phone call in 1965, when his Boston & Maine train derailed on flood-damaged tracks in Andover, Massachusetts. He and the former Ruth Burns had been separated nearly thirty years.

Following her parents' breakup, Smoki began working at the age of nine in a Brookline laundry where her mother had taken a job to get off welfare. Unbeknownst to Smoki and her future husband, young Master Edwin Conant Bacon was often chauffeured from Boston for riding lessons at a stable not far from her shop.

She got her nickname in the usual capricious way. Teenaged girlfriends took to calling her by the handle of a basketball referee called Smokey. The more she complained, the more often they tagged her with his nickname. Soon it became hers.

According to maternal family lore, the Burns genealogy went back to the great eighteenth-century Scottish poet. If great-grandfather Robert Burns had indeed been a descendant of his famous namesake, the family had no record of it. After arriving in Canada from his native Glasgow in the late nineteenth century, Smoki's grandfather John Burns was disinherited by his father. The reason was said to be his choice of wife. In 1890 at the age of twenty-six, he married an eighteen-year-old Canadian woman named Abbie Hendrigan, or Hendrichan on some documents. Although the ceremony was Methodist, rumor had it Abbie was at least part Jewish.

After Brookline High School, Smokey Ginepra attended Boston art schools on scholarship, specializing in illustration.

The fairy tale blossomed for her in October 1956. She was a technical illustrator at the Massachusetts Institute of Technology and living on Beacon Hill when she met a Bacon of Commonwealth Avenue. Their engagement was announced two months later at a dinner party thrown by her fiance's parents at the Ritz.

Following the May 1957 wedding, the newly minted

Smoki Bacon became a name to contend with. Under the wing of Polly Bacon, she entered high society as eagerly and energetically as she had left the Farm for Boston. In fact, as Smokey Ginepra she had for years been a volunteer in a variety of civic organizations. As Smoki Bacon she suddenly found herself being asked to serve on their boards.

She was, in the words of a Boston society columnist, "one of the most active members of Boston's social set." It was a reputation that won her both everlasting admiration and contempt.

To her critics, she was a girl from the wrong side of the tracks, exploiting the Bacon name. Friends saw her as genuinely committed to the arts and charity.

Off the society pages, Ed's closest confidants heard him complain increasingly that his wife was deeply compassionate toward everyone under the sun but him. He also complained of being on the short end of quarrels with Smoki and more than once presented a scratched face as evidence.

Smoki's defenders saw her rather as a woman struggling and working to keep house and home afloat with little help from an improvident husband.

However, their troubles were unknown outside a close circle of family and friends. Boston society was as tight lipped as it was exclusive.

A friend of the Bacons had once referred to James Blaikie in a furtive whisper as "different." It was one of the more polite terms of disdain for an interloper in the Yankee vocabulary. Ironically, the garrulous young man with an ambiguous smile was not necessarily Ed's social inferior by birth. Blaikie certainly did not have as high to climb in his upward mobility as Smoki had in hers.

Born on August 16, 1945, the day after World War II ended, James Blaikie was the only child of a comfortably middle-class couple who fit in nicely with their solid Waltham neighbors. The former Alma Stocker and James Francis Blaikie, Sr., a U.S. Army sergeant stationed in Massachusetts, had come to parenthood late by standards at the time. The thirty-six-year-old housewife and forty-four-year-old father happily made up for lost time. They lavished their bright and energetic little boy with playthings and attention. Permissiveness reigned as a way of encouraging creativity. His mother, a warm and shy woman, began reading to him at an early age, and as a preschooler Jim was devouring books beyond his years.

Teachers at his neighborhood public school found him highly intelligent. However, their praise for his work got peculiar results. Once a teacher had commended him, he leaned on the oars and coasted to above-average grades. To him superiority meant progress with the least possible exertion, even if it meant falling short of his potential.

Regarded by some as a class clown, he struck neighborhood boys as a loner. His enviable summer job selling refreshments at Fenway Park was arranged by his father, who managed a parking lot at the baseball stadium. The experience illustrated James Senior's guiding philosophy that who you knew was as important as what you knew.

The family attended St. Jude's Catholic Church, and while a student at Waltham High School Jim was active in the Catholic Youth Organization. After graduating in 1963, he helped his father run the parking lot at Fenway Park, raising money for college.

At Northeastern University in Boston, the Blaikie quickness got Jim better than average grades and his political instincts began to flower. He won election as pledgemaster, social chairman, and then president of his fraternity. On the threshhold of late-1960s social activism, he was recognized by his fraternity brothers for his energetic volunteerism. He worked with mentally handicapped children and helped raise scholarship funds for the needy. His fraternity brothers considered him a model of charity. Yet he complained the university was impersonal and dogmatic.

Not much taller and no trimmer than he had been as a youngster, the business major restlessly trod the urban campus like an undergraduate Napoleon, complete with hairstyle. He found his appropriately stunning empress in fellow Northeastern student Kathleen Goodrow. It seemed to friends that Kathy, with her dazzling eyes and feline smile, gave Jim a purpose that had been lacking in his life.

His gregarious nature appeared to draw her out of some secret place and Kathy's reserve had the effect of moderating his friskiness. Despite her father's objections, they were married at St. Jude's in Waltham in the spring of 1968, shortly before his graduation. They took a Brookline flat in one of the Boston area's numerous student ghettoes.

That year Jim's father suffered a stroke and began the first of several lengthy stays at the VA Hospital.

Out of college, Jim joined millions of ex-students facing the draft. But he put in for a deferment as the only son of a debilitated military veteran and marked time that summer as a salesman for a chemical company in Waltham. In the fall he took a job at a travel agency in suburban Newton and within a year was a sales representative for an insurance company. His entry-level salary was a then-respectable $8,000 a year. He befriended a secretary, and when she went to work for Bacon insurance in 1970, he received an introduction to the agency's head.

Jim was pitching his company's group policy plans to agents, and Ed Bacon became one of his prospects. The recent college graduate and the tolerably dignified forty-year-old Brahmin hit it off.

By 1971, Jim and Ed had struck up an informal business relationship. Bacon wanted Blaikie for two reasons: to help pay operating expenses and, for a share of agency billing, to do the legwork. Ed was the man with the contacts and the savvy. Jim made personal visits to the companies, servicing current group accounts and drumming up new ones.

As volunteer treasurer of McGovern's Massachusetts campaign committee in 1972, Jim rented office space at the Bacon agency for his campaign work and continued feeding money into the business. Blaikie claimed the money came from his personal savings.

After tangling with Blaikie over the campaign deficit, Lou Kane made his dislike of Blaikie known but Ed Bacon continued the business relationship.

In fact, Ed was always circumspect with his brother and close friends on the subject of his junior associate. If Ed knew, he never related certain facts about Blaikie that would not have improved their opinion of him. According to Massachusetts Insurance Commission records, Blaikie was not and never had been registered to sell insurance in the state. A supporter of antiwar, nonviolent candidate McGovern, Jim Blaikie owned a nine-inch black- and silver-handled switchblade knife and a .38-caliber Smith & Wesson revolver that was not registered in his name.

A friend knew he carried the gun wrapped in a towel under the front seat of his car.

Chapter 9

In the first week of September, pressure from Smoki and the Louis Kanes resulted in the Bacon case reaching the Boston police homicide unit. It came down from the police commissioner with a request for a reevaluation. Sergeant Detective John Maillet recalled his conversation about it with private detective Tom Cunningham the previous month. Maillet, a tall and rugged man of fifty, volunteered to look it over.

At his desk, he turned the pages of district police and medical examiner's reports in the unhurried manner of a man reading his Sunday paper. Nothing about the report of responding officers appeared out of line with suicide. A month earlier they had found Ed Bacon's body, undisturbed surroundings, and an apparent suicide note at the Bacon agency on the waterfront. However, looking through the file, Maillet found a photocopy of the note but nothing to confirm its authenticity.

A twenty-four-year veteran of the Boston police department, with four years as a detective, John Maillet knew a can of worms when he saw one, and he was looking at one. There was no conflict between authorities and families worse than one over a suicide ruling. When a person has clearly been murdered, survivors see law-enforcement officials as their allies. However, in a contested suicide the law is seen as part of the problem. Making matters worse, police and the medical examiner are caught in a

Catch-22. Without evidence from investigators of foul play, the medical examiner rules suicide on the basis of forensic evidence. The police investigate no further because the case is officially a suicide. It's the kind of tail-chasing that can go on for months if not years.

Telephoning Tom Cunningham as promised, Maillet told the private investigator the Bacon case had come his way and he was looking into it. A former FBI handwriting expert at Cunningham's firm was examining the so-called suicide note.

"Also, since I talked to you," Cunningham said, "a guy at the Bacon agency found a container labeled cyanide in Bacon's file cabinet. He and the brother swear it wasn't there the day after the body was found."

"The brother?" Maillet asked.

"Frank Bacon. President of his own computer company. Very successful."

"No motive there?"

"He's the one pushing the investigation," Cunningham said. "He's thinking a kid from Brookline by the name of James Blaikie killed Bacon. Bacon's business associate."

"What the hell is a *business associate?*"

"He wasn't actually a partner of Bacon's. It was more like he shared the office."

"Why does he kill Bacon?"

"Sixty-four thousand–dollar question."

Maillet snorted. Never having seen an angel get anywhere in this job, he preferred devil's advocacy. "Tom, the family has to know Bacon's relationship with Blaikie better than anyone else alive, and they think Blaikie killed him, but they don't have any idea why?"

"It's a tough one, John."

"What about the wife?"

"Well, she agrees with her brother-in-law it was murder. As far as the inheritance goes, apparently the kids get the money."

"Kids," Maillet said, and flipping through the file,

he saw Ed Bacon had died at the age of forty-four. "They've got to be what, teenagers?"

"Yeah, two daughters."

After agreeing to stay in touch with Cunningham, Maillet thought about his three girls, two of them around the ages of Bacon's daughters and the oldest nineteen. With him they were trying to deal with the worsening medical condition of their mother. How long could his wife keep up her increasingly painful struggle with cancer? Besides lighting candles, saying rosaries, and otherwise hoping against hope, what the girls did most was try to understand her fate. Why was their once-vivacious mother confined to a wheelchair? How could this happen to a soul as good as her?

He figured the same kind of questions must be going through the minds of the Bacon girls.

Over the next two weeks he met with the district police officers who had been at the death scene. To believe murder, they pointed out, you had to accept that the killer left poison behind for Bacon to ingest and departed from the office before Bacon died. There was the problem of the body blocking the door and the back door locked from the inside.

In a telephone conversation with Sergeant Detective Maillet, attorney Davlin told of the Bacon family's apprehensions.

"They firmly believe Ed was murdered," Davlin said, "and, as I'm sure you can appreciate, they are concerned about their own security. If someone did indeed kill Ed, who knows why he did and whether he might strike again?"

"I'll tell you, counselor," Maillet said, "I'd like to meet with the family. They might have some information that could help."

Davlin agreed and after speaking with Frank and Smoki, he called Maillet back to schedule a meeting later in September at his law office.

The whipping posts and stockades described in *The Scarlet Letter* once stood near the downtown corner of

Washington and State Streets. However, no physical sign of Puritan justice thereabouts had survived three centuries. The museum piece of an old State House with its stepped facade and wedding-cake tower was one of the few buildings in the vicinity to have lasted more than two hundred years. It was dwarfed by the nearby 28 State Street Building, a nondescript bank and office building like any in modern New York, Chicago, or Los Angeles.

Entering the lobby of the skyscraper, Sergeant Detective John Maillet anticipated a difficult meeting with the Bacons and their attorney. He did not expect them to appreciate anything he had to tell them.

The rangy plainclothesman wore a serious expression as he got into an elevator, but the lines of his face suggested a playful smile was never far below the surface of his ruddy complexion.

Maillet was known to have an ever-sunny disposition, even while uttering useful hints for long life to a felony suspect seeking avenues of escape. Eight years before he had given such free medical advice to the notorious mobster Joseph Barbosa after arresting him for possession of a weapon on a Boston street. Barbosa took the hint and came quietly, but he later sang his heart out about his gangland connections. The Federal Witness Protection Program was created to preserve his invaluable vocal cords. Barbosa's dramatic court testimony decimated the New England mob and, for busting him, Maillet won a police department commendation for "meritorious police duty in the face of danger."

Although Maillet had drawn his .38-caliber Smith & Wesson revolver in many such arrests, he was not only proud but grateful that he had never fired a shot at a single soul. Even a legal killing, he understood from the experience of fellow officers, stayed with a person. He attributed his blood-stainless record to good, overpowering teamwork, as in the Barbosa case. His philosophy was simple—the less a suspect thought he had a chance to shoot his way out of an arrest, the less chance there was for a shoot-out.

In the twenty-second-floor law firm of Hennessy, McCluskey, Earle & Kilburn, a secretary showed Maillet into Zal Davlin's spacious office. Inside sat a grim-faced Smoki Bacon, Frank Bacon, and Lou Kane. Cordially introduced by Davlin, Maillet had the impression he had entered a window of the venerable Brooks Brothers clothing store down Berkeley Street from police headquarters. Wearing a Donegal tweed jacket purchased in Ireland, he took a seat and listened attentively as Zal outlined the family's differences with the suicide findings.

Maillet thought he saw intensity at the breaking point in the widow's darting eyes. Frank's gaze seemed intelligent, reasonable, and determined; and Lou Kane demonstrated the relaxed confidence of an authentic military man. Maillet knew Kane was the husband of a deputy mayor and had been instrumental in the case being reopened.

But when Zal finished his summary of Ed Bacon's inheritance and generally high spirits, Maillet had no intention of pleasing his audience.

"I've been back over the investigation," he said, "and I have to tell you the police saw nothing at the Bacon agency to indicate there was a crime involved. If and when something new comes to light, it might be a different story. But, hard as it might be to accept now, it appears Mr. Bacon killed himself."

"Sergeant Maillet," Smoki said almost imploringly, "I was married to Ed Bacon for seventeen years. Surely I would have seen some sign that he was in a depressed state. Or Frank or my daughters or Lou, his best friend, would have."

Maillet nodded benignly. "Mrs. Bacon, family are sometimes the last to know. You've got to understand I have to see evidence of a crime. So far there isn't any."

Lou Kane spoke up. "It is inconceivable to us that a suicide ruling could have been made with so many holes in the case. Where did the cyanide come from? Did Ed write the so-called suicide note?''

Maillet nodded. ''Mr. Kane, I'm not here to defend or criticize anybody, but the note is being analyzed now and so is the substance found in Mr. Bacon's office. Maybe something will come out of those tests.''

Frank Bacon had the feeling the detective considered them a bunch of Back Bay swells trying to clear a precious family name of disgrace. ''Sergeant Maillet,'' he said unemotionally, ''Ed's secretary found a coffee mug and a blood-spattered handkerchief at the Bacon agency the day after his body was found. Were they there when the police investigated? I don't know. I do know that container labeled cyanide wasn't there that day. And I think the reason is the person who killed my brother planted it there.''

''And that person is this Mr. Blaikie, your brother's associate?'' Maillet said.

''I suspect it was,'' Frank said evenly.

Maillet came as close as ever he did to appearing ill humored. ''And what might his motive have been, Mr. Bacon?''

''For one thing,'' Frank said, ''my brother was trying to get him out of the agency. Blaikie simply wasn't performing.''

''Mr. Blaikie wasn't a partner, I understand,'' Maillet said.

''That's right!'' Smoki's words sliced into the conversation. ''He was not and never was.''

Maillet's eyes questioned everyone. ''If he had no standing in the company, what did he have to gain by killing Mr. Bacon?'' Following the silence, Maillet resumed with an edge to his amiable tone. ''There's no motive, and there's no evidence of a murder. Suspicions and your belief that Mr. Bacon wouldn't kill himself don't amount to a case.''

''There is something else,'' Frank said. ''I have heard that Jim's mother died at her home in Waltham last year and her death was ruled a suicide. The information I have is she shot herself to death and Jim was alone with her in the house at the time. I think this could be a pattern.''

A crease formed over one of Maillet's eyebrows. "I'll check it out,'' he said, scrawling on his legal-size pad.

Back in New Hampshire that afternoon, Frank was feeling as angry and frustrated as he had ever been in the month since his brother's death. When he got a telephone call from an unusually excited Zal Davlin, Frank wondered what other calamity could have occurred in the past few hours.

"Frank,'' Zal blurted, "who do you think I just got a call from?''

"Try me, Zal, and I'll let you know,'' he said patiently.

"Jim Blaikie.''

"Oh, and what does the illustrious Mr. Blaikie have to say for himself?''

"Frank, listen to this. Blaikie said Kemper is sending me the check for Ed's $50,000 life insurance policy. You know, the policy we couldn't find in Ed's office. Blaikie said the check is payable to *him!* To *him,* Frank, not Smoki and the girls.''

The words hit Frank like a blast from water tossed on white-hot sauna stones.

"Frank,'' Zal continued emphatically. "Blaikie was expecting the check to go directly to him. He found out from Kemper they're sending it in my care because I wrote to them as a trustee of Ed's estate.''

"This sounds a little like the motive Sergeant Maillet was saying we needed this morning,'' Frank said. "If and when the check comes, will you let Maillet know about it?''

"I will.''

"How did you leave it with Blaikie?''

"He said he would call me early next week to see if the check arrived.''

As they rang off, Frank had a hunch they might finally get some cooperation from the police.

* * *

When Smoki received word from Zal of Blaikie's claim to the insurance policy, her last shred of doubt about Frank's murder theory vanished. She had been correct in her sense that it was the worst of all possibilities. Natural death and then suicide had been devastating and punishing in turn, but the thought of Jim Blaikie, or anyone, killing her husband was unbearable.

She could only imagine physical torture, but now she knew the mental variety. It surpassed the victim's capacity to express pain. Was that when you crawled into a fetal position, she wondered fearfully, and whimpered like an injured animal? She had to get a grip on herself. Wanting to be more certain about the possibility of murder, she decided not to tell the girls immediately. Better, she felt, to wait for developments next week. Besides, she was too upset and fearful to talk about it.

The following Monday, September 23, the $50,000 Kemper check showed up in Zal Davlin's mail. It was indeed made out to James F. Blaikie, Jr. The accompanying letter to Davlin from a Kemper claims representative in Long Grove, Illinois, indicated the beneficiary check was for Bacon's life insurance policy number 613600. The number matched the one Ed Bacon had given Zal a month before his death. The Kemper letter concluded, "Please deliver the check to Mr. Blaikie as soon as possible."

In a telephone conversation with the insurer's policy service office, the mystery of how James Blaikie had come in line for the check was partly solved.

In its files Kemper had a form, ostensibly signed by Ed Bacon on July 1, 1974, indicating that Blaikie was to replace Ed's family as primary beneficiary. Eighteen days later, the change-of-beneficiary form was received by Kemper. On July 24, Kemper approved the beneficiary change and mailed an acknowledgement of it to Ed at the Bacon agency on Commercial Wharf. Five days later he died.

Following his telephone conversation with Kemper, Davlin pondered a chilling question. Had Ed actually signed the beneficiary change and, if not, had the acknowledgment ever reached him?

Davlin got the call he was expecting from James Blaikie, who did not speak of the check but asked if he could see Davlin that afternoon. Blaikie said he had papers from the Bacon agency, which he believed Zal as executor of Ed's estate should have. Zal said nothing about the check, but suggested Jim come around at three o'clock that afternoon. Davlin did not relish the thought of being alone with a man whose mother and business associate had allegedly commited suicide within a ten-month period, but as Ed's trustee he had to meet with him.

Hearing by telephone from Zal of what seemed a motive for murder, Smoki was filled with a mixture of raw anger and bitter satisfaction. At the very least, there appeared to be hope James Blaikie would be brought to justice, if indeed insurance fraud could be proved. Finding out whether that signature was actually Ed's was the next step that Zal planned to take, and she felt certain it was a forgery.

Frank also could not believe his brother had signed the policy over to Blaikie. But whether or not Ed had done so, Frank believed the document had been a virtual death warrant. Once Blaikie had it approved by Kemper, Ed Bacon was worth far less to him alive than dead.

Jim Blaikie showed up at three o'clock, and Zal Davlin was struck by the young man's nonchalance.

After handing over a sheaf of Bacon agency papers and bills, Jim casually asked, "Do you have my check from Kemper, Zal?"

"Yes, I do, Jim," Zal said. "Can you tell me what the money is for?"

"It was one of two matching policies that Ed and I had," Jim said. "So if one of us died, the other would get insurance proceeds."

"Oh," Davlin said. "And where is the other policy?"

Jim replied that he did not know where it was. "I assume it's somewhere around Ed's office," he said.

Amazingly to Davlin, Jim had the Kemper policy that Zal and Frank had been unable to find at Ed's office two days after his death. Zal did not bring up the incident. Davlin made a photocopy of the policy and handed the original back to Jim. Again Jim asked for the Kemper check, saying he had been paying agency expenses and was short of cash.

"I feel that as a trustee of Ed's estate my giving you the check would be a conflict," Zal said. "After all you're claiming the agency owes you money, and we're really across the table from each other on all of this."

Zal said he wanted to think about it and suggested Blaikie call him later in the afternoon.

Jim amiably said he would and left. Zal Davlin discussed the matter with a partner of the firm, who agreed Davlin should not turn the check over to Blaikie but send it back to Kemper.

In telephone contact again with Kemper's policy service department, Zal asked if there was any record of the kind of matching Bacon and Blaikie policies Jim had described. It was not an unusual arrangement between people in a business to indemnify each other. The Kemper service department told him that there had been a $32,000 Kemper policy in Blaikie's name with Bacon as beneficiary. It had been taken out by Blaikie in 1971, the year Ed bought the $50,000 coverage in question. However, Blaikie's policy had lapsed for nonpayment of premiums after one quarter. Furthermore, the beneficiaries of Ed's policy from day one had been his family, until the beneficiary change of July 1974.

Davlin told the Kemper representative that he was returning the check. Asked if he had any objection to Kemper sending it directly to Blaikie, Zal said that was Kemper's business, but as the Bacons' attorney he would write Kemper of his serious questions concerning the purported change of beneficiary. Davlin was assured that under the circumstances, Kemper would first clear the matter with its legal department.

Zal Davlin thought he would be surprised if Ed had actually made the change. Looking down at the copy he had taken from Blaikie, Davlin would not hazard a guess whether the signature was indeed Ed's. It looked as though handwriting experts would be sorting that one out.

When Blaikie telephoned that afternoon, Davlin told him of the law firm's decision to send the $50,000 check back to Kemper.

The late Edwin Bacon's business associate was not happy. He reiterated his desperate need for the money, claiming agency bills had to be paid.

After ringing off with Blaikie, Davlin studied the change-of-beneficiary form again. On it, Blaikie as the new beneficiary was designated as Ed's "business partner," which he was not. Since Ed had made it clear Blaikie was only an informal associate, it seemed inconceivable Ed would have approved that language. And it certainly was odd that Kemper would have approved a document witnessed *only* by the person who stood to gain from it, James Blaikie.

But there was also something positively eerie about the prosaic form with its "Federal Kemper Life Assurance Company" masthead.

James Blaikie's name was typed in as the new beneficiary, along with his address, in a swanky part of Brookline, Massachusetts. If Ed had not given Zal Davlin the number of that policy, the attorney would not have known to write Kemper about it. The check would have gone directly to Jim Blaikie at his home address. Blaikie would be $50,000 richer today and the Bacon family none the wiser.

It was as though Ed Bacon had reached up from his grave and pointed a finger at James Blaikie.

Informed by Zal Davlin of Blaikie's claim to the insurance benefits, Sergeant Detective Maillet considered the information provocative indeed. It had the nasty smell of a murder motive. He telephoned Kemper, got confirmation of Zal's account, and was promised a copy of the beneficiary-change document.

Late in September, Maillet got the results of the state police laboratory analysis of the substance found in Ed Bacon's file cabinet three weeks after his death. As indicated on the label, it tested as *potassium* cyanide. However, Maillet noticed, the lab had earlier identified the poison in Bacon's remains as *sodium* cyanide.

Maillet visited the state police chemist, who explained that sodium and potassium cyanide, both deadly poisons, cannot be distinguished in their dissolved state in the human body. Both sodium and potassium are naturally present in blood. In either event, he said, it is the cyanogen that is the lethal half of both compounds. Bacon could have ingested either potassium or sodium cyanide and died within seconds or minutes.

Maillet confirmed with Frank Bacon and Rick Adams what he had heard from Zal Davlin. All three men clearly recalled the cyanide had not been in Ed's file cabinet the first day police allowed them back inside the agency.

Filling in his younger partner, Detective Thomas Cashman, Sergeant Maillet said, "I find it hard to believe all three of them would have overlooked a pound-size can marked cyanide. It sounds to me, Tommy, like someone planted it so it would be there *after* the responding officers left the office."

"And *after* the ME ruled suicide by poisoning," Cashman offered.

"That's right, Tom." He stroked his chin. "He wanted people to find things *when* he wanted them to. Not before. He's either a cagey sonofabitch or a lucky one. Tell you what, I think we're going to take a ride out to Waltham and have a talk with our brothers out there. Frank Bacon tells me he heard this

Blaikie's mother passed away last summer. Also suicide."

"Don't tell me poisoning," Detective Cashman said.

"Yeah," Sergeant Maillet said. "The lead variety, I hear."

Chapter 10

On the last day of September, the rolling wooded countryside west of Boston was becoming a splendor of scarlet and gold. Sergeant Detective Maillet drove with his partner, Detective Thomas Cashman, out the Massachusetts Turnpike and headed north on the Route 128 beltway to Waltham.

Meeting with Waltham deputy police chief John Rooney in his office that morning, Maillet quietly looked over the file on the death of Alma Blaikie.

According to the incident report, James Blaikie claimed to have been in the second-story attic at the time his mother shot herself, but he had not heard the report of the .38-caliber weapon from the basement.

After handing the three-page report to Cashman, Maillet hefted the black .38 revolver from Deputy Chief Rooney's desktop. It was a curious firearm, composed of a Smith & Wesson barrel and cylinder and a Harrington & Richardson frame.

''Lunchbox Special,'' Maillet said of the gun. It was jargon for firearms composed of defective parts smuggled out by employees of gun factories. He found the trigger pull so abnormally hard that he wondered if an ailing sixty-four-year-old woman would have had the strength to fire a shot with one hand. She could hardly have held the eight-inch, two-pound revolver with two hands and fired it directly into the bone behind her right ear. Of course, if she knew how to work the double-action revolver by cocking the hammer, the slightest pressure on the trigger would have fired the gun.

The half-dozen 8-by-10 four-color photographs of Mrs. Blaikie's body on the basement floor raised additional questions in Maillet's mind. She was lying in a twisted position, face down and on her left hip. Whether she had fired from a standing or kneeling position, Maillet tried but could not visualize how her right arm could be extending straight back until the hand rested, palm up, over the crook of her right knee. Directly below the right hand, the revolver lay on the floor. A .38 with its considerable recoil requires a firm grip to keep the weapon from flying up and out of hand. Yet if suicide was to be believed, she had fallen from the fatal shot with the gun still in her hand as her arm somehow reached backward, and the gun fell straight down to the floor.

Maillet asked about the pool of water extending from the washing machine and encircling the body. Deputy Chief Rooney explained that it was an older machine and did not have an automatic filling mechanism. External hot and cold water valves had to be turned on and off manually. Assuming she would not have stood there and watched the overflow, it must have happened after she died. The water had been turned off by the time police arrived.

The photograph that brought a frown to John Maillet was a closeup of the note on the floor near Alma Blaikie's blood-soaked head of hair. Without a signature, it read:

I can't stand how I am anymore

From his files Maillet withdrew a photocopy of the unsigned note found almost a year later under Edwin Bacon's body:

I CAN'T STAND IT ANYMORE

Of course, neither note could be used in connection with the other case in any prosecution. The Boston detectives were there only to confirm Frank Bacon's story about Alma Blaikie's death and they had done so.

On the half-hour drive to Back Bay Boston and police headquarters, Maillet glanced at Cashman. "This is working up to something, Tom."

"I think you're right, John. The notes are incredible."

"If you substitute cyanide for the gun, the Bacon case is a rerun of Alma Blaikie's death," Maillet said. "Assuming one person writes both notes, he figures one worked the first time so why not try it a second time. Besides, who would believe someone planting notes that much alike?"

"A woman sets out to do her laundry," Cashman said, "starts filling the washing machine and shoots herself."

"Before turning off the water," Maillet added with a humorless smile. "Sound like maybe someone didn't know how the machine worked. He plugs her from behind while it's filling up. He's planting the note and the gun and the thing is overflowing. Funny, you didn't see any laundry basket or hamper in the pictures, did you?"

"No, I didn't," Cashman said.

"You never know, though, Tom. People do strange things when they decide to kill themselves. Remember the lovely woman who shot herself in bed? She tugs down her nightie and shoots herself in the chest so the wound is below her neckline."

"Yeah, and some people fly without leaving a note behind."

"All the same," Maillet said, "let's chip away at this one some more."

The following day they returned to Waltham and interviewed one of Blaikie's neighbors. Jim had told Waltham police he thought his mother had been visiting the woman on the morning of her death. The sixty-five-year-old widow said she had not seen Alma Blaikie that morning and was shocked to learn her friend of twenty-six years had committed suicide. Her impression was that Mrs. Blaikie had been recuperating very nicely from her heart attack the previous April, taking her daily walks as prescribed by her doctor. It was after such a stroll that Alma had come around the day before her death, their last visit together. Having to restrict her household activity and visits to her husband at the VA Hospital in Bedford had been a bother for Alma, but she had never talked of suicide. Jim, the neighbor said, had come to see his mother at least once a week and seemed very close to her.

That afternoon Detective Cashman telephoned Alma Blaikie's doctor, who also expressed surprise that she had taken her life. He said he had treated her for an apparent heart attack in April and found her to be a jovial person who was making a rapid recovery. As Jim Blaikie had told investigators, the doctor had put her on medication. The physician said the last time he had seen her, two months before, she had shown no signs of depression.

That afternoon Sergeant Detective Maillet drove through Callahan Tunnel under Boston Harbor to the East Boston offices of Ogden Security, the investigative firm hired by the Bacons. Private detective Tom Cunningham had news for him. The company's handwriting consultant had made his report on the purported Bacon suicide note. Comparing it with specimens of Bacon's handwriting provided by his family, the former FBI document analyst believed the note had been hand printed by Bacon, but said he could not be certain.

"That," Maillet said, "would blow holes in any prosecution."

Cunningham was waiting to receive Ed's fingerprints from Harvard University, a source suggested by Frank Bacon. Ed had been fingerprinted there as a member of Harvard's Reserve Officers Training Corps. The private detective wanted the prints compared with any on the mysterious cyanide container.

The following day Maillet and Cashman drove to the

respectable southwestern Boston suburb of Dedham. At the Norfolk County Registry, a limestone building with imposing Corinthian columns, they pulled the records on Blaikie's Brookline house. He had purchased it the previous spring for $74,500 and had two mortgages on it for almost the entire amount. The house alone, Maillet calculated, had to be costing Blaikie more than a thousand dollars a month. If James Blaikie had been on his way out of the Bacon agency for lack of performance, where was he coming up with his money?

Outside the registry, Norfolk County Courthouse rose like a scaled-down Capitol Hill across lightly trafficked High Street.

"No wonder he can't wait to get that $50,000 Kemper check," Detective Cashman said as they headed for their car.

"Unless that beneficiary change is legit," Maillet said with a scornful grin, "he's going to be waiting a long time."

The check was farther than ever from Blaikie's reach. Zal Davlin returned it to Kemper insurance with a cover letter telling of his and Smoki's surprise that it had been payable to James Blaikie. Bacon, the attorney wrote, had told him a month before his death that his family were the beneficiaries of record.

To make matters worse for James Blaikie in the first week of October, a Boston bank was demanding the contested $50,000 check from Kemper. Jim, who had pledged it as collateral, had missed loan payments for the second month in a row. He was having trouble coming up with money for his house and other payments that month.

The five thousand dollars borrowed from friend David DeWilde the previous summer was about gone, and David was looking for his money. Jim's excuse, that the Bacon family had tied up the Kemper check, was wearing thin.

Blaikie was saved by confusion at the Bacon agency. Ed had handled revenues and two months after his death there still was no new procedure in place. As secretary, Pat Haskell had received her orders from Ed, who had instructed her when to make payments on the insurance policies of their commercial clients. She would retain a percentage as agency commission and pay the premium on whatever coverage the client had—group life, employee health, or liability.

James Blaikie stepped into the void and picked up the October check from the New England Nuclear Corporation, a major Bacon client. Ed had deposited such checks in the agency account at the New England Merchant's Bank and then instructed Pat to pay premiums from it. Instead, Blaikie deposited the $6,223 check in the Bacon–Blaikie joint account at the Harbor National Bank on October 11. He did not forward New England Nuclear's group life insurance premium to the underwriter in Texas that month. Figuring it would take at least several weeks before the insurer started screaming for its money, Blaikie did not expect New England Nuclear to realize what had happened for at least a month.

He wrote checks on the Bacon–Blaikie account and deposited them in his own personal account. He was then able to get David DeWilde and half a dozen other creditors off his back. Temporarily.

Chapter 11

Sergeant Detective John Maillet wanted to get some ducks lined up before questioning James Blaikie and so far he did not have any. Blaikie was not officially a suspect, because no crime had been proven. But he was the subject of Maillet's investigation into Bacon's death. The life insurance policy was the key. If Blaikie turned out to be the rightful beneficiary, there was not much a homicide detective had to talk about with him. Especially in view of the purported Bacon suicide note, which so far was not looking like a forgery. The fact that it resembled the Alma Blaikie note carried no prosecutorial weight. Her note could not be introduced in any grand jury investigation into the Bacon case, or in any trial that might follow.

Maillet did visit the Bacon agency for talks with Pat Haskell and Rick Adams, who confirmed information already in his possession. He purposely ignored Blaikie on the principle that if Jim had anything to worry about, Maillet wanted him to start worrying big-time. Sometimes you could smoke or spook a criminal into a revealing move just by being there and not saying a word to him.

Early in October, Maillet received a copy of the July 1 beneficiary-change application from Kemper and it contained an intriguing revelation. At the bottom right of the form, which assigned $50,000 in benefits to James Blaikie, was the ostensible rounded signature of Edwin C. Bacon. Curiously, on the lower left was the scratchy signature of the only witness to the signing, and it was James F. Blaikie, Jr.

There's a golden opportunity for a murderous bastard, Maillet thought, if, of course, there's a murderous bastard around.

Kemper had received the change form on July 19, and approved it on July 24, mailing an acknowledgment to Bacon that day. He died on July 29, and no one at the agency or in the Bacon family knew if he had received the acknowledgment or where it was.

Interviewing Al Powers, Sergeant Detective Maillet heard of Edwin Bacon's last known conversation, a very routine one, sometime before ten o'clock on the night of Bacon's death.

The Somerville contractor repeated to Maillet what he had told Smoki Bacon upon arriving at the Bacon house to estimate a painting project on July 30, the day Bacon's body had been found. Nothing out of the ordinary had come up in his talk with Bacon.

Maillet got an unflattering opinion of Bacon from a former associate of his at an insurance agency where both had worked before Ed started his own company. He groused to Maillet in a telephone conversation that Bacon was argumentative to a fault, "very fussy in small things," and difficult to do business with. According to him, Ed was highly intelligent but unimpressive as a salesman and a businessman.

"To tell you the truth," he told Maillet, "I don't think Ed killed himself, because he'd rather stay alive and go on irritating people."

After the call Maillet wondered if one of the details that Bacon had bugged people about might have been a *small thing* like a change-of-beneficiary form. In the wrong hands, the simple piece of paper could end a man's life.

At the Bacon agency, Smoki found it ever harder to meet payroll and other expenses as income continued to fall off. Getting in afternoons after her morning job, she did not see much of the man she considered her husband's murderer. When she did, she avoided him.

Blaikie was pressing hard with a claim for some $30,000 against the agency. Since Frank held the business as collateral for his loans to Ed, he agreed to meet with Blaikie in late October. Zal Davlin, not entirely joking, advised Frank over the telephone to keep his eyes on Blaikie's hands at all times.

"I don't think I have anything to worry about, Zal," Frank replied. "My dead body doesn't represent money to him."

"Frank," Davlin scolded, "be careful anyway. We don't know what we're dealing with here."

Frank laughed, but when he met with Blaikie at the Rusty Scupper, he was not a little apprehensive. Sitting across a table from him at a quaint waterfront pub, Frank thought it absolutely surreal to be having drinks with a man he believed had poisoned his brother.

Jim seemed nervous but, with a shade of his patented grin, almost as congenial as ever. But the mouth across his baby face became a gash of pity. He expressed sadness over Ed's suicide but said he was not surprised by the medical examiner's ruling and the discovery of cyanide in Ed's office. Ed had been extremely depressed in recent months, he said, really down about the business and money problems. Ed was about as miserable as he had ever seen him, Jim lamented.

Frank listened to what he regarded as rubbish and locked Blaikie in a stony gaze. But he followed Zal Davlin's advice not to provoke Blaikie with a debate on Ed's death.

"To business," Frank said briskly. "What's this about money?"

Jim blinked. "Well, I've got $36,000 coming to me. Eight thousand in commissions and $28,000 that I loaned Ed. I've got the records. That's partly the reason Ed signed the Kemper policy over to me. As business insurance."

"The insurance money is in Kemper's court," Frank said cooly. "As for the agency, you've got to put in a claim to Zal Davlin. He's handling everything as attorney for the estate.''

The tense meeting ended with Blaikie looking more uptight than he had been at the beginning and Frank relieved that no tables had been overturned.

Driving away from the waterfront, he marveled at the composure of the man ten years his junior. He's under investigation in connection with my brother's death, Frank thought, and he's having a routine business conference with me. If this guy isn't innocent, he's a pretty smooth operator.

Blaikie did telephone Davlin and the attorney told him essentially what Frank had suggested: Kemper would decide on the check. Jim should send Davlin a formal claim against Bacon's estate for alleged investments in the agency and commissions purportedly due to him. Blaikie would be in line with some thirty other creditors, including Frank Bacon, who was out nearly $50,000 in loans to his brother. It was looking as though Ed's personal and business debts would amount to more than $100,000 and his available assets to less than $2,000.

By November, Blaikie himself was another month deeper in his fiscal quagmire. He still did not have the Kemper check he had pledged as loan collateral at his bank, where he had missed his third installment in a row. He was two months in arrears on his car payments.

To his relief, the New England Nuclear Corporation's insurance company in Texas had not notified the agency about nonreceipt of the October premium. It was just a matter of time. The question was how much time. And where would he come up with money to get through November?

Hilary Bacon, just turned fourteen, was in the third form or high school freshman year at the Winsor School, and Brooks was two years ahead of her at the girls' academy near the Fenway. They lived at home and walked the mile and a half to school when their mother did not drive them or they did not take the subway. Aware of suspicions about James Blaikie, they were more apprehensive about their safety and their mother's than they let on. If he had killed their father, they privately reasoned, might he not strike against the family again?

As autumn deepened, the stroll to the Fenway station or alongside the winding stream toward home in the Back Bay became more unnerving. Sometimes they left school separately at dusk and distant human figures ahead or footsteps behind increased their anxiety. At home they developed a kind of early-warning system without their mother's knowledge. At night when Brooks or Hilary thought she heard a noise in the century-old house, she went down the third-floor hallway to the other's room and knocked on the door. After getting a reply, she would pause at the dimly lighted staircase and listen for footsteps on the second floor, where their mother's bedroom was located. Then it was back to bed until the next sound, real or imagined.

For the younger Hilary, there was an additional and very private psychological burden. She still did not believe her father was dead and continued nightly to peer out a window whenever a car pulled up in front of the house, expecting her father to emerge from it.

At least one acquaintance of James Blaikie's outside the Bacon family had purchased a handgun.

Frank and Smoki decided the time had come to get Blaikie out of the agency and thought it would be easier to relocate it than try to remove him from it. To reduce the possibility of a confrontation, they arranged to move the agency lock, stock, and barrel from Commercial Wharf to nearby Lewis Wharf at night.

Invoking his rights under his formal security agreement with Ed, Frank wrote Blaikie that he was acting to "exercise dominion to preserve and protect" his assets and interest in the agency. James Blaikie would not have a key to the new location.

On November 7, Frank sent a letter by certified mail to Blaikie's Brookline address. The transfer of the agency to Lewis Wharf went off without incident that night and Frank posted a copy of his letter on the door of the former Commercial Wharf offices.

Blaikie responded the following day by paying an excited visit to the agency secretary at her Boston apartment. With Patricia Haskell was her six-foot five-inch sweetheart, Ron Beal. To a perplexed James Blaikie, Pat pleaded complete ignorance about the Bacon family's actions. Beal, an amiable giant, shook his head with a look of sympathetic puzzlement about the goings-on, and Blaikie left Pat's apartment in a dark mood.

At the insistence of Sergeant Detective Maillet, Pat was to telephone him if Blaikie ever showed up at the new location of the Bacon agency.

Jim did not come to the agency that day. Instead, he did a repeat performance of his October caper and picked up the New England Nuclear Corporation's November check. He deposited the client's $6,372 in the Bacon–Blaikie account and again wrote checks to his own account. For the second month in a row, the Texas insurance company was not going to receive New England Nuclear's premium payment.

Again, the maneuver went unnoticed at the Bacon agency.

On November 11, Frank Bacon brought a photocopy of the Kemper change-of-beneficiary form to Elizabeth McCarthy, a Boston handwriting specialist recommended by Zal Davlin. At her Court Street office near the old State House, Frank also handed over to the elderly and dignified woman several of Ed's signed and canceled Harbor National Bank checks. She asked him nothing about the questioned document or his reason for wanting the apparent signature of Edwin C. Bacon examined. As the Vassar and New England Law School graduate would say in her lectures at Harvard and other law schools, she told Frank she believed the "collateral issues" in a case were immaterial to a handwriting expert.

Observing that the handsome young man appeared

very anxious, Ms. McCarthy told Frank she would have a preliminary opinion for him within two weeks and their brief meeting ended.

She was as good as her word and on Monday, November 25, Frank received her report in the mail. His eyes raced down the one-page letter to the key section. "I do see in the questioned signature a slow, hesitating writing line which is one of the common earmarks of forgery. In contrast to this slowly drawn line, Mr. Bacon has a very quick, sharp slim writing line."

She added that if the original of the beneficiary form were provided her, she would be able to give a final opinion on its signature.

Slapping the report with the back of his hand, Frank thought, *Well, Mr. Blaikie, we seem to be a step closer to figuring out exactly what in the hell is going on.* He telephoned Zal Davlin, told him of Ms. McCarthy's tentative finding, and asked Zal to get the original of the document from Kemper.

Davlin learned Kemper had contracted a handwriting analyst who was examining it. When he had finished, Kemper would send it to Davlin.

He did not have to wait long. The week after Thanksgiving, Zal heard from Kemper that its expert had reached a conclusion.

Donald Doud of Milwaukee, Wisconsin, once chairman of the document section of the American Academy of Forensic Sciences, had examined purported Edwin C. Bacon signatures on both sides of the Kemper form. The "Edwin C. Bacon" on side A was clear; the one on side B, where a signature was not necessary, had been "partially blocked out by lateral applications of a fibre tip pen," Doud wrote in his November 26, 1974 report to Kemper.

He explained that when a transparency of the signature on side A was superimposed over the signature on side B, "the two signatures appear as one." Terming them "unnaturally similar," he said that "the hand is not like a printing press that stamps out identical signatures time after time, and this unnatural sameness between two signatures is compelling evidence of forgery by tracing.''

Furthermore, he reported, the genuine specimens of Edwin C. Bacon signatures provided by the Bacon family ''differ significantly from those on the questioned application.''

Doud concluded that ''the evidence is strong that Edwin C. Bacon did not sign his name to either Side A or Side B of the questioned Application for Change of Policy.''

That day, another handwriting report was issued. An Arlington, Massachusetts graphoanalyst consulted by James Blaikie's attorney wrote that the Kemper form had been signed by Edwin Bacon.

Teresa M. Sacco, an examiner of questioned documents, said she found ''all the known habits of Edwin C. Bacon'' in the beneficiary-change signature. She focused on the capital letters *E* and *C* and the small letters *a, c,* and *n,* finding them consistent with known specimens of his signature.

''It is my opinion,'' Ms. Sacco concluded, ''that the writer of the disputed document and all the documents used for comparison were all written by the same hand, namely Edwin C. Bacon.''

To Sergeant Detective Maillet the Bacon and Blaikie experts canceled each other out, but the forgery conclusion reached by the Kemper handwriting analyst bolstered his suspicions about Blaikie. Ogden Security analysis indicated none of the latent fingerprints on the metal cyanide container matched a copy of Ed Bacon's fingerprints.

''A man about to end it all takes pains to keep his fingerprints off the can of poison,'' he said to Detective Tom Cashman. ''Then he spoons cyanide into his coffee and puts it where? Not in the filing cabinet, because it wasn't there two days later. But it is three weeks later.''

''And why does he want to hide the cyanide anyway?'' Cashman joined in at the homicide unit. ''If he wrote the note, he sure wasn't trying to hide the fact he killed himself.''

"Yeah, Tom. The note. He clutches it as he's dying, falls on it and it's barely wrinkled? We've got to have that paper checked for fingerprints. I think the FBI ought to have a look at the note and the Kemper form."

While Detective Cashman sought an exemplar of Alma Blaikie's handwriting from her former neighbors, Sergeant Detective Maillet got specimens of Bacon's handwriting from his widow. Getting a sample of Blaikie's handwriting also turned out to be no problem.

Checking by telephone with Brookline police, Maillet learned they had no criminal record on Blaikie, but they did have a file on him containing his 1971 application for a hackney license. Blaikie had hand printed the information and signed it.

The Brookline police promised a contented Sergeant Detective Maillet it would be sent to him.

Detective Cashman scored with greeting cards from friends of Alma Blaikie's.

If the Bacon case was a homicide, it involved a major insurance company, a disputed document, and a questionable suicide note. The paper trail was crucial and that meant lawyers and Maillet wanted an assistant district attorney in on it from the beginning. This was no murder for money in a cash register.

Early in December he had his material together and decided to drop in on a young Suffolk County prosecutor whose work he liked. In the cigar-cured domain of the district attorney's offices at the courthouse in Pemberton Square, Maillet's choice was no gentleman. However, twenty-eight-year-old Alice E. Richmond, a magna cum laude graduate of Cornell University two years out of Harvard Law School, was an assistant district attorney on her way up.

Moreover, along with Boston College Law School graduate Fran Burns, Richmond was among the few female prosecutors in the country dealing with violent crime. The reason was venerable Suffolk County District Attorney Garrett Byrne. For more than a decade he had been in the forefront nationally among district attorneys, promoting women to front-line positions. Asked why by a *Boston Herald* reporter, he had once chuckled at the question and replied: "They are tops—dedicated, aggressive and efficient," and, "they work like hell."

Sixteen months into her job, smart and stylish Alice Richmond was known for finishing up twelve-hour days that had started in the morning with trials on assault, rape, and murder cases.

The transplanted New Yorker was in her cramped office with a scenic view of a brick wall.

"Counselor," Maillet said at her office doorway. "How's by you?"

"Good, Sergeant," she said, with a pretty smile. A long-haired blonde with confident blue eyes, she repeated his old-time Boston greeting. "And how's by you?"

"Good, good. I've been working on the strangest damned case." He tapped the folder under his arm. "Have you got a minute to talk about it?"

"Sure, John, have a seat and tell me all about it."

As he outlined the case, from the discovery of Bacon's body to the suspected forgery of the insurance form, her eyebrows rose more than once. She looked back and forth at the photocopies of the nearly identical purported suicide notes.

"As you say, John, strange," she said at last. "What's this Blaikie like?"

"Smart, smart-ass, or both, depending on who you talk to. Champagne taste on a beer budget, if that. Big house in Brookline. Pretty wife."

"How does she figure in this?"

"She doesn't, as far as anyone can tell. People who know them think he's afraid of losing her and plays big shot to keep her."

"What's he up to now?"

"Well, he got broomed out of the Bacon agency last month and Tom Cashman and I can't see where he's bringing in any money."

Richmond agreed he should request an FBI analysis of the papers and handed them back to him.

"Keep me up to date on this, will you, John?"

He got up from his chair. "I will, counselor," he

said, raising his hand in farewell. He left satisfied that if this can of worms ever headed for the grand jury, he'd have an assistant DA up to speed on it.

With Christmas three weeks off, another matter of life and death weighed on John Maillet. After three-and-a-half years of gradual deterioration, the condition of his cancer-stricken wife, Colette, had sharply worsened. At her request she was at St. Elizabeth's Hospital on the city's west side. Their daughters—Michelle, a nursing student; Colette, in high school; and Kathleen, an elementary schooler—despaired of a house without their mother, but, soldierly, they accepted the necessary. With their father they were bracing for the end.

Chapter 12

Weeks before Christmas 1974, James Blaikie was running on empty. No longer with the Bacon agency, he was receiving calls from irate creditors at his Brookline residence. It was the only major possession he was not in immediate danger of losing. He was three months in arrears on his car payments and four months behind on a $12,000 loan, among other debts at the Harbor National Bank in Boston. Three parties were demanding the Kemper insurance check for $50,000—the bank, the Bacon family, and James Blaikie. His attorney was not hopeful about getting the money soon and his claim against the Bacon agency was getting nowhere.

Blaikie again turned to longtime friend César David DeWilde for help.

With smoldering good looks, the long-haired and bearded DeWilde bore a striking resemblance to the late rock idol Jim Morrison of The Doors in his hirsute days. At twenty-seven, DeWilde was the age Morrison had been when the singer died, reportedly of a heart attack, in 1971. A sinewy six-footer, DeWilde did nothing to discourage superficial comparisons with the creator of *Light My Fire*, *L.A. Woman*, and *The End*, which were still popular three years after Morrison's death, and were destined to remain so.

DeWilde and Blaikie had gotten to know each in the late 1960s through DeWilde's then fiancee, Ruth Whitney. Ruth was going to Northeastern with Kathy Goodrow and her popular fraternity boyfriend, James

Blaikie. The couples occasionally double-dated. Politically liberal Jim Blaikie and free-spirited David DeWilde saw eye to eye on issues that were tearing the nation apart, personal liberty among them.

Jim and Kathy were married in 1968, the year of his graduation; Ruth and David the following year.

The DeWildes and Blaikies continued their friendship, and David's estimation of Jim only grew as the McGovern campaign official spoke of being a partner in the Bacon agency. The image was bolstered by Jim's Bacon–Blaikie stationery, modish attire, and, especially, his air of confidence.

In the summer of 1973, the DeWildes joined the Blaikies for a cruise out of Boston Harbor on Jim's thirty-foot Pearson sloop, and the picture of affluence was complete.

David DeWilde's friendship with James Blaikie outlasted his marriage to the woman who had introduced them.

The following spring, David and Ruth divorced, but he remained close to their five-year-old daughter, Paris. She often stayed in a charming room he had appointed for her in his Brighton apartment. When she was with her mother, he telephoned nightly to hear her voice and be certain she knew he was thinking of her.

Following his family's tradition of higher education, the Florida-born DeWilde had attended college but foreign cars were his passion. He had turned it into a thriving auto repair business in Brighton.

With its minimal rents and like amenities, the unpretentious neighborhood on the city's west side was a mecca for a waning counter-culture. Dope for every appetite was still as available on or off the street as organic food and antique clothing were in converted "straight" stores.

David DeWilde led an extraordinarily directed life in this milieu of aimless vanities. Some around him were acid-tripping to the nearest psychiatric ward or setting out with a trust fund to found a new religion in the Yucatan. But DeWilde was his own man and making a good living. In an era when most mechanics did not own metric tools and called the Toyota a "Toy," he always had an imported car waiting for a hairline tuneup or seamless body repairs.

Ironically, the hip DeWilde was partial to Brooks Brothers suits when he dressed up while straight-looking James Blaikie affected a modish look. Incongruous as the pair seemed to mutual friends, DeWilde in December 1974 was again contemplating a loan to Blaikie, for a considerable amount. When DeWilde casually told a close friend that Blaikie wanted to borrow some serious money, she advised him against it simply because she did not think it a good idea to loan money to friends. But DeWilde ignored the advice and loaned Blaikie $6,000, which Jim was supposed to repay by February.

Blaikie's Christmas spirit was steadily improving.

The morale of the Bacon family received no such boost. Instead, developments before the holiday only deepened their alarm.

Searching for a carton of company records, a book-keeper employed part time by the Bacon agency came across something peculiar in the storage room behind the agency's former quarters on Commercial Wharf. He was looking for records inadvertantly left behind in the November move.

What he found gave him pause.

Stuffed between two of many corrugated cardboard boxes was a bundle of what seemed to be navy blue woolen fabric. Lifting it, he saw it was a blazer rolled up in a ball. Such a jacket had belonged to Ed Bacon and the bookkeeper wondered what on earth it was doing there. Then he felt a tad queasy and quickly left the building, carrying the article as he had found it.

At the agency's new location on nearby Lewis Wharf, Smoki Bacon immediately recognized the Brooks Brothers blazer as Ed's. She had assumed officialdom in all its secret wisdom was holding onto anything Ed had left behind in the office. But it had been behind his office, not in it.

In the inside left breast pocket was his appointment book with meetings scheduled beyond the date of his death. In the right outside pocket was his set of keys, including those for the house and their cars.

Like Smoki, Frank considered it utterly absurd to imagine that Ed had gone out of the agency to the storage room in back, rolled up his blazer, and stashed it between some boxes. For what conceivable reason?

In a telephone conversation with Sergeant Detective Maillet, Frank said as much. "My brother didn't give a damn about business, Sergeant, but he was so fastidious about his clothes, they could go back in the window at Brooks Brothers. If you ask me, Blaikie hid the blazer before he poisoned Ed. He was in a hurry to separate Ed from his car keys."

"In case the poison didn't kick all the way in," Maillet said, "and your brother started thinking about getting to a hospital."

"Exactly, Sergeant," Frank said. "The wharf is out of the way and deserted at night. But whatever the reason, the blazer was back there with the boxes, five months after Ed's death."

"Because Blaikie was afraid he might be seen removing it."

"Yes," Frank said. "For all he knows, a police officer will be there the next night or the next, waiting for him to come waltzing out of the building with Ed's blazer."

Maillet and Frank agreed Blaikie would have had a problem getting the blazer back inside the office after Ed had perished. His body had been pressing against the door.

"Blaikie might have thought of tossing the blazer in through the crack in the door," Frank said. "But wouldn't it look strange lying there in the morning? A man poisons himself and carries a suicide note *and* a blazer to his death?"

"Yeah," Maillet said. "In fact, that blazer in a heap on the floor might get a cop thinking it was the sign of a disturbance."

"The last thing a killer wants a cop thinking."

"Especially," Maillet said, "when he wants the cop thinking suicide, from start to finish."

After his conversation with Sergeant Maillet, Frank could not get the position of Ed's body out of his mind—the head against the door near the middle, the body stretched almost straight back. Given the six-inch opening in the door, Frank figured someone reached through it and slipped the so-called suicide note under the chest area of the body. Could the portly Blaikie have done it, he wondered, or had a thinner accomplice planted the note?

The second unseasonably cheerless revelation came in a bombshell of a telephone call to the Bacon agency the week before Christmas. An executive of the New England Nuclear Corporation, the agency's largest client, grumbled to Patricia Haskell that he had just received an incredible message from the Republic National Insurance Company of Texas. New England Nuclear was two months in arrears on its employee group insurance premium. In October and November, he said, New England Nuclear issued the Bacon agency two checks totaling $12,600. They had come back cashed, the client huffed, and he wanted to know at once how it was the agency had not forwarded insurance payments to Texas.

A shocked Pat Haskell mustered a businesslike voice and promised to find out what had happened. She immediately telephoned the withering news to the Bacons. Alerted by Smoki, Zal Davlin brought it to the attention of Sergeant Detective Maillet and then called New England Nuclear. He explained to the executive that the agency had been in disarray since Ed's death and he was looking into the missing money. Accounts were so fouled up, he confided, there was no telling when the matter could be cleared up.

A personal friend of Ed's, the executive was understanding.

The only good news, by default, came days before Christmas in the final report of Elizabeth McCarthy, the handwriting expert hired by the Bacons. Confirming her earlier finding, she wrote, "It is my opinion that Edwin C. Bacon did not sign his name on the Change of Beneficiary form" and "that the signature is therefore a forgery."

The evening of December 20, the Maillet girls left their mother's room at St. Elizabeth Hospital and John stayed with her until she had fallen asleep under medication shortly after nine o'clock.

He was on duty that cold, wet night and quickly found himself involved in three homicide investigations, one of which resulted in his arresting a suspect. At his office, he worked until dawn, typing up his reports of the previous night's mayhem.

At seven o'clock that gray morning his wife's sad eyes came to mind and he thought he'd better call the hospital. A nurse suggested he drive out.

At St. Elizabeth's half an hour later, he was in his wife's room. He held the hand of sweet Colette Mullaney, kid sister of his buddy growing up in Roslindale, a sturdy neighborhood on Boston's far south side. Then he kissed her goodbye.

She had passed away in her sleep at the age of forty-six.

James Blaikie dressed up as Santa Claus for David's daughter, cheerfully admitting he did not need a pillow to achieve his convincing look.

Two days after a solemn Christmas, Smoki Bacon received word from Zal Davlin of the Kemper insurance company's decision on the contested $50,000 check.

"The good news, Smoki," Davlin said over the telephone, "is that Kemper is not sending the money to Jim Blaikie and they're suing him."

"Zal, why do I get the feeling the bad news is going to be much worse than the good news?"

"Because you're right. Kemper is not sending the money to you either, and they are suing you."

Following a silence, Smoki said, "Zal, I must have lost my sense of humor somewhere along the way."

"Well, you better find it in a hurry," Davlin said firmly, "because what I'm saying is Kemper is trying to wash its hands of the whole matter. They're seeking a restraining order in Suffolk Superior Court to prevent you and James Blaikie and his bank from going after them for the money. They also want the court to order you to fight it out among yourselves."

"Zal, how can they do that?" Smoki said, her voice rising. "I mean Kemper's own handwriting expert said that beneficiary-change was a forgery. Kemper approves my husband's death warrant, and now they're saying we can't even go after them for the money. We've got to go to court against Blaikie?"

"You've got it, Smoki. Kemper's position is that it was reasonably sure the signature was Ed's. Until, of course, he was dead and their handwriting expert said otherwise."

"For god's sake, Zal, you can't go into a bank to cash a five-dollar check without having your signature verified. And Kemper is saying they don't have to verify signatures involving thousands of dollars in insurance? That means anybody with a life insurance policy in this country is liable to have someone forge their name and kill them. That's crazy."

Zal Davlin chuckled angrily. "Why do you think there are more and more cases where the murderer finagled insurance the victim knew nothing about?"

"Yes, Zal, I've read about it. Another one of those things that happen to the proverbial someone else."

But Kemper was rubbing more salt in her wounds as far as she and Zal Davlin were concerned. The company was also requesting of the court that its legal expenses connected with the lawsuit be paid out of the insurance benefits.

"Great," Smoki said, almost able to laugh. "I'm paying Kemper to sue me over money that legally belongs to me and the girls. Then I have to battle in court with Blaikie over who the money belongs to. Is this what is meant by the security of life insurance and American justice?"

In a soothing voice Zal assured her that his answer

to the Kemper lawsuit would include the counter-claim that the beneficiary change was forged. He would not hazard a prediction on the outcome of the case but counseled her to keep up her spirits.

On the Friday of the first week of a dreary new year, widower John Maillet received the FBI laboratory report on the Edwin Bacon and Alma Blaikie papers. Reflecting the ambiguity of the case, it was another split decision.

Of the Kemper beneficiary-change application, the FBI wrote:

> It was determined that the Edwin C. Bacon signature is a forgery and was not written by EDWIN C. BACON.

However, regarding Bacon's putative note "I CAN'T STAND IT ANYMORE," the report was inconclusive, stating:

> It was not determined whether any of the hand printing was prepared by either EDWIN C. BACON or JAMES BLAIKIE, JR., because of the presence of hand printing characteristics that could not be explained on the basis of the limited amount of hand printing available for comparison. It was found that the hand printing is more consistent with the characteristics of BACON and more inconsistent with the hand printing characteristics of BLAIKIE. It is further pointed out that the hand printing appears to be a very normal hand printing and contains no evidence of disguise, distortion, or forgery.

About the note "I can't stand how I am anymore," found by Waltham police in front of Alma Blaikie's body, the FBI concluded:

> It was not determined whether any of the handwriting was prepared by either JAMES F. BLAIKIE, JR., or ALMA BLAIKIE, because of the lack of sufficiently significant characteristics. The handwriting

characteristics present suggest that the handwriting may have been prepared by ALMA BLAIKIE. The handwriting is also very normally written and contains no evidence of distortion or disguise.

On Maillet's mental scorecard, the conclusive FBI finding on the insurance form was a home run. However, the inconclusive finding on the so-called suicide notes was one for the umpires to rule on if the case ever got before a jury.

The report ended with the note that the findings of a fingerprint examination of the Bacon and Blaikie papers were to follow under separate cover.

That afternoon Sergeant Detective Maillet apprised the district attorney's office of the FBI report and mentioned he had talked about the case with Alice Richmond. The assistant DA in charge of assignments asked her to look into it. Maillet supplied her with a copy of his file.

The following week Richmond met with Frank Bacon in what seemed to him a large closet of an office. Surprised by her young age and even younger appearance, Frank wondered if she were the best or merely the only available prosecutor for the nagging Bacon case. However, appreciating any action at all, he concealed his doubts behind a cordial and trusting expression.

As she succinctly laid out what she saw as the strengths and weaknesses of a murder scenario, his concern vanished. There was obvious intelligence glittering in the eyes across the desk from him. *This woman is top drawer,* he thought to himself.

"What do you make of the case?" he asked.

"Gut reaction?"

"Yeah."

"I think the FBI report on the insurance form is *very* incriminating. Do the inconclusive report on the suicide note and the medical examiner's suicide ruling help Blaikie? You bet they do. To convict him of first-degree murder, a jury has to believe beyond a reasonable doubt that your brother did not write that note or was duped into writing it. Somehow wrote it with no intention of killing himself.'' The index fingers of her clasped hands went to her pursed lips.

''And the magically appearing can of cyanide and Ed's blazer.''

She leaned back. ''Defense will argue lots of people had access to the office, Mr. Bacon.''

''Frank,'' he said.

''Alice,'' she responded.

''Alice, do my wandering eyes deceive me or is that the medical examiner's report on your desk?''

''Your eyes don't deceive you. Haven't you seen it?''

His dry laugh ended with a sneer. ''They have shown us *nothing* and told us not much more.''

She handed him the file. When he got to the autopsy findings, he began chuckling. Alice thought for an awful moment he might be having a hysterical reaction to the starkly clinical analysis of his brother's earthly remains.

''This is remarkable,'' he said, looking up with a sardonic grin. ''You'd have to have known Ed to appreciate it. The man was an absolute hypochondriac. One skip of a heartbeat, one twinge in his side and he was sure he was suffering from some terminal illness. But according to this,'' Frank said, weighing the report, ''he was in perfect health. Except, of course, for the ravages of cyanide.''

Relieved he was in control, Alice Richmond smiled sympathetically.

All traces of irony disappeared from Frank's face, though, as he looked over the several photographs of his brother lying face down on the floor of his office. Closing the folder and placing it on Richmond's desk, Frank looked away. ''Alice,'' he said in a soft voice, ''if someone did this to my brother, I want him to pay for it.''

She paused and said, ''Frank, I can promise you I'll do whatever can be done to find out what happened and act accordingly.''

He responded with a vulnerable smile. ''You know

something, Alice, I believe you will, and that is all I am asking.''

She did not say so but he struck her as a man of his word.

Later in January, at the new location of the Bacon agency on Lewis Wharf, secretary Patricia Haskell was once again stunned by a chance finding. Finishing up the task of organizing papers and accessories brought there from Commercial Wharf two months before, she got to a box filled with the contents of James Blaikie's former desk. Since he had been kept in the dark about the move, he had not had the chance to remove his things. They had been packed and taken from the old office with everything else.

In the box she found something upsetting. It was an ordinary white scratch pad, but on several pages ''Edwin C. Bacon'' had been hand written over and over again.

Informed of the discovery, Sergeant Detective Maillet had still another request to make of FBI handwriting experts: to determine, if possible, who had repeatedly written Bacon's name as though practicing his signature.

Chapter 13

Early in January, Smoki Bacon and Zalman Davlin responded to the Kemper lawsuit. As cotrustees of her late husband's estate, they denied the validity of Ed's signature on the beneficiary change and demanded Kemper pay the $50,000 in benefits to Smoki and her daughters.

David DeWilde was also preoccupied with a financial matter involving James Blaikie.

The year started out well enough with this odd couple—hip DeWilde and straight Blaikie, in the facile terms of the day. David and his attractive friend Judith Fillippo, an artist for a Boston-area greeting card company, had an enjoyable outing with Jim and Kathy Blaikie at the dogtrack in Seabrook, New Hampshire, early in January. The foursome did not do badly with two-dollar long-shot bets, and everyone seemed in good spirits.

Apart from Jim and Kathy for a moment, David took the opportunity to tell Judith how pleased he was that she seemed to get along well with the Blaikies. He considered them good friends and he thought it would be a good idea if she asked Kathy out to lunch sometime.

David might have been less congenial had he known just how shaky his friend's financial and legal condition was.

On Thursday, January 9, Assistant District Attorney Alice Richmond got on Blaikie's paper trail. If Ed Bacon had been murdered, his death was about money.

She telephoned the Boston bank where she knew Blaikie had pledged Bacon's Kemper policy as loan collateral and deposited the New England Nuclear checks. Blaikie's loan officer at the bank was indignant about her inquiries concerning a client, and she informed him a subpoena for Blaikie's records would be forthcoming. After the conversation, she imagined the bank would call Blaikie and shake his tree but good.

She figured right. The loan officer picked up the phone, reached Blaikie, and told him about the call from Alice Richmond. He demanded Blaikie come in the following Monday for a serious discussion about his overdue accounts.

Whether or not David DeWilde was aware of Jim's banking problems, he told Judith nothing of them in a telephone conversation on the morning of January 10th. However, he seemed to her a changed person, irritable and aloof. She could not remember his acting that way in the year she had known him. She asked what was troubling him and he grumbled that he wanted to be left alone.

In the afternoon he called her at work with an apology but soon became agitated and upset again. She was too confused and hurt by his mercurial behavior to see him that night.

The following day, a Saturday, they met by chance in Harvard Square, where she was shopping with her roommate, and they talked in his car. He mumbled something about a deal that was heavier than he had thought it would be. He said he did not want her involved in it in any way. Her impression was that he was frightened.

That evening at his Brighton apartment he brusquely announced it was time they stopped seeing each other. She left on the verge of tears and when she reached home, the telephone was ringing. It was David, begging her to return, and, although she thought better of it, she went back to his apartment.

On Sunday morning, January 12th, an extremely nervous and visibly shaken David DeWilde paced his apartment and told Judith he was increasingly worried about his financial arrangement with Blaikie. DeWilde was no longer referring to it as a loan but vaguely as a "deal," a deal involving as much as $12,000 of his money.

He received two telephone calls from Jim that morning, but Judith noticed that the conversations did nothing to improve David's mood. The couple had been invited to the Blaikies' to watch the Super Bowl game between the Pittsburgh Steelers and the Minnesota Vikings, but did not go. That night Judith and DeWilde went to dinner at the ardently funky restaurant in the Orson Welles Theatre complex near Harvard Square in Cambridge, but he was too upset to eat. Inconsolable, he said he feared the deal with Blaikie had gone wrong, terribly wrong, and he grimly foresaw a financial disaster in his future.

Within a matter of minutes, he was alternately affectionate and hostile, telling her they were finished one moment and, in the next, asking her to marry him. She tried to ignore his mood swings, hoping in an instant he would become the lovable man who had just as quickly vanished.

On Monday, January 13th, James Blaikie had a tension-filled conversation with the loan officer at his bank. He gave Jim an ultimatum. His arrearage on four loans, totaling $21,000, would no longer be tolerated and if he did not immediately bring them up to date, they would be called. Two of the loans were for the Blaikies' cars. At the same time, a credit company was looking for three months' payments on the couple's Yamaha grand piano, and the January installment on the sailing sloop was overdue.

That evening David DeWilde received two telephone calls at his apartment and he perked up considerably. He hugged Judith and told her he thought everything was going to be all right with Blaikie and the money after all. All smiles, he told her he would make a lot of money and take her on a trip to Jamaica.

Judith stayed the night and the next morning, Tuesday, January 14th, dawned brutally cold. She left for work in her car and around eleven-thirty that morning telephoned David at his shop, a rented bay in a commercial garage. He said he was going to meet with Blaikie for lunch and expected to get his money then. But to Judith, David sounded far from relieved. Rather, there was anxiety in his voice again. He said he did not expect anything to go wrong, but if it did, he might not see her that evening. They could meet later. Hesitantly, he said something that she did not think was funny—he wondered aloud if he would return from his luncheon engagement.

Around 12:15 P.M. DeWilde received a call from James Blaikie and, after hanging up, appeared joyous. To a friend at the garage, who was aware of the troublesome deal, DeWilde announced, "He's got it, man. Jimmy's got it!"

Five minutes later, DeWilde was playing nickel poker with friends when he got another call at the shop. On the phone he said, "Oh, you want me to come over there? O.K."

After winning the game and scooping up a few bucks in change, DeWilde left the garage shortly before twelve-thirty P.M. It was a ten-minute drive southwest from gritty Brighton to dignified Fisher Hills in Brookline.

The tall shrubbery in front of Blaikie's looming gray house was spidery in the miserly winter light. David DeWilde turned into the driveway.

At Boston police headquarters that January afternoon, Sergeant Detective John Maillet had in his possession the FBI Laboratory report on the fingerprint analysis of the alleged Edwin Bacon suicide note and the Kemper beneficiary-change form. The FBI on January 10th had written Maillet that "no latent prints of value for identification purposes were developed on the specimens."

The results on the insurance form were not surprising to him. Whether or not Bacon had signed it, it was not the kind of paper a person was going to clutch. But the lack of fingerprints on the unwrinkled so-called suicide note was another matter. Bacon supposedly held it and fell on top of it in the final convulsive moments of his life, if suicide were believable. Add in a can of cyanide without Bacon's fingerprints, Maillet thought, Ed's rolled-up blazer in a storage room behind the Bacon agency, and an FBI-certified forgery of an insurance document.

At the Bacon agency on Lewis Wharf the afternoon of January 14th, Smoki was once more feeling the effects of her husband's death. And the sheer sense of loss was not helped by the sorry spectacle of his business going under. No matter how she and Pat Haskell, a goodhearted trooper, pored over accounts and stretched them, it did not seem likely that the firm was going to make it through the winter.

Continuing to work mornings as a graphic artist at Bolt Beranek and Newman in Cambridge, Smoki was spending her afternoons at the agency but taking no money out of it. There was none to be had.

As to Ed's own insurance, the Kemper policy was in limbo, but she was expecting payment soon on the two other policies totaling $200,000. Frank and the other trustee of Ed's inheritance exercised their discretionary powers in accordance with the late Pauline Bacon's guidelines and were paying some of the household expenses on Fairfield Street.

Looking at immediate agency expenses, a disheartened Smoki Bacon saw a payment for workmen's compensation was due that week and, of course, salaries for Pat Haskell and their part-time bookkeeper. The income column indicated the agency was going to be in the hole again that month.

Smoki was chillingly haunted, as she had often been since Ed's death, by terrible recollections of a poverty-stricken childhood. In these moments she actually felt like the girl in the tenements, surviving on handouts from Back Bay Brahmins.

Around two o'clock that afternoon, James Blaikie arrived at the Sea & Surf Restaurant in suburban Framingham, thirteen miles west of Brookline. He joined

Kathy at a table where she had been for two hours and had finished eating. He had a couple of drinks.

That afternoon David DeWilde did not return to his shop in Brighton and he did not make his nightly telephone call to his daughter, Paris.

The little girl and her mother were surprised.

The following morning, a worried Ruth DeWilde called her former husband at a Brighton number that rang at both his apartment and his auto repair shop. There was no answer. She telephoned a mechanic at the shop adjacent to David's and learned of his scheduled meeting with Jim Blaikie the previous afternoon. She telephoned Jim several times before noon and got his answering machine.

Unbeknownst to her, James Blaikie was making an $800 cash payment against his arrearage at his bank in Boston. His loan officer had been on the verge of calling in his loans since their heated discussion two days before.

After hearing from Ruth, David's fifty-four-year-old mother became concerned about him. Patricia Wynn, who had remarried years after the death of his father, drove to Brighton from her suburban home and called on David's landlady. The two women entered David's apartment on the second floor of the frame house and found no one there. Like the rest of the modestly appointed flat, the charming room for his daughter's visits showed no sign of disturbance.

At Boston police headquarters, Pat Wynn was told a young man's overnight absence did not a missing-person case make.

Early in the evening Ruth DeWilde reached James Blaikie by telephone and urgently asked if he knew David's whereabouts.

"Oh, I haven't seen him," Blaikie said. "Why, is he missing?"

"Gee, you're the last person that I can trace him to," Ruth said. "I can't seem to make David go any further than your house."

"David did come here on Tuesday," Jim said

calmly. According to Blaikie, DeWilde had paid a brief visit about an auto insurance matter. Jim had left his keys in his car at Coolidge Corner, the account continued, and David had given him a lift to the popular Brookline shopping and entertainment center. After dropping him off, David had driven north on Harvard Street, toward Brighton, Jim said.

Still unable to locate her former husband, Ruth called Jim Blaikie again two hours later and pressed for details.

Sounding impatient, he said, "I locked my keys in my car at Coolidge Corner so I had to go back to my house and get a spare set. So I called Dave and told him to come to my house about the registration paper."

"Then what happened?"

"Well, he came over."

"Well, what then? Did he park out in front or on the side?"

"He parked in the driveway on the side of the house."

"Then what?" she asked anxiously.

Jim repeated his earlier story and added that he thought David was going to visit a friend.

The conversation ended with Blaikie promising in a helpful tone to let Ruth know as soon as he should hear from David again.

For the second evening in a row, DeWilde called neither his daughter, Judith Fillippo, nor his mother. The telephone at his apartment continued to go unanswered.

The Bacons, who had no knowledge of David DeWilde, did not know that James Blaikie's friend was missing. DeWilde's family and friends were similarly unaware of the Bacon affair. In response to Patricia Wynn's information, the *Boston Globe* ran a short article on the disappearance of her son. Otherwise, nothing about either case was reported in any of the Boston news media, for neither officially involved a crime. If any journalist did know about them through the grapevine, no one did any reporting on them. The death of a Back Bay man, presumably due to natural causes, was no more newsworthy than the alleged disappearance of a young Brighton man.

However, the Bacon and DeWilde circles were nearing one another in their separate pursuits of James Blaikie.

Assigned to check out the DeWilde disappearance, Brighton detective Thomas Moran at first figured he had one more case of an unpredictable young man who blows town for a week in Atlantic City or Acapulco. A photo of David DeWilde, provided by his family, did nothing to dispel the hunch. The good-looking young man could not have much trouble finding diversions.

The boulder-jawed Moran, a strapping Navy veteran of the Pacific theater in World War II, knew something about youthful wanderlust. He suspected that within days, DeWilde's distraught ex-wife would get a phone call from somewhere south. Mexico or New Jersey. Before anyone knew it, DeWilde would be back in Boston, either broke from the crap tables or laden with Mexican souvenirs for his daughter. That was usually the way vanishing acts ended, harmlessly if not happily.

Meeting David's mother six days after the disappearance, Moran was not surprised to learn DeWilde had not returned. At Brighton District Court, where the detective was testifying in another case, Patricia Wynn told him that her son still had not communicated with anyone.

"He left his shop unlocked and vanished," Pat said with a deeply troubled look. "It just isn't like him, Detective. I feel strongly that he was either kidnapped or murdered."

The forty-six-year-old detective, a brawny six-footer, looked down at the trim and attractive woman in her mid-fifties, and he was struck by the intelligence and intensity in her light blue eyes.

"Mrs. Wynn, I can appreciate your concern," he

said in a soothing voice. The phrase came out *yo-uh con-suhn* in the dialect of his native Dorchester, a section of closely knit neighborhoods and triple-decker houses on Boston's south side. "But I hope you understand it's not unusual for people to take off and come back in a week or so. It happens a lot."

Pat Wynn, a Massachusetts Yankee with a degree in French from Cornell University, did not take her eyes off Moran's. When he had finished, she spoke right up. "Detective, my son's friends tell me he loaned a lot of money, as much as $12,000, to someone he knows. This *friend*, James Blaikie, has a yacht and an expensive house and no income that anyone knows about. Jim admits he saw David the day he vanished and he's the last person who has seen him as far as we know." She said that according to Blaikie, David had arrived at Jim's house in a friend's car. She gave Moran its Massachusetts registration number.

Moran was as impressed by her self-control as much as by her information. She did not strike him as an alarmist, as many in similar situations did.

"I'll tell you what, Mrs. Wynn," he said. "David's been gone less than a week, but I'll look into this as much as I can. And you let me know if you hear anything, will you?"

"I will," she said, brightening a little at his attentiveness. She gave him the telephone numbers of David's former wife and current female friend. Then, looking up at him, she added, "Detective Moran, you won't forget about my son."

It was not a question. "No, I won't," he said. "You have my *wuhd* on it."

Back in the courtroom, waiting for his case to come up, he wondered where he was going to find the time to investigate a case that should take the lowest priority in his workload. Moran figured the time would once again come out of his family life. His wife had already reached sainthood for bringing up their seven children while he worked a detective's hours.

The following morning, Moran visited David's auto repair shop on Cambridge Street in Brighton and saw the gray Volvo described by Pat Wynn parked out front. However, a friend of DeWilde's in an adjacent garage informed Moran that DeWilde had driven away in another car, another Volvo owned by a customer.

Moran put out a revised description of the missing automobile and registration number over the police telex. He also turned for help to a corps of city workers unrivaled for their knowledge of Boston's streets, parking-control officers. Moran chatted up Brighton district meter maids when they gathered in the station that afternoon, asking them to be on the lookout for the missing vehicle.

The first break came later that afternoon, a week after DeWilde's disappearance.

Shortly after four o'clock, Moran received a telephone call from David's attorney. Patricia Wynn had urged him to bring new information about her son to Detective Moran's attention.

The attorney said he learned at David's Brookline bank earlier in the day that his client had not made any deposits or withdrawals from his account since the day of his disappearance. The last time David had been to his safe-deposit box at the bank in Coolidge Corner was the morning of January 10, four days before he vanished.

The vault attendant claimed there was someone with DeWilde who fit the description of James Blaikie.

And DeWilde disappears the following Tuesday, Moran thought to himself. He had the feeling a rodent might be nosing its way out of an alley.

On the phone with Ruth DeWilde, he repeated the description of the man reportedly seen in the bank with David. DeWilde's former wife said it sounded like Blaikie. She had pictures of him.

"Beautiful," Moran said. "I'll be right over."

Following a two-minute drive east to her Linden Street apartment, Moran was soon looking at a photograph of James Blaikie the yachtsman. Except for the smirk, Moran thought, the cherubic face might have come off a church ceiling. In the color snapshot taken by Ruth two summers before, Blaikie was at the helm of his sailboat, and he certainly looked like the sandy-haired person described by the vault attendant at DeWilde's bank.

Also pictured in the cockpit of the boat were David DeWilde and Jim's wife, Kathy, who did not appear at all happy.

The following morning a Brighton meter maid had in mind dear Detective Moran's request to be on the lookout for a 1970 Volvo. For a cop who treated her brigade respectfully, she'd go to bat. Shortly after eight o'clock, she went directly to the short and narrow Brighton Street, where she could have sworn she'd been ticketing a similar car the past week or so. Sure enough, there stood the grime-covered sedan near number 5 Royce Road, one of the brick apartment buildings on the little-traveled street. As she approached the rear of the car she felt a rush of excitement. The registration matched the number given her by Moran.

She hastened half a block north to Commonwealth Avenue, a major crosstown thoroughfare, and telephoned the district police station.

"Detective Moran," she said breathlessly. "I found that Volvo, and all I can tell you is there's no one inside. The trunk I don't know about."

"You're a *dee-uh*," Moran said in a grateful baritone.

Within five minutes the detective was driving up to the car. Royce Road was a mile northwest of Coolidge Corner, the Brookline intersection where Blaikie was saying DeWilde had dropped him off on the afternoon of January 14. The car was parked one and a half miles northeast of James Blaikie's Brookline house.

Moran saw nothing out of the ordinary in the front or rear seats. In cold weather, the lack of telltale odor did not necessarily mean there was no body in the trunk.

He radioed for a tow truck and the car was hauled to the parking lot behind the Brighton station. After forcing open the trunk, he found only a spare tire and assorted tools inside. There was nothing to suggest David DeWilde had ever been in the vehicle.

When Moran telephoned the news to Patricia Wynn, it further confirmed her belief David was dead. If he had not driven off somewhere in the car, how had he gotten away? Moran was agreeing with her more and more.

He briefed his superior officer, Sergeant Detective John Doris, who agreed the case merited further investigation. With every day that passed it was looking less like a kid off on a ramble.

On the telephone with Brookline police, Moran reported finding the missing car and asked what if anything they had on James Blaikie. He learned that Blaikie had no criminal record, but police had an old hackney license application of his. A Boston detective had asked for it the previous month as an exemplar of his handwriting.

When Moran heard it was John Maillet, two thoughts sprang to mind. He and Maillet had worked out of the South End station together years before, and his former bowling teammate was currently in homicide.

Told Maillet was investigating Blaikie in connection with the fatal poisoning of a Boston man, Moran growled, "Sonofabitch. This fuckin' Blaikie sure is the man of the hour."

Two investigations of separate cases involving James Blaikie were about to link up.

At his desk in the homicide unit in late January, John Maillet was surveying material gathered at the chemical supply company where the cyanide found in Bacon's office had been purchased. A receipt showed that not one but two one-pound cans of potassium cyanide had been sold over the counter to "Bacon & Blakey" of Commercial Wharf for a total of $5.25 on July 16, 1974, two weeks before Bacon's death.

Maillet gazed at the photo of James Blaikie from his hackney application and at one of Ed Bacon, supplied by his widow. The salesman at the chemical company had not picked out either one from an array of a half-dozen mug shots.

Later in the day his phone rang and he was talking to Sergeant Detective John Doris of Brighton, Tom Moran's superior. Doris told of the DeWilde investigation crossing the path of the Bacon case at the Brookline Police Department. Doris briefed Maillet on DeWilde's disappearance and the detectives agreed they could well have two murders on their hands. Considering Moran a good cop, Maillet was happy to hear he was working on the DeWilde case. Maillet would stick to the Bacon poisoning.

After hanging up, Sergeant Detective Maillet dialed Alice Richmond. With homicide, Brighton, and Brookline on Blaikie's case, the sonofabitch could crack, Maillet thought. Or he could split.

At his office, Frank Bacon got a call from Alice Richmond, who told him she had just learned something amazing and thought he might find it interesting.

Frank responded, as he did to all adult eagerness, with the Bacon reserve. "Oh, and what's that, Alice?"

"Guess what I just heard?"

"What, Alice?" Frank asked, leaning back in his chair.

"Does the name David DeWilde, a guy from Brighton, mean anything to you?"

"No, Alice, it doesn't," Frank said. "Should it?"

"No, but guess what?"

"What?"

"He's been reported missing and the police are looking for him."

"Hmm." In his experience when Alice Richmond warmed up to a subject, she always had a reason, and he had a feeling this was not going to be an exception.

"And guess who the last known person to see him was?"

Frank had a hunch she was going to say what she did next.

"James Blaikie."

Frank did not sound surprised. "And what was the

money angle this time?'' he asked, adopting his rule of thumb on James Blaikie—he was a threat only if your death was profitable to him.

"Blaikie supposedly owed him as much as twelve thousand dollars."

"There you go," Frank said and he laughed bitterly. "Now I've got a question for you. Can some official somewhere in all his wisdom declare a missing person a suicide?"

"Why do I get the feeling you're being cynical?" she asked.

"Perhaps because I've tried everything else, Alice, and it's the only attitude that makes sense anymore."

Having met David DeWilde's attractive former wife, Moran was further impressed by the quality of the missing man's taste in women when he met Judith Fillippo, also in her late twenties.

At her Brighton apartment eight days after the disappearance, the dark-haired beauty reiterated the alleged Blaikie–DeWilde money connection. She hardly knew James Blaikie, but recalled how upset David had been about a "deal" with him.

She spoke of David's mercurial mood swings in the days before his disappearance. He seemed to her a changed man. One minute he wanted nothing more to do with her and the next he wanted to marry her and set out on a Jamaican honeymoon.

Asked when this behavior started, she told Moran it was the Friday morning before Super Bowl Sunday. She remembered because she had called him at his shop about weekend plans and he had shocked her by saying he was too busy to see her.

Moran silently recalled that as the day Blaikie had been seen with DeWilde at his bank shortly after nine in the morning.

Driving through the bleak January night back to the Brighton station, Moran figured that meeting in the safe-deposit section had been critical. Within three hours of leaving the bank, the lovable David is a changed man, spurning his girlfriend on the telephone.

Something had gone very wrong.

Four days later he doesn't take Judith to Jamaica. He falls off the face of the earth.

The following day, Sergeant Detective John Doris agreed with his Brighton detective that it was time for a heart-to-heart with James Blaikie. Despite suspicions, Moran had no probable cause to suspect a crime had been committed. In his conversations with Blaikie's neighbors, no one knew David DeWilde and no one recalled seeing his car approach or leave Jim's house. Knowing Blaikie could simply tell him to fuck off when he requested a talk, Moran thought he had a sure-fire way to get him into the Brighton station.

"Mr. Blaikie," he said briskly over the telephone. "This is Detective Tom Moran of the Brighton police."

After a moment, James Blaikie pleasantly said, "Yes, Detective. What can I do for you?"

"I'm calling about David DeWilde," Moran said, letting the name sink in.

"Oh?" Blaikie said, sounding surprised.

"Yeah. I am told by Mr. DeWilde's family that you're the last known person to see him, and I'd like to have a talk with you about him. I can go to your house right now." With tongue in cheek, Moran waited for the expected reply.

"No," Blaikie said.

"Well," Moran said, nodding to himself. "You can come down here to the station."

Now was when Blaikie could tell him to take a flying leap, but Jim said, "Yeah, sure. How about if I came to see you there tomorrow, in the afternoon?"

"Fine," Moran said, "I'll be here."

I wonder why, Moran thought, *Mr. Blaikie doesn't want a visit by one of Boston's finest. Maybe he's afraid I'll track something on the carpet.*

The face that greeted James Blaikie at Brighton station shortly after two o'clock on the afternoon of January 24 was not merely rock solid. It announced confrontation.

"Hello, Mr. Blaikie," Moran said coldly as Jim approached him in the cramped detective room. "Have a seat."

Blaikie sat down next to Moran's desk and looked up with the expression of a bored undergraduate.

"Mr. Blaikie, you have come here of your own volition and, as I said on the phone yesterday, I am seeking information concerning one David DeWilde. He has been missing for nearly two weeks, since January 14th. Was he at your house that day?"

Blaikie nodded affirmatively, looking as mystified as anyone. "I know, Detective," he said, "and I want to do what I can to help find him. But as I've told his mother and former wife and others, I haven't seen him since he came to my house and gave me a ride to Coolidge Corner. I'd locked my keys in my car there earlier in the day."

Exuding confidence, Blaikie said that after getting a lift to his car from David, he had driven to the Sea & Surf Restaurant in Framingham, where he had met his wife for lunch around two o'clock.

Staring stone-faced at Blaikie, Moran asked coolly if he knew where DeWilde might possibly have gone after dropping him off. Blaikie repeated that DeWilde had traveled north on Harvard toward Commonwealth Avenue. However, he added that David had a female friend who lived near Ken's Pub, which was on the corner of that Brighton intersection.

"That's interesting, Mr. Blaikie, because we found the Volvo David was driving. It was parked on Royce Road."

Blaikie looked surprised. "Oh, where's that?"

"Behind Ken's Pub," Moran said, allowing skepticism to shape his grin.

Appearing as though it were news to him, Blaikie went off on a discussion of the car, suggesting it was the vehicle David had come to see him concerning insurance papers.

Moran cut him off. "Jim, what's this I hear from Dave's friends about a lot of money you owe him?"

"I don't owe him anything," Blaikie insisted. "I got a loan of several thousand dollars from him last summer but I paid it back."

Moran's gaze locked in on Blaikie's in the ambient drone of voices and the ring of a nearby telephone.

"Thank you for coming in," Detective Moran said at last, getting up from his chair. He meant the words, for he had gotten something out of his first chat with James Blaikie. He had Blaikie saying he didn't owe DeWilde money and DeWilde's friends saying he did. Either several people very close to DeWilde were all wet or Blaikie was lying.

As James Blaikie receded from his view, Moran thought to himself, *That arrogant little bastard killed his friend.* Then Moran thought of Patricia Wynn's imploring eyes and revised his estimation. *He killed a fine lady's son.*

Chapter 14

Geographically, the comfortable suburb of Brookline should have been a section of Boston. However, the birthplace of John F. Kennedy and residence of newly elected Governor Michael Dukakis had never joined the city. Instead it wedged between Boston's Back Bay on the east and Brighton on the west, leaving the two Boston districts connected on the north by a narrow strip alongside the Charles River. Brookline and Brighton police routinely cooperated on cases that began in one jurisdiction and crossed into the other. Working on the DeWilde disappearance, Brighton Detective Moran and Brookline Detective William McDermott were no strangers to each other.

Like Moran, the younger McDermott thought it would be a good idea to pay respects to James Blaikie every chance they had. They did not want him to think police had lost interest in him and his missing buddy.

Late in January, a tall and muscular Detective Billy McDermott moved unhurriedly up the brick steps of the house on Fisher Avenue. He spoke to an amiable James Blaikie on the front portico.

"I was in the neighborhood," McDermott said evenly, "and I thought I'd see if you've heard from David DeWilde at all. Can I come in and have a talk with you?"

Blaikie vaguely shook his head no and said he too was worried about DeWilde, but had no idea where he was.

"Well, Mr. Blaikie, you'll let me know if you hear

from him, won't you?'' Detective McDermott said, letting contempt show in his dimple-producing grin.

"Sure," Blaikie said with the emphatic nod of a helpful citizen.

On the telephone with Detective Moran, McDermott said, "Tom, I'm not so sure David DeWilde ever left Blaikie's place."

"I'm with you on that, Billy," Moran said. He thumbed through his notebook. "DeWilde leaves his garage in Brighton around twelve-thirty, which gets him to Brookline by, say, a quarter to one. Blaikie's saying he met his wife at the Sea & Surf around two. Let's say someone can place him there. That means he had forty-five minutes, tops, to kill DeWilde, dispose of his body, and dump his car in Brighton."

"Which leaves him half an hour to get to Framingham," McDermott said. "The body could be somewhere on his property. Blaikie has around half an acre of enclosed land, but it was hard as rock in the cold weather."

Without sufficient information to get a search warrant, Moran and McDermott decided on the next best thing. They would continue paying as many visits as possible to the Blaikie residence or simply park in front of the house. It was a perfectly legitimate tactic, for Blaikie was admittedly the last known person to have seen DeWilde.

If Blaikie had not already removed David from his property, Moran and McDermott certainly did not want him to do so now. They wanted him to squirm under the pressure of living with the body and they wanted it there when they finally cracked him. The more often he saw one or both detectives or their cars, the less likely he was to risk driving from the house with human remains in the trunk. For all he knew, squad cars would converge on him with lights flashing and sirens shrieking. For all he knew, any time Moran or McDermott climbed the brick stairs to the front door, one of them could be armed with a search warrant.

The police were feeling as much suspense as they imagined Blaikie was.

So were DeWilde's people. Friends of David's, from Yankees to ethnics, upper- to working-class, rallied around his former wife and his mother. Some took to calling Blaikie and demanding to know where David was. Others drove into his driveway, parked, and rattled trash cans. One especially determined youth peered in through Blaikie's windows.

Hearing of his exploit, Pat Wynn said she appreciated his concern about her son but she begged him never to do anything of the dangerous sort again. Blaikie might shoot him as an intruder. She did not want any more casualties than she already counted in this horrible situation. When this friend spoke of a plan to waylay Blaikie and force information out of him, she firmly forbade him to do anything of the sort. She would never countenance abduction or torture for any reason, not even a solution to her son's disappearance. The young man reluctantly promised to honor her moral standards.

Patricia Wynn herself drove to James Blaikie's house and parked in front, hoping she could be seen from an upper-story window. As she sat in the car by the hour, she increasingly felt the presence of her only son, handsome and vivacious as his late father, at her shoulder. Her mind wandered back to her nineteenth year and a 1939 cruise from New York to Cuba with her parents. On board for the return trip she met a dashing Belgian of French descent, César deWilde, fifteen years her senior. A widely traveled engineer, he was returning from an assignment in Costa Rica, supervising the installation of a diesel engine in an irrigation system. Speaking with him, a petite and attractive Patricia Spear appreciated the French she had learned as she never had before. They remained in touch and married in 1943. Four years later César David was born to them. Three years after his birth, the husband and father died of cancer.

Alone where she had never expected to be, doing what she had never imagined doing, Patricia deWilde

Wynn gazed through the wintry half-light at the Blaikie house. David, his father in him, was at her side. He asked, as only a son can ask a mother, to remember him always, but he need not have asked.

No one felt the urgency of cracking the DeWilde case more than Tom Moran. It was like close games he remembered playing as a linebacker on the Dorchester High School football team. Determination rose with every passing second and deep reserves of energy automatically kicked in. But it was not a personal victory he wanted as much as answers for David's family.

Moran wanted a look at DeWilde's safe-deposit box. To justify a request for a search warrant he had the contradiction between DeWilde's friends and Blaikie concerning money. Blaikie denied the debt that others believed he owed DeWilde. But Moran also came across something tangible to present to a judge.

In David's apartment he found a curious manila envelope on the desk beside the telephone.

Five inches by eleven inches, it was empty but there were notations on the outside. Several names and addresses appeared, along with the number of a Delta flight, number 403, from New York to Boston. One of the names was identified as "courier" and another as "buyer."

Checking, Moran found that the only flight 403 Delta ever had was not from New York to Boston but from Chicago to Memphis. No other airline had a New York–Boston flight by that number. A visit to the Back Bay address listed on the envelope determined no one by the name of *Ned Woodman* lived there.

In light of David's repeated references to a *deal* with James Blaikie, the envelope with bogus information struck Moran as odd in the extreme. Some of David's acquaintances were known to police as drug dealers. Referring to $12,000, had David been talking to friends about money he had loaned Blaikie, who claimed to be making a drug connection? Blaikie scores and repays DeWilde, presumably with interest.

Blaikie telephones phony information about a Delta

flight and Ned Woodman to DeWilde, Moran further speculated. David thinks the *deal* is coming down when in reality Blaikie is just setting him up for the kill.

DeWilde's words, after he got off the phone at his garage on January 14 were, *He's got it, man. Jimmy's got it!*

To Moran it all reeked of a murderous con job.

Pat Wynn came into the Brighton station for one of her frequent inquiries about progress in the case. She let slip the fact that she too had been staking out Blaikie's house.

Staring at her with a mixture of concern and admiration, Moran said, "You are one ballsy broad." Immediately he blushed and muttered, "I'm sorry, I forgot I was talking to a lady."

"Tom," she said with a sweet grin, "I consider that a compliment."

Police got a search warrant and on the morning of January 28, Moran met with Brookline detective McDermott at DeWilde's bank in Coolidge Corner.

Moran presented the vault attendant with separate photographs of several men. Among them was Ruth DeWilde's photo of James Blaikie on his boat, with the images of her ex-husband and Jim's wife masked. The attendant immediately picked out Blaikie as the man who had been with David on his last visit to the safe-deposit section.

Moran shot a look at McDermott, who nodded with a humorless smile.

Among the articles they found in the metal box was an ordinary number 10 envelope on which was written:

```
12/12/74
   loaned (6,000) to James Blaikie
      due February 12, 1975
         César David DeWilde
            ($9,000 left)
1/3/75 ($3500.00) deposit (not from J. Blaikie)
```

The envelope was empty.

"And Blaikie denies there was a loan," McDermott said.

Moran looked over the note. "And when you look at these figures, you've got the kind of money David's friends are saying he talked about. A deal with Blaikie involving more than six grand."

Moran said he intended to talk to Sergeant Detective John Doris at the Brighton station about questioning Blaikie again. "As far as I'm concerned, Billy, he's a suspect in the DeWilde case."

On the telephone early the following week, Detective Moran again invited himself to Blaikie's house for a chat and for the second time Jim opted to meet him at the Brighton police station instead. Blaikie said he would appear with an attorney. Moran told him by all means to bring counsel along and asked if Kathy could also join them. Jim said he would discuss the request with his attorney.

However, Blaikie arrived alone at the station on the afternoon of February 6.

"Hi, Jimmy," Moran said coldly and he ushered Blaikie into the detective room. "Where's your attorney?"

"I didn't think I'd need one," Blaikie said with a blasé shrug.

Leaning against the wall behind Moran's desk with his arms folded was Sergeant Detective John Doris. Moran's imposing superior officer did not acknowledge Blaikie's arrival but stared at him impassively. Introducing Doris, Moran sat at his desk and Blaikie took a seat beside it. He had to look to his left to see Moran and up to his right to see Doris.

"Mr. Blaikie, I am investigating the disappearance of David DeWilde," Moran said with an official ring to his statement, "and you are a suspect in the case."

Moran then read an inscrutable James Blaikie the so-called Miranda warning, informing him that he had the right to remain silent, that anything he said could be used against him in court, and that he had a right to an attorney, a public defender if private counsel was unaffordable.

"Do you understand what I just read you?" Moran asked.

Blaikie replied, "Yes."

"Are you willing to talk to us about the case?"

Again Blaikie responded in the affirmative and said, "I want to do everything I can to find David."

A discussion followed in which Blaikie did not veer from his earlier accounts of DeWilde's January 14th visit to his Brookline house.

"When is the last time before the fourteenth you saw Dave?" Moran asked casually.

"At his garage the latter part of the previous week," Blaikie said.

"Are you sure?" Moran asked.

"I'm positive," Blaikie said.

Moran asked if he had gone with DeWilde to his bank on January 10th.

"No," Blaikie said. "I'd been to the bank with him on other occasions, but I'm sure I didn't that day."

Sternly, Moran said, "The vault keeper at the bank identified a picture of you and said you were with David in the vault on Friday the tenth."

Puffing on a cigarette, Blaikie seemed to be plumbing his memory. "I did go with him that day."

"What kind of business did David do there?"

"I don't know."

"You mean you went into that small room with him and didn't see what he did?"

"No, I didn't."

Detective Moran did not conceal his estimation of Blaikie. As he had in their first interview, he asked Blaikie if he owed DeWilde money.

With a weary look, Blaikie repeated, "No. I paid back all my loans and at this time David owes me six thousand."

"Well, Jim," Moran said, "since we talked a few weeks ago, I've talked to Dave's close friends again and they still say you owe him a great deal of money." Getting no response, Moran leaned toward Blaikie. "Jim, I read a note that was in Dave's safe-deposit box," Moran said, consulting his notebook. "It's dated December 12, 1974, and it indicates you owed David six thousand dollars that was going to be due on February twelfth.''

The detectives observed Blaikie color and light another cigarette.

''All right, I lied,'' he said, looking downcast. ''I had a lot of financial problems. I was deeply in debt.''

Noticing Blaikie perspire heavily, Moran looked at Sergeant Detective Doris, who nodded.

Blaikie added, ''I was afraid if I told you I'd be suspected of killing him.''

''Who said he was *dead?*'' Moran shot back, nearly lunging from his chair.

Blaikie recoiled with a look of shock.

Still standing, Sergeant Detective Doris weighed in. ''How do you know he's dead? Right now he's only a missing person.''

Blaikie said he had spoken with David's mother and friends, who had not seen him in three weeks and suspected he was dead.

Pressed by Doris on how DeWilde happened to come to Blaikie's house on January 14th, Jim said, ''I called David at work and told him I had the money I owed him.''

''The six thousand?'' Sergeant Detective Doris asked.

''No,'' Blaikie said, ''a fifty-dollar bet I owed him from the Super Bowl.''

''You mean,'' Doris said with a derisive smile, ''when you called Dave at his auto shop and said you had the money you owed him that you were referring to a fifty-dollar bet and not the six grand?''

''Right,'' Blaikie said.

''That is unbelievable,'' Doris said.

''That's the way Dave was,'' Blaikie said weakly. ''He would always get excited when he was going to get money.''

''Jim,'' Detective Moran said roughly, bringing Blaikie's gaze back to him. ''I'm not talking about the six grand here. I'm talking about an additional twelve grand—that's what transpired at the vault.''

Blaikie shook his head no.

Moran pressed on. "You mean all those friends of David's I talked to are all lying? They tell me he talked about $12,000 or more that he loaned to his friend with the big house in Brookline, with two cars, and how he acted uptight that weekend after the tenth. You're telling me that DeWilde got that excited that Tuesday about fifty bucks on the Super Bowl?"

"Yes," Blaikie said.

The two detectives stared at him.

"Tell me again what happened when Dave DeWilde came to your home on January fourteenth," Sergeant Detective Doris insisted.

Blaikie ran one hand across his damp brow while holding a cigarette in the other and retold his story, unhappily. "He arrived shortly after noon and I paid him the fifty-dollar Super Bowl bet I owed him," he repeated. "I asked him for a ride to the Purity Supreme on Harvard Street where I had left my car with the keys locked in it."

Blaikie had referred to a supermarket in Brighton, which was nearly a mile north of Coolidge Corner, where he had told David's mother and ex-wife and police that DeWilde had dropped him off. Moreover, the supermarket was less than a mile from DeWilde's auto repair shop.

"You mean to tell me," Sergeant Detective Doris said, "the last time you saw Dave was shortly after noon on a busy street in Brookline only a short distance from his place of business?"

"Yes," Jim said.

"Mr. Blaikie, if a complete stranger lured him to a house on Royce Road and murdered him," Doris said, referring to the street where DeWilde's car had been found, "we'd have found the body by now. The only reason to hide the body is to cover the murder."

"Yes," Blaikie said, appearing distracted, "you're right."

"I think you are lying," Doris said heatedly. "I think you killed DeWilde. Not only that, I think you killed your business partner. Tell us where the body is. David's mother won't rest until she knows where the body is. Tell Detective Moran where the body is so the mother will at least get some peace. At least call David's mother. Send an anonymous note stating where the body is.''

Although quivering, Blaikie stuck to his story. He was apparently the last known person to have seen DeWilde but his friend had been alive and well on Harvard Street at the time.

The Brighton detectives ended the questioning and watched an extremely nervous-looking suspect trudge out of the detective room.

''He killed him, all right,'' Moran said.

''Yeah,'' Sergeant Detective Doris said. ''All we need is a body.''

Later that week Moran acquired copies of Blaikie's telephone bills and spotted a Tempe, Arizona number. He recalled DeWilde's friends telling of Blaikie's fondness for the area, where he had traveled several years earlier. Shortly before his disappearance, DeWilde had voiced concern that his purported $12,000 investment might vanish with Blaikie in the desert air.

Moran called the Tempe number and found it belonged to a former Massachusetts resident. He told the detective he and Blaikie had belonged to the same fraternity and remained in touch since college. He insisted he did not know David DeWilde and had no idea where he might be. But he promised to let Moran know if Blaikie got in touch with him again.

Jim's friend did not wait to hear from him. He telephoned Blaikie in Boston and told of Detective Moran's call concerning a missing Boston man by the name of David DeWilde. Jim blithely claimed DeWilde was a friend who had not been paying alimony and had skipped town.

David DeWilde had been missing nearly six weeks when James Blaikie surprised Detective Moran on February 24 by telephoning and requesting a meeting. At the Brighton station the following morning, James Blaikie looked dapper but disturbed when he confronted Moran with a supposedly hypothetical question. "Could I be criminally responsible if I allowed my telephone to be used in a deal," he asked, "if I accepted phone calls from a person and relayed messages to another person, even if I suspected the deal was illegal, and I didn't know anything about the merchandise involved?"

With a dubious look, Moran replied it would be difficult to prosecute anyone without the contraband as evidence. Blaikie somberly asked if they could meet again that afternoon. Moran, fascinated by what he considered a cock-and-bull story, said they could.

At three-thirty Blaikie returned and, smoking a cigarette, told Moran in a confessional tone that DeWilde had asked him to take telephone messages from someone named Ned Woodman. Blaikie claimed to be a middleman in a mysterious deal between DeWilde and Ned. According to Blaikie, he had no idea what the commodity was. He then added another new dimension to his statement. After dropping him off on January 14th, DeWilde was going to meet this Ned at Brandy's, a pub in nearby Brighton.

"Why didn't you tell us that before?" Moran asked, stringing Blaikie along.

"I was afraid you would suspect me of something."

"Suspect you of *what?*"

"David's disappearance."

"What did you have to be afraid of?" Moran shot back.

"Look what happened to David," Blaikie said with a wounded look.

Moran did not let up. "Mr. Blaikie, as far as I'm concerned, you are trying to frustrate this investigation."

"Detective Moran," Blaikie said patiently, "two days after David's disappearance I received a call from someone named Ned and he said if I mentioned his name, he would kill me and my wife."

"How did you know it was this *Ned?*"

"By his voice," Blaikie said.

From the file on his desk, Moran removed the narrow manila envelope found next to the telephone at David DeWilde's apartment. "Ned Woodman" was one of the names on the envelope, but Moran did not tell Blaikie he had found no one by that name at 49 Hereford Street. However, Moran mentioned the name and address and Blaikie appeared flustered by the detective's knowledge of them.

His cool facade was melting and he said it happened to have been his own address several years earlier.

Moran thought to himself, *This sonofabitch is digging his own grave. I just wish to hell he'd hurry up.*

They were joined by Sergeant Detective Doris and Blaikie worriedly told them someone had shot BB pellets through the window of his car in his driveway. He asked the detectives if they could provide him with protection.

It was hard to tell from Moran's expression whether he wanted to punch Blaikie or laugh in his face. Sergeant Doris sardonically advised Blaikie that as a resident of Brookline he would have to talk to police there about protection.

Blaikie asked if he could leave and Moran shrugged permission.

"Well, if I'm killed," Blaikie said dejectedly as he got up from his chair, "I want you to know what the story is."

"Jim," Moran said with a tinge of mock concern in his growl, "please, don't get killed until we find David."

Blaikie gaped at him and loosed a pained smile as he turned to leave.

Inquiring of Brookline police, Moran learned Blaikie had reported damage to his car from BB pellets on February 4, but had expressed no fear of a threat to his safety.

Blaikie's elaborate song and dance about the nefarious "Ned Woodman" further convinced Moran he was right about the scam. Blaikie had concocted the name to entice DeWilde into bankrolling a nonexistent drug deal. DeWilde went looking for the payoff at Blaikie's house and bought the farm instead.

Moran decided to canvas Blaikie's neighborhood once more. He wanted an ally there and he found one.

A dear old Jewish lady with a view of Blaikie's driveway in the posh neighborhood had not seen any unusual goings-on across Fisher Avenue. But she promised to let the rough-hewn Boston detective with the charming smile know about any extraordinary activities across the way.

Moran left her with a hunch that some day she was going to report something important to him.

Chapter 15

In his ongoing investigation of the Bacon death, Sergeant Detective Maillet found additional pieces to the James Blaikie puzzle. Seven months after the death of his mother, Jim's seventy-three-year-old father died in March 1974 at the Veterans Administration Hospital in Bedford. The retired army sergeant had been a stroke patient there on and off since 1968. The cause of his death was listed as bilateral bronchopneumonia, or double pneumonia.

Because one effect of cyanide poisoning is to fill the lungs and other organs with fluids, Maillet made inquiries about the elder Blaikie's death. No autopsy had been performed and the hospital maintained the confidentiality of its visitor list.

Maillet did find out that Jim Blaikie sold the family house in Waltham for $33,000 and received $6,845.42 from his late father's VA life insurance coverage. That total of nearly $40,000 apparently helped explain how in April 1974 Jim was able to come up with more than ten thousand dollars in cash for a down payment on the Brookline house.

That left him with $30,000 from his parents. Since Ed Bacon had stopped sharing commissions with him at the insurance agency the year before, the question was if and where Blaikie had come up with any other money. And how did this picture square with the $28,000 he claimed to have invested in the agency since 1972? Maillet and the other detectives along with Assistant District Attorney Alice Richmond wondered where he was getting money and what he had been doing with it.

Intriguing to police as well as Richmond was Blaikie's pattern of spending as indicated by bank and other records.

What did Blaikie do after Ed Bacon had frozen him out of the commission pool in May 1973? He bought a $15,700 sailboat in June.

In August, his mother died, leaving him a $33,000 house. In December, Kathy, who was not known to be working full time, got a new car. In March 1974, Blaikie's father died, leaving him nearly $7,000 in insurance.

The following month the couple bought a $74,500 house and a $4,000 grand piano. Two months later, in June, Jim bought another new car.

At that point there was no indication of his earning more than a thousand dollars in all of 1974 at the Bacon agency, following a year in which he had done no better. According to the records, Blaikie's heavy borrowing on all of the above had gotten him around $100,000 in debt. His monthly expenses were topping $1,000.

On July 1, 1974, a month after the purchase of the second new car, the suspect Kemper insurance form was signed by James Blaikie as witness, making him the new beneficiary of Ed's $50,000 policy.

Kemper received the form in Long Grove, Illinois, on July 19th, approved it, and mailed an acknowledgment of the change to Ed Bacon on July 24th.

Five days later, Edwin Bacon, who had just inherited a small fortune, was dead of cyanide poisoning.

Unknown to the Bacons at the time, Blaikie filed a claim of death to Kemper on August 9th.

On September 17th, Kemper sent Blaikie a check for $50,000, and the fat was in the fire.

Two New England Nuclear checks totaling some $12,000 were deposited in the Bacon–Blaikie account in October and November. Blaikie wrote checks to himself from that account.

Blaikie borrowed $6,000 from David DeWilde in

December, and in January DeWilde vanished from the face of the earth.

Authorities observed that James Blaikie had an amazing knack of spending himself into catastrophic debt and then coming into money. *Until* the Bacon affair. The $50,000 insurance benefits did not get to him.

If Blaikie had gotten the money, he might not have needed to strike a deal with DeWilde, and David might not be among the missing.

The FBI said the crucial Kemper document was a fraud and New England Nuclear was insisting that checks it handed over to Blaikie had been cashed, but its insurance underwriter had not received its premium payments. The words forming in the mind of Alice Richmond were *forgery, embezzlement*, and, not once but twice, *murder. Time I met this Mr. Blaikie,* the assistant district attorney thought.

Although Brookline was in Norfolk County, De-Wilde's residence was the Brighton district of Boston and within Suffolk County, Richmond's bailiwick. She wanted to question Blaikie on the disappearance of his friend as well as on the death of his business associate on Boston's waterfront.

Richmond telephoned Jim, asking him to come to the Suffolk DA's office at Pemberton Square for a talk about the DeWilde and Bacon cases, and he agreed to a meeting.

She also invited Frank Bacon.

Shortly before the interview on March 5, a Boston police detective attached to the district attorney's office removed all the ashtrays from Alice Richmond's office. Although Detective John O'Malley, Alice, and Frank Bacon were smokers, they were willing to defer their habit for a reason. They understood from Brighton detective Moran that Blaikie got to smoking heavily under interrogation, and they wanted to see how he reacted without a cigarette ritual to punctuate his answers.

Blaikie showed them soon after his arrival by firing

up a cigarette and flicking ashes into his cupped hand. Accompanied by an attorney for the first time in a meeting with investigators, he and his counsel sat across the desk from Richmond and Bacon at her side. Detective O'Malley stood near the door. With no ashtray in sight, Blaikie put his cigarette out on the floor.

After reading him the Miranda warning, Richmond brought up the Bacon case. Blaikie's attorney advised him he did not have to answer questions pertaining to the New England Nuclear checks and the Kemper beneficiary-change form.

Abruptly the lawyer and then his client got to their feet, gathered their coats, and filed past Detective O'Malley and out the door.

After a silence in which three cigarettes were lit, Bacon said, "I guess Mr. Blaikie did not enjoy the conversation."

Richmond smiled dryly, shuffling the papers on her desk. "And I thought I had fairly good social skills."

"I don't know if you could see it," O'Malley said, "but from where I stood I could see his knees pumping up and down. He looked like he was running the hundred-yard dash stuck to his chair."

"Did you get the feeling from what he *did* say that he thinks he can talk his way out of anything?" Alice said, rising from her chair.

"Or at least walk away from anything," Frank said.

"If we ever get him on a witness stand, he'll croak himself," Richmond said, looking from Detective O'Malley to Bacon. "I'm convinced he killed your brother, and I've got a feeling David DeWilde's body could rise with the spring thaw."

In March winter still showed no signs of releasing Boston from its grip. David's former wife left a desperate message for Jim on his answering machine, begging him to tell where David was. Ruth Whitney DeWilde did not get a reply.

Jim and Kathy were virtually beseiged and their fortress was crumbling. The grand piano and two cars were on the verge of repossession. Blaikie's creative sale of his mortgaged boat was unraveling as he had not made a payment on the vessel since December. The Blaikies had managed to keep a roof over their heads but after missing their March mortgage payments they were two months in arrears on the house.

The detectives figured the Blaikies had to be near the snapping point.

Hopelessly behind in all their debts, the Blaikies signed a purchase-and-sale agreement for the house on April 19th.

Later that month, Brookline detective William McDermott climbed the stairway to the front portico of the Blaikie residence and Kathy answered the door. She joined him on the landing and looked haggard, not at all well.

He said hello with a dash of a cordial smile and she barely returned his greeting. Something appeared to be weighing heavily on the mind of the dark-haired and petite beauty.

"Mr. Blaikie wouldn't be in, would he?"

"No." Her answer was almost inaudible. She leaned on the top of the stair railing, not casually but as though steadying herself.

"I just wanted to ask if you've heard from David DeWilde," McDermott said. "He is still missing, you know."

With a hundred-yard stare, she simply replied, "No."

Their ritual ended with her vaguely promising again to let him know if they should hear from DeWilde. Billy McDermott returned to his car, thinking, *That woman is scared.*

It was the last time he would see the attractive twenty-eight-year-old Kathy Blaikie.

She and James Blaikie vanished.

Chapter 16

The Bacons received the troubling news of the Blaikies' late-April disappearance in the wake of closing the Bacon Insurance Agency. As primary creditor under his 1969 loan agreement with Ed, Frank planned to sell agency assets, including group and individual insurance accounts, lest they evaporate entirely. As it was the assessed value did not cover half the money owed him.

Including investments in Ed's luckless business ventures, Frank's brotherly generosity had cost him close to $175,000. Yet Smoki rankled at his control of Ed's stake in undeveloped land purchased by the brothers with several other shareholders. Ed had signed over his twenty percent of the property to Frank as partial collateral for the loans. In social settings the ice between liberal Smoki and conservative Frank was occasionally broken by sharp political exchanges. The debates over Kennedys and Republicans struck some observers merely as excuses for verbal combat. Mutual friends began seeing Frank and Smoki separately.

It was not so easy for Brooks and Hilary. They were caught in the middle between a mother and uncle they loved. Neither Smoki nor Frank competed for their loyalties, but the girls deplored dissension in the family as one more result of their father's death. If he had not died, they felt, none of this would be happening. They would also have a teacher, tennis instructor, and affectionate confidant at home if he had not died.

And their days would not be filled with free-floating anxiety about a killer abroad.

Detective Tom Moran knew exactly what James Blaikie was up to.

On April 24, his hunch about the alertness of the little old Jewish lady on Fisher Avenue had proved correct. She saw a moving van pull up in front of the Blaikie house and immediately telephoned the news to her favorite Boston detective.

With the name of the transport company, Moran was able to find out the Blaikies were shipping their possessions to a warehouse on Black Canyon Highway in Phoenix, Arizona.

Moran was not surprised by the destination.

He again telephoned Blaikie's former fraternity brother in Tempe and learned Jim had recently called him. Jim had said he planned to drive from Boston and make a stop in Washington to interview for a job with Representative Morris Udall of Arizona. Udall was mounting a presidential bid, and Blaikie was hoping to parlay his McGovern campaign experience into yet another Democratic run for the roses.

Moran said that Jim was a suspect in the two-month disappearance of David DeWilde and a groan came over the line from Arizona.

In a telephone call to Udall's Washington office, Detective Moran confirmed that Blaikie had been interviewed there. Asked why he was inquiring, Detective Moran stated his official reason and a Udall aide thanked him profusely for the information. Blaikie had gone on to Arizona expecting to talk about a position on the congressman's Phoenix staff.

Moran was starting to feel like a Navy gunner, receiving word of the enemy's position and firing away.

The Blaikies' itinerary was as tortuous as the events sending them on their odyssey.

After Washington, they drove on in Jim's car with less than two hundred dollars to their name until they reached Albuquerque, New Mexico. Telephoning Tempe, Jim learned without explanation that his college friend could not take him and Kathy in and knew of no temporary job for him. Dejected, the Blaikies turned around and began the arduous 2,000 mile drive back to Boston.

Jim's shaky buddy telephoned Moran about Blaikie's call, and the grateful detective alerted Brookline police to the possibility of Blaikie's return from New Mexico. All he and Billy McDermott could figure was Blaikie was heading back home to get some money together somehow.

However, the couple eluded police. Upon reaching Massachusetts early in May, they did not go back to the Brookline house even though final papers had not been passed on it. Instead, they slipped into a motel in nearby Newton, another western suburb of Boston.

Unaware his college friend was in touch with Moran, Blaikie again called Tempe, telling of his plan to fly to Phoenix on May 18th. When Moran heard of the date and flight number, he was concerned that if Blaikie hit the skids again in Phoenix, he could well go underground. But the detective had no warrant to stop him at the Boston airport and no hope of getting one.

On May 18th, Jim and Kathy left the Newton Motor Lodge, still owing $300 on a bill from their ten-day stay. They drove in Jim's Ford LTD to Logan International Airport in Boston Harbor and left the car in a parking garage. With less than a hundred dollars, they boarded a flight for Phoenix.

Detective Moran notified police in Phoenix that a suspect in a Boston missing-person case and his wife were on their way there.

The following day, a deeply perplexed James Blaikie drove in a rented car to Tempe and told his college friend he was staying in a Phoenix motel while seeking a job and apartment. Blaikie borrowed twenty-seven dollars and left. Later in the day Detective Moran got the news, including the name of Jim's motel. Moran telephoned the information to his Phoenix counterparts.

Jesus, he thought as he put down the phone at the

detective room in Brighton, *Blaikie is tapping a friend for his spare change. The sonofabitch is running on empty.*

Moran was right. Eleven days later, James Blaikie tripped himself up. He made the kind of blunder that Boston and Brookline detectives hoped their pressure would drive him to.

Among the felonies reported to Phoenix, Arizona police on Thursday, May 29, was an armed holdup in the parking lot of the Biltmore Fashion Park.

A day later, a young man fitting the robber's description held up two local dry cleaners at gunpoint. The *modus operandi* was the same in both cases. The gunman came into the shop while the attendant, a female in each instance, was alone. Pointing a steel-blue revolver at the woman, he demanded all the money in the cash register and promised not to harm her if she cooperated. In the 8:00 A.M. and 12:30 P.M. holdups, they complied and handed over their cash, sixty-five dollars and eighty dollars respectively. Without firing a shot or laying a hand on either woman, the gunman fled.

The following morning shortly after ten o'clock, a Phoenix patrolman was cruising west on Camelback Road near the Biltmore when a late-model sedan coming in his direction rang a bell. He thought the driver and vehicle matched the description of the parking lot thief and his rented getaway car. The officer pursued the suspect vehicle and four blocks away his warbler brought the car to a halt. With a hand on his service revolver he rousted the driver out.

The patrolman found a .38-caliber revolver under the front seat and took a quaking James F. Blaikie, Jr. into custody.

Questioning Blaikie that morning, a Phoenix police detective had the feeling he was not talking to a complete stranger. Without telling Blaikie, he realized his holdup suspect was a suspect in the missing-person case that Boston Detective Tom Moran had been calling about.

Later in the day when Moran got news of Blaikie's arrest, he got a few glances in the detective room with a hearty "Damn!"

Not only did he know where Blaikie was, he was behind bars. Considering there was currently no way to lock him up in Boston, Moran figured a Phoenix slammer was as good for Blaikie as Charles Street Jail.

Blaikie professed no knowledge of the parking lot holdups and was not charged with them. But he sheepishly related that he had held up the two dry cleaners and also a Scottsdale motel the previous day. He put his total haul at roughly $120, which was $49 shy of the actual amount.

Appearing contrite, Blaikie said he and his wife had arrived in Phoenix mid-May after they had "suffered financial reverses" in Boston. They had run out of money before he could find a job, he said. "I even visited Our Lady's Catholic Church in Scottsdale," Blaikie claimed. "I guess I became desperate when we had no money for food or lodging, and the unfamiliar hot weather started to bother me."

He said he had purchased the revolver, a Smith & Wesson .38 Special, several years earlier from a friend.

"I went out in my rented automobile with the thought of robbing some place," he glumly told investigators. "I was trying to find a place where there weren't many people around, because I didn't want anyone to get hurt. I was driving around for several hours."

Blaikie said he held up the desk clerk at the Scottsdale motel and an hour later passed a dry cleaner where he noticed a lone woman behind the counter. Several hours after robbing her, he held up the lone female attendant at another cleaner.

He told police he deeply regretted this and wished he could apologize to his victims.

Blaikie said his wife knew nothing of his crime spree, and in a later conversation with an overwrought Kathy Blaikie, police were persuaded she had no involvement in it.

* * *

With James Blaikie in Phoenix, Brighton Detective Moran conferred with Sergeant Detective Maillet of Boston Homicide and Brookline Detective McDermott on their next move. Still lacking probable cause to obtain a search warrant for Blaikie's house, they arrived at another legal way to enter it. Request permission from its new owner.

On June 6, a local bank executive took possession of the house. In the afternoon three days later he permitted the three detectives on his property for the purpose of investigating DeWilde's disappearance.

Inspecting the rolling grounds of shrubbery and tall trees, they were not surprised to find no hint of a grave. They had never thought Blaikie could or would get very far digging into January's frozen soil.

In the attic, they found plasterboard that appeared of a later vintage than the rest of the walls. The owner planned to remodel the area and allowed them to break into the curious sections with a hammer and wrecking bar. The openings revealed only empty spaces.

The party descended to the second floor and saw no evidence of tampering with any of the walls or stains of any kind. The first floor was likewise unremarkable.

The owner led police through the kitchen and down wooden stairs into the dimly lighted cellar. Toward the rear was a boiler area with two furnaces. The newer one was an oil burner. The other, a coal burner, was empty.

Making their way forward along the concrete floor in the direction of Fisher Avenue, police saw an unlighted section at the front of the cellar. It was littered with numerous trash barrels, cardboard boxes, and plastic market bags. The detectives rummaged through and about the various containers, finding paper refuse, an old rug padding, unused plastic trash bags.

Detective Moran glanced about the cellar and asked for permission to break up this floor.

The owner gawked at the detective and with a pained look surveyed the concrete expanse. "Have a *heart,* officer,'' he groaned. ''No, I won't allow it.''

Moran asked again and was refused again.

Appearing near the end of his patience, he marched out of the basement.

The police followed him into the pleasant spring air and entered the garage. Kathy's car was no longer there, taken by the bank like Jim's. Several corrugated cardboard boxes on the garage floor contained assorted insurance material and records along with personal effects. The owner confirmed the boxes were not his and presumably had been left behind by the hastily departing Blaikies.

The papers were the only potential evidence found that day.

Three days later, Blaikie hit a brick wall.

On June 12th the Suffolk Superior Court in Boston ruled against him in absentia in his quest for the $50,000 benefits from Edwin Bacon's Kemper life insurance policy. However, the court also threw a roadblock in the path of the other remaining defendant in Kemper's 1974 Christmas lawsuit, Smoki Bacon. Blaikie's bank, to which he had pledged the insurance proceeds as loan collateral, dropped out of the contest. The judge ruled in favor of the insurance company, ''perpetually and permanently'' granting it relief from any legal action by the two parties in their pursuit of the $50,000 benefits.

Blaikie and Bacon would have to vie in court for the money, at their own expenses.

Kemper placed the $50,000 in a court-held fund, which would go to the winner. The company's action was not unusual. Businesses faced with competing financial claims frequently ask courts to order such an arrangement

Hearing of the ruling from Zal Davlin, Smoki Bacon reacted with a mixture of rage and disbelief. ''Do you mean, Zal, that the court ruled in *favor* of an insurance company that approved a phony beneficiary change, a change that its own handwriting expert says is a forgery?''

"I'm sorry, Smoki."

"Don't you be sorry, Zal. It's Kemper and the court I'm furious with."

"There's more," he said. "The court has awarded Kemper $1,500 in attorney's fees, which will come from the $50,000."

Smoki laughed bitterly. "That figures, Zal. Thanks to Kemper, Ed was murdered, and now I'm paying *their* expenses for suing *me*. So this is the justice we were all brought up to believe in."

"What can I say, Smoki? The good news is Blaikie's attorney is withdrawing from the case. In any event, I'll initiate a suit immediately, claiming the Kemper benefits rightly belong to you."

The following June day, James Blaikie suffered his second legal setback of the week. He pled guilty to the two felony counts of armed robbery in Phoenix and was returned to Maricopa County Jail to await sentencing.

With the help of Jim's college friend, Kathy Blaikie found an apartment and a part-time job. She also asked him to write a letter on her husband's behalf to the Maricopa County probation department.

Facing Kathy at his house, he balked at the suggestion. He and his wife were not delighted by Jim's grotesque descent on their city as a gun-toting holdup man.

However, Kathy would not hear of his reluctance. Nor would she beg for help. Fixing her dark eyes on him, she spoke instead in an urgent and accusatory tone. If he did not speak up for Jim, she said, her husband would certainly face five years in prison and his supposed friend would have the weight of that knowledge on his conscience.

He relented and wrote a glowing endorsement of Blaikie's character.

In his June 28 letter, he described Blaikie's criminal activity in Phoenix as "totally out of character" and "a desperate act, one which I am sure he regrets." Concluding, he said that with Kathy back on her feet the Blaikies now had "a foundation in Phoenix on which they can build a future . . . a strong marriage and a close friend more than willing and capable of helping."

A probation officer took the letter under advisement and interviewed Blaikie. In his report to the judge who was to pass sentence in Maricopa County Superior Court, the officer stated that Jim was "well-oriented" with an "excellent" academic background and

> *it is felt that the defendant has an excellent positive attitude. His goals at this time are to obtain a position in the insurance field, establish a home for his wife, and conduct himself as a law-abiding productive citizen in the future. It is felt that the defendant does not pose any future criminal threat to society. It is further felt that the defendant would be amenable to probation, and that he would subscribe fully to the terms and conditions of a long-term probationary period.*

In July, a year after the death of Edwin Bacon and six months after the disappearance of David DeWilde, sentence was passed on James Blaikie for the armed robberies in Phoenix. He was ordered to serve forty-five days in Arizona State Prison and a ten-year probation after his release.

Chapter 17

Rather than a triumph, Frank Bacon considered Blaikie's imprisonment a travesty. For robbing people with a lethal weapon he gets a total of *three months* behind bars, half of them awaiting trial. The news only reinforced his view that the criminal justice system was a pathetic charade. Liberals got satisfaction from it, attorneys got money, criminals got vacations, and victims got screwed.

He bitterly mused that by late August, Blaikie would be out of prison and running for South America, or for governor of Arizona.

The Bacon family was right back where it had started a year earlier.

Alice Richmond could not get permission to seek a murder indictment in the Bacon death although she firmly believed her case against Blaikie was strong. Suffolk County District Attorney Garrett Byrne saw the evidence as too circumstantial and would not give her the go-ahead.

Smoki and Frank were incredulous. The insurance beneficiary-change application, a forgery according to the FBI, pointed to an obvious motive as far as they were concerned. Blaikie claimed to have witnessed the signing of the document. What other reason would the alleged forger have had but to murder for the proceeds of the insurance? Then there were the discoveries they considered incriminating: the magically appearing can of cyanide in Ed's office, the scratch pad among Blaikie's possessions with "Edwin C. Bacon" repeatedly written on it, and Ed's blazer hidden in the agency storage room.

If such evidence were weak, the Bacon circle wondered how the district attorney could ever prosecute a murder. Some suspected that Democrat Byrne was reluctant to prosecute a party member, but Richmond did not think politics were involved. Although she disagreed with Byrne's decision, she respected him.

Contemplating ways to turn up the heat on Blaikie, Frank hit on publicity. If any reporter knew about the questions surrounding Ed's death, not a word had been printed.

A name in Boston journalism that came to Frank's mind was that of a boyhood friend. William O. Taylor II, the *Globe* general manager, was a great-grandson of Civil War General Charles H. Taylor, who in 1873 had become the first of the family to publish the newspaper. The general had rescued a year-old publication from collapse and marched it to greatness. Bill Taylor, destined to be the family's fourth generation of *Globe* publishers, had gone to Boston's exclusive Dexter School with Frank and Ed in the 1940s. The trio had been chauffeured in a limousine back and forth between the Back Bay and classes.

He had not seen much of Taylor over the years but nevertheless called him at the *Globe*. The newspaperman was intrigued by the broad outline of the Bacon and DeWilde cases and said he would pass the information on to a reporter.

The next day, Frank received a telephone call from the *Globe*'s top crime reporter, Richard J. Connolly. Frank briefed him on the case and Connolly said he did not know what if anything would be published. But he was going to investigate the matters thoroughly. In the ensuing weeks, he spoke with Smoki Bacon, DeWilde's family, and all the officials involved in both cases.

By mid-August, Connolly saw an astonishing drama had been smoldering in obscurity for a full year. His next step was to try for an interview with James Blaikie.

The day Blaikie was released from Arizona State Prison in late August, Richard Connolly knocked on the door of the parolee's Phoenix apartment and introduced himself as a *Boston Globe* reporter. Connolly said he had come to Phoenix in connection with the Bacon and DeWilde cases and wanted to interview him.

Blaikie readily agreed and met the reporter in the lobby of his hotel the following morning.

Over coffee in the dining room, Connolly explained that he was not certain at that point what he was going to write, but as far as he was concerned everything Blaikie might tell him was to be for the record and reportable.

Blaikie agreed and Richard Connolly became the first news reporter to interview him about the death of Edwin Bacon and the disappearance of David DeWilde.

Two weeks later, the first of Connolly's three articles appeared in the Sunday *Globe* of September 7.

It was a blockbuster.

The headline read: A YEAR LATER—WAS IT MURDER?

At length, in forty-five column inches on three pages, the exclusive laid out the Bacon case from Ed's mysterious death to the questions that continued to surround his Kemper life insurance policy. Included were a picture of Smoki with the caption "Doubts suicide," and a photo of Ed with the underlying question, "Was he murdered?"

"From all that was apparent in the life of Edwin Conant Bacon, he did not expect to die on the night of July 28, 1974," was Connolly's lead. "The forty-four-year-old Harvard-educated insurance executive and Back Bay society figure had given no indication to his family and friends that he intended to commit suicide."

Connolly then unloaded with detailed accounts of ongoing probes by Assistant District Attorney Alice Richmond and Sergeant Detective Maillet.

Thirty-year-old James Blaikie was named in public

for the first time in connection with the case. Connolly reported his recent arrest and incarceration for armed robbery in Arizona as well as his background as a Northeastern University graduate and treasurer of the local McGovern for president committee in 1972.

The following day's installment also opened on page one, with the headline, WAS $50,000 SIGNATURE A FORGERY?

It included quotes from Connolly's interview with James Blaikie in Phoenix.

Referring to the questioned Kemper document, by which Blaikie had replaced Edwin Bacon's wife and daughters as beneficiaries of his $50,000 life insurance policy, Blaikie was quoted as saying: "I saw him sign it. I witnessed his signature."

The second article continued:

Of those who talked with Bacon on the day of his death, only Blaikie felt that Bacon was depressed and capable of suicide. . . .

"I liked him," Blaikie said of Bacon, who grew up on Commonwealth Avenue, Back Bay, the son of a wealthy book publishing firm executive.

"He was a funny guy from an old Yankee background. But he'd rather have a 'Big Mac' than sit down at a formal dinner. But looking back, he was always up and down. One day the world was about to end. The next day he was up and everything was fine.

"He always talked about how depressed he was," Blaikie said. "He'd say he didn't know why he bothered to go on . . . He was kind of a lonely guy. He'd stay at the office for hours and hours.

"The last few days," Blaikie said, "he was really down. I would have stayed if I knew how bad he was . . . He must have been thinking about this [suicide]."

Blaikie said he left the office about 5 p.m. on July 29 and that Bacon, as usual, remained late. His body was discovered the next morning.

About the reportedly forged beneficiary-change application, Connolly wrote:

Blaikie told *The Globe* that he saw Bacon sign the form in his office on July 1, 28 days before his death.

"It surprised the hell out of me," Blaikie said.

He quoted Bacon as saying: "I want you to have this [the $50,000 policy]. I want you to be protected. If anything happens to me, I don't want my family to screw you out of it."

"I said, 'Don't be ridiculous. You're a young guy. Nothing's going to happen to you.' "

"I saw him sign it," Blaikie said. "I witnessed the signature. He told me not to tell anybody about it. He gave me the policy when it came back . . .

"I had a good relationship with Ed," Blaikie recalled the other day. "I don't know . . . I thought I knew him better than anybody else.

"When he died, everything fell apart with me," Blaikie said.

Referring to his Phoenix holdups, Blaikie reportedly told the *Globe:* "I was desperate—really. This was a stupid thing to do. It didn't help me at all."

Blaikie's public defender in Phoenix was quoted as saying: "He was the most personable, likeable robber I've ever met."

The next day, *Globe* reporter Connolly focused on the DeWilde case in the last of his three-part series on James Blaikie.

The installment on September 9th included a photo of a bearded DeWilde with his young daughter, Paris, and a picture of Assistant District Attorney Alice Richmond, identified as "probing Bacon case." Like Connolly's reporting on the Bacon death, it was an exclusive.

After outlining the twenty-seven-year-old Brighton man's disappearance the previous January 14th, Connolly reported that the case was being investigated by

Detective Thomas Moran of the Brighton division, "who said he is convinced that DeWilde is dead."

Connolly wrote that Blaikie said he had $6,000 that DeWilde wanted on January 14. However, Blaikie's statement continued, DeWilde did not request the money because he understood Blaikie needed it for his court case involving Bacon's contested insurance policy.

The end of the article and series read:

He wonders what will happen next in what has become known as the Bacon case.

A strange case?

"I know it," the central figure replies.

Within three September days, the *Boston Globe* series blew the lid off the Bacon and DeWilde affairs. The question of what had happened to James Blaikie's former business associate and his Brighton friend became the focal story of the New England news media. Wire services carried it across the country.

It was more than Frank Bacon had hoped for. James Blaikie was under the glare of publicity at last.

District Attorney Byrne agreed with Alice Richmond that she should proceed immediately with the Bacon case.

On the morning of September 16 she sought secret indictments against Blaikie on several charges, including forgery and embezzlement. It was the first official action taken against him in connection with Bacon. However she still did not have Byrne's green light to go after a murder indictment.

Bacon attorney Zal Davlin's grand jury testimony concerned the reported forgery of Edwin Bacon's Kemper insurance policy number 613600. Davlin said that in his meeting with James Blaikie and Frank Bacon at the Bacon agency two days after Ed's death, Blaikie claimed not to know of either the existence or the whereabouts of the policy. Yet, Davlin said, in September he received from Kemper a benefits check on that policy for $50,000, payable to James F. Blai-

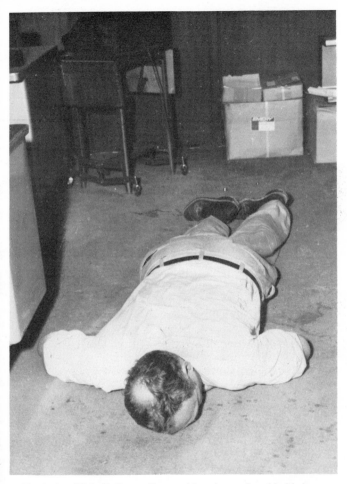

The body of Edwin Conant Bacon, 44, as it was found in his insurance firm on Boston's waterfront.

Four years out of Harvard, Edwin's younger brother, Francis Lyman Bacon, already had a reputation for innovation in computer systems.

Smoki Bacon [*second from left*] and husband, Edwin [*center*], at the penthouse of friends on Beacon Hill.

Edwin Bacon on the dock at his brother's summer house in New Hampshire, a year before his death.

Harvard-man Edwin Bacon and his artist wife, Smoki, at Boston's exclusive Waltz Evening in the Copley Plaza Hotel. (*Boris and Milton, Boston*)

James Blaikie and the former Kathleen Goodrow leave a Waltham, Mass., church after their wedding ceremony.

At the wedding reception, bride Kathy gets a hug from mother-in-law, Alma Blaikie.

James Blaikie in the cake cutting ceremony at his and Kathy's wedding reception.

James Blaikie, David DeWilde, and Kathy Blaikie cruise Massachusetts Bay on the Blaikies' sailboat.

APPLICATION FOR
CHANGE OF POLICY IN

JUL 19 1974 25 A

☐ FIDELITY LIFE ASSOCIATION, A Mutual Legal Reserve Company, | Long Grove,
☒ FEDERAL KEMPER LIFE ASSURANCE COMPANY, | Illinois 60049

Kemper
INSURANCE

INSTRUCTIONS

THIS FORM IS TO BE USED FOR ALL POLICY CHANGES, except for change of existing policy to a Family Policy or the addition of the Dependent Children's Rider to an existing policy, in which case a regular application should be submitted, giving evidence of insurability on all dependents proposed for insurance as well as the Insured.

USE THIS SIDE OF THE FORM (CD-15-1A) ONLY FOR THOSE CHANGES REQUIRING NO EVIDENCE OF INSURABILITY.

USE THE REVERSE SIDE OF THE FORM (CD-15-1B) FOR CHANGES REQUIRING EVIDENCE OF INSURABILITY, such as a change to a lower premium plan, an increased amount of insurance, additional benefits or riders, rate reduction, or when the change applied for in any way results in an increased amount at risk.

BENEFICIARY AND OWNER. The beneficiary and owner on any new policy shall be the same as on the original policy unless change is requested on the proper forms.

SIGNATURES. This application (Form CD-15-1A) must be signed by the Owner and any Irrevocable Beneficiary or Assignee. The reverse side (Form CD-15-1B) must be signed by the Owner, the Insured if age 15 or over and other than the Owner, by the applicant for the Payor Benefit and by any Irrevocable Beneficiary or Assignee.

Application is hereby made to change Policy No. 613600 _____ on the life of Edwin C. Bacon _____
as designated below, effective July _____ 1st, 19 74, and said Policy is hereby surrendered to the Company for such change.
       (Month)

☐ CHANGE From _____ , $ _____
         To _____ , $ _____
   with register date _____ 1st, 19 ____ . Any cash value released on account of this change shall be applied as follows:

☐ REMOVE ☐ Waiver of Premium ☐ Double Indemnity ☐ Payor Benefit ☐ _____

☒ CHANGE OF BENEFICIARY. For any policy issued on or after June 1, 1964, the Company hereby waives the requirement of the policy for endorsement at the home office for the purpose of this change of beneficiary, but agrees to so endorse said policy if requested by the owner.

All prior beneficiary designations and settlement directions are hereby revoked and the following are designated as beneficiaries under this Policy:

		Relationship to Insured
Primary	James F. Blaikie, Jr.	business
	244 Fisher Avenue, Brookline, Massachusetts 02146	partner
Contingent	Edwin C. Bacon Trust of August 28, 1973, Adelaide R. Bacon and	
	Zalman O. Davlin, Trustees or their successors.	

☐ CHANGE OF NAME. Application is hereby made to change the name
of the Insured of this Policy from _____
_____ to _____
_____ because of:
☐ Marriage to _____ on _____
☐ Other (explain, giving date of event) _____

☐ OTHER (Specify) _____
_____
_____
_____
_____

If a change in premium mode is desired, circle new mode: A S Q M __

☐ CORRECT DATE OF BIRTH. The date of birth of _____
         (Name)
_____ was incorrectly stated
on the application for this Policy as being _____ .
This certifies that the correct date of birth is _____ .
Application is hereby made to correct the policy and make any adjustment in premiums and/or reserves made necessary because of this correction.

HOME OFFICE ENDORSEMENTS (do not write in this space)

APPROVED 7/24/74

FKLA mg

It is understood and agreed that (1) this application shall be considered an amendment to the original application and shall form a part of the policy, and that (2) the change requested shall not be effective until approved and recorded at the Home Office of the Company and any required additional premium has been paid.

Application made at Boston _____ State Mass _____

Edwin C. Bacon _____ Signature of Owner

this 1st ____ day of July ____ 19 74. Address 50 Commercial Wharf Boston, Ma 02110

Witness James A. Luhil jr _____ ☐ Check here if above is change of address

Form No. CD-15-1A-C 3-73 THE POLICY OR A LOST POLICY WAIVER MUST ACCOMPANY THIS APPLICATION

The notorious beneficiary-change application for Edwin Conant Bacon's $50,000 life insurance policy. The FBI concluded his suspect signature was a forgery.

In Arizona to bring James Blaikie back to Boston, Detective Thomas Moran [*left*] and Sergeant Detective John Maillet, both of the Boston Police Department, visit the Grand Canyon while Phoenix authorities complete rendition papers.

Alice Richmond has a pat on the back for onetime courtroom opponent Edward F. Harrington. Richmond was prosecutor and Harrington, a future federal judge, was defense counsel in two blistering Blaikie trials.

Francis Lyman Bacon escorts his daughter, Avril, to her wedding ceremony in 1988.

Smoki Bacon and her daughter Hilary attend the signing of an insurance-fraud prevention bill by Massachusetts Governor Michael Dukakis in January 1990. State Senator Paul Harold was a sponsor.

James Blaikie is escorted from Brookline, Mass., Municipal Court after his arraignment for the murder of longtime friend David DeWilde. (*Boston Herald*)

kie, Jr. Blaikie later told him, Davlin stated, that Bacon had chosen to change the beneficiary and on July 1, 1974, signed a form in Blaikie's presence, making him the primary beneficiary of the policy instead of Bacon's wife and daughters.

The grand jury was shown the form bearing the signature of James Blaikie as the acknowledged witness and the signature he had alleged to Davlin and, later, the *Boston Globe* to be Edwin Bacon's.

The grand jurors heard the FBI finding that the "Edwin C. Bacon" written on the form was a forgery by simulation, and not the genuine signature of Bacon.

Pat Haskell testified that as secretary at the Bacon agency she did all of Edwin Bacon's typing, did not type the information on the beneficiary-change form and did not receive the acknowledgment of the change sent to the agency by Kemper on July 24th.

Haskell also told of discovering the scratch pad with "Edwin C. Bacon" written in it several times among Blaikie's effects two months after he was severed from the agency.

The FBI had found the writing bore characteristics common to the Bacon signature on the Kemper form, which the agency considered a forgery.

Turning to the question of embezzlement, the grand jury heard testimony from an executive of the New England Nuclear Corporation. He stated that following Bacon's death, the company's October and November 1974 insurance premium checks totaling $12,000 were personally picked up at its offices by James Blaikie. However, according to company records, it was advised by its Texas underwriter in December 1974 that it was two months behind on payments for its employee group coverage. The executive said the checks had come back canceled, paid to the Bacon–Blaikie account at the Harbor National Bank. According to him, the Republic National Insurance Company of Texas did not receive its premium payments.

An assistant cashier from the Harbor National Bank presented records confirming earlier testimony that the New England Nuclear checks had been deposited in the Bacon and Blaikie account at this institution. The books also indicated that between October 11, 1974, and November 12, 1974, James Blaikie wrote checks from that account either to himself or to his personal account and a joint checking account with his wife at the bank.

Zal Davlin stated that these constituted unauthorized conversions of agency funds for which the Bacon firm was never compensated.

A stenographer and notary public testified. He had given James Blaikie his oath and recorded his answers in a February 5, 1975 deposition concerning the Kemper insurance policy. Reading from his certified copy of the deposition, he quoted Blaikie as saying he was a licensed broker of insurance in the commonwealth. The chief administrative clerk of the Massachusetts Insurance Commission then stated he was unable to find any record of Blaikie ever having been licensed as an insurance agent or broker in the state.

With testimony completed, Frank was making his way out of the grand jury room with Zal Davlin and Pat Haskell when Alice Richmond at the prosecutor's desk looked up from her papers and caught his eye. She slipped him a plucky grin and thought she detected a hint of approval at a corner of his reserved smile. He nodded to her.

My god, she thought, *did I just get the Yankee equivalent of three cheers?*

Later that day, the grand jury handed up five indictments against James Blaikie. He was charged with forgery of the Kemper insurance form, uttering a forgery upon presenting it to Kemper as authentic, larceny by embezzlement, perjury in presenting himself as a licensed insurance broker, and selling insurance without a license.

Alice Richmond immediately pressed machinery into motion to generate a warrant for Blaikie's arrest by Phoenix police.

By Friday, the Phoenix police had received the Suffolk County warrant and the following morning, September 20, shortly before two o'clock, James Blaikie answered a serious knock at the door of his apartment on North Thirty-sixth Street. Appearing stunned, he did not resist arrest by Phoenix police officers. He quickly found himself back in Maricopa County Jail, less than a month after completing his prison sentence for armed robbery.

When local and Boston media reached his former neighbors, they spoke of him only as a pleasant young man of apparent leisure. He was remembered as someone who frequented the swimming pool and tennis courts of the comfortable apartment complex.

In his *Boston Globe* story on the arrest, Richard Connolly recounted the death of Blaikie's mother:

When a *Globe* reporter showed Blaikie a copy of his mother's note in Phoenix on Aug. 29, he said it was the first time he had read it.

He said she was affected by her husband's condition and had told her son: "I'd rather have someone shoot me than end up like your father."

"I knew she had been down," Blaikie said.

"My 'Mum' was alone and couldn't get around," Blaikie said.

"Touching story, isn't it, Tommy?" Sergeant Detective John Maillet said on the telephone with Brighton detective Moran.

"Yeah," Moran responded. "I can hardly wait to offer my sympathies in person."

The two officers were preparing to fly to Phoenix and bring Blaikie back to face the forgery and embezzlement charges.

Suddenly, in the wake of Connolly's *Boston Globe* series, there did not seem to be anything the Suffolk County government could not accomplish in days that it had failed to do in previous months. The first week in October, the superior court ruled on the lawsuit that Smoki Bacon and Zal Davlin had filed in June, seeking the contested benefits from Ed's Kemper life insurance policy. The Harbor National Bank, to which Blaikie had pledged the benefits as loan collateral, had dropped its claim to the scandal-tainted policy. That had left James Blaikie and Smoki Bacon as the possible recipients of the money. Taking into account the forgery findings on the beneficiary-change document, the judge ordered the $50,000 to be turned over to Smoki Bacon, the beneficiary originally designated by her husband in 1971.

However, the poisoning death of Edwin Bacon, which fifteen months earlier had given rise to the very issue of the money, remained an official mystery. Likewise, the nine-month disappearance of David DeWilde, who was related to the Bacon case only by the presence in his life of James Blaikie.

James Blaikie was officially wanted in Boston only for a handful of white-collar crimes.

Chapter 18

Blaikie decided surrendering on the Boston charges was preferable to languishing in an Arizona jail cell and waived his right to contest extradition. On October sixth, Sergeant Detective Maillet and Detective Moran boarded a plane in Boston and flew to Phoenix with a warrant for Blaikie's arrest on the forgery charges.

As a technician with the old Army Air Corps, Maillet had flown into nearby Luke Field and visited Phoenix several times during the war. He had worked on bombers in the states before heading for the Philippines.

The sun-drenched scene reminded Moran of a case that had brought him to Phoenix the previous December. A local man had been charged in Boston with the vicious assault and attempted rape of a Brighton woman and Moran with another detective came to Phoenix to arrest him. He had nearly torn off one of the woman's nipples with his teeth and kicked her repeatedly in the vagina. Moran did not enjoy long flights with his likes.

In his room at the Aloha Phoenix Motel near the airport, Moran telephoned Blaikie's college friend, who did not sound happy to hear the voice on a local call. But, he agreed to meet with the detectives at his Tempe house the next day.

The following morning Maillet telephoned county authorities from his motel room. They said their paperwork on Blaikie should be complete the next day, Wednesday, and promised to have him ready for a Friday departure.

In Tempe Blaikie's anxious former fraternity brother greeted the detectives coolly. He said he and his wife had not resumed their friendship with the Blaikies after Jim's release from prison five weeks earlier.

Moran commended him for reporting Blaikie's Phoenix movements in the previous six months. The young man seemed relieved to hear the detectives were taking Blaikie back to Boston.

The next day, the Boston detectives met with the Phoenix police lieutenant in charge of Blaikie's case. He handed Maillet the revolver Blaikie had admitted using in the May armed robberies. Maillet signed for the steel-blue Smith & Wesson .38 Special and the six live rounds police had found in it.

That afternoon they paid a visit to Kathy Blaikie at the insurance company where she worked as a secretary.

She came to the lobby with a numb expression and asked if they could meet later outside the building. The detectives agreed to wait for her in their car in the parking lot.

Kathy showed at 4:40 P.M., looking highly distraught. Moran got out of the passenger side and let her into the rear of the car. He returned to the front seat where Maillet was leaning against his door and looking back at Kathy.

She haltingly said she had no knowledge of her husband committing any of the alleged or suspected crimes they were investigating, neither the forgery and embezzlement in connection with Edwin Bacon nor the disappearance of David DeWilde. "I've been with him for ten years, and I still can't believe he would be capable of stealing, let alone killing anyone," she said, looking more shaken with every word.

"Mrs. Blaikie," Detective Moran said evenly,

"your husband admits that he borrowed money from Dave DeWilde and he's the last known person to see David. Is there anything you can tell us to help find him?"

Tears came as she shook her head no and she spoke of hating to return to her apartment. "It feels like the walls are closing in," she blurted. "I've been thinking about suicide."

After she calmed down, Maillet gave her the number of their motel and suggested she telephone if she should need any assistance or have anything further to say.

She nodded and weakly got out of the car.

Maillet watched the slender young woman walk away with her head down and he aimed a glowering smile at Moran. "Prick."

"John, you've gotten soft since you made sergeant. I had questions to ask her."

"You think she knew anything?"

Moran paused and considered her behavior. "I don't think so, John," he concluded.

Maillet agreed.

That evening, the detectives took several turns telephoning her apartment. She did not answer at home and left no message at their motel.

On Thursday they drove the 180 miles north to the forested south rim of the Grand Canyon. Neither had seen it before.

A couple of tourists, the rangy Maillet in a pink short-sleeve shirt and the broad-shouldered Moran wearing a blue cardigan sweater, leaned against a railing and silently looked down on the Colorado River some 5,000 feet below and out across the endless majesty.

Maillet regretted that his wife, gone ten months, would never see the incredible sight. He acutely felt the spiritual dilemma that had been mounting within him since Colette's death. How, he wondered, could the creator of all this take away a person as good and innocent as she? He knew the answer, but hearing of the divine mystery at Mass was different from living under its weight.

"Unbelievable," Moran said, squinting in the sunlight. *David DeWilde disappears in Boston,* he thought, *and nine months later I'm looking at one of the great wonders of the world.*

"A lot prettier than Columbus Avenue on a Saturday night in August, eh, Tom?" Maillet said, managing a grin for their old crime-ridden district.

Moran reached out. "You'd swear you could touch the other side."

Friday morning, shortly after seven o'clock, Sergeant Detective Maillet drove the rental car to the airport. With him he took his suitcase, which contained his service revolver and Blaikie's .38, both unloaded. He also had Moran's suitcase, with his unloaded .38 inside. Maillet was not concerned about Blaikie pulling anything with him and Moran, and, like airline pilots, he preferred not having guns in the cabin.

A deputy sheriff picked up Detective Moran at the motel and drove him to Maricopa County Jail. A clutch of photographers, television cameras, and reporters had already gathered at the exit.

Inside, a somber James Blaikie was brought into the holding area from his cell. Moran said, "Hello, Jimmy."

Impassively Blaikie said, "Hi, Detective Moran. How are you?"

"I'm *fine,*" Moran said.

Not having seen him in eight months, Moran was surprised to find him perhaps ten pounds lighter than the 215-pounder he remembered.

"Jim," Moran said, "I have an indictment warrant for your arrest on the charge of forgery in Suffolk County. When you get back, there will be additional charges read to you."

Blaikie nodded.

Squeezing handcuffs around Blaikie's uplifted wrists, Moran read him his rights under the Miranda warning. A uniformed sheriff's police officer led Moran and his prisoner down a corridor and outside.

With Blaikie held at either arm by Moran and the Maricopa County officer, the trio quickly passed a phalanx of newspeople cordoned off from their route to a cruiser. The press corps shouted questions to Blaikie about the missing David DeWilde and the Suffolk County indictments but got no response.

Moran ducked Blaikie's head under the roof of the vehicle and slid into the backseat on Blaikie's right. A young sheriff's police officer got in on the left side.

Moran noticed his baby-faced prisoner was smiling subtly. He reminded the detective of a youngster who knows he has done something wrong and will be punished. But there was something about the expression that Moran had never before seen on a kid or an adult in trouble. It was a curl of the lip, a hint of pride.

This sonofabitch really thinks he is superior, Moran thought to himself as the car sped away toward the airport.

Maillet was waiting in front of the American Airlines terminal when the cruiser pulled up half an hour before the nine o'clock flight to Boston. Moran stepped out and Blaikie followed.

The Boston detectives thanked the Maricopa County officers for their help and with Blaikie between them proceeded at a casual pace into the terminal building. The prisoner's coat was draped over his handcuffs.

The trio boarded ahead of the other passengers and found their seats near the back of the plane on the left side.

"Let me explain something," Maillet said. "Detective Moran and I want to take off the cuffs. We don't want you to be embarrassed or scare anybody on the plane."

Blaikie nodded with a bored expression.

"Now, in return for that courtesy, you're going to

be courteous, too," Maillet said in a patient monotone. "Right?"

Blaikie said nothing.

"Right?" Maillet said.

"Yes," Blaikie said.

"Good," Maillet said, "because Detective Moran or I don't want to have to break you in half. Isn't that right, Detective?"

Moran nodded, removed the cuffs and took the window seat. Blaikie sat between him and Maillet.

When breakfast trays had been cleared, Detective Moran again read Blaikie the Miranda warning and asked if he wanted to answer questions concerning DeWilde.

Blaikie said yes and did not swerve from his earlier professions of ignorance about DeWilde's whereabouts.

Maillet leaned forward and toward the prisoner, catching Moran's eye. "Mr. Blaikie," he said in a deep, quiet voice.

Jim stared at Maillet.

"I'm not going to talk to you about the Suffolk indictments in the Bacon case. They are matters for the court now. But I can and will say something to you about David DeWilde. As you know, you're a suspect in his disappearance."

The man in the middle nodded.

"You know, when you were arrested for those robberies in Phoenix, you had a gun with you," Maillet said. "You're a smart man, but you made a big mistake. I've got that gun in my suitcase. Detective Moran knows that DeWilde is dead and you killed him and I know. When we find his body, the bullet we get out of his body will match that gun and we will nail you."

The rumble of Maillet's voice segued into the sound of the engines and Blaikie stared at him mutely.

Maillet had what he wanted.

If ever he had to testify in the DeWilde case, he could state he accused Blaikie point-blank and the suspect remained calm, saying absolutely no-thing.

The jury would decide whether Blaikie was cold blooded.

Chapter 19

Handcuffed again, James Blaikie appeared to enjoy the attentions of New England news media when he deplaned at Logan International Airport with the Boston detectives that evening. Sergeant Detective Maillet figured Jim thought the left side of his face the more photogenic, for he seemed to present it to the cameras as much as possible.

The next time pictures were taken of Blaikie that day, he had no choice in the matter. They were mug shots, one frontal and one profile, at Boston Police headquarters. He was then taken to Suffolk County Jail. Known by its location at the foot of Beacon Hill, Charles Street Jail became Blaikie's residence that night.

It was still home for him a month later as he was unable to make $25,000 bail.

Apparently he would be spending Thanksgiving in the nineteenth century granite fortress near the Charles River north of Beacon Hill. Kathy Blaikie, who had not communicated with the detectives since her October interview with them, remained in Phoenix.

Alice Richmond was relieved to have Blaikie back in town on the Suffolk County indictments for forgery and embezzlement. But she was less concerned about those charges in the Bacon case than with Ed's death itself. If convicted only of the white-collar felonies, Blaikie could be back on the street within five years.

District Attorney Byrne was not relenting in his refusal to permit her to seek a murder indictment against Blaikie. Nearly sixteen months had passed since Bacon's excruciating death by cyanide poisoning. David DeWilde's case was ten months old.

Given the protracted length of the cases, the twenty-nine-year-old Richmond had gotten to know the Bacons and DeWildes better than any other family survivors in her two years of prosecuting violent crime. She felt deeply for them. Mourning had to be terrible when you did not know how or if your loved one had died.

At her office on the dreary Monday afternoon of November 24, Alice Richmond was not planning to be home in New York for Thanksgiving dinner three days later. Instead, she had accepted an invitation from a friend's family in the Boston area.

In Brookline that evening, a busy bank executive was expecting family for his first major holiday in the house he had purchased from James Blaikie five months before. In the front of the basement, which he had cleared of debris, he was cleaning a paint brush, idly stroking it back and forth against the concrete foundation. In the illumination of a recently installed light bulb, something on the floor caught his eye and he felt a chill slide down his back.

The next day he dialed the telephone number given to him by Sergeant Detective John Maillet the previous June, and he reached the homicide unit at Boston police headquarters.

Early the following afternoon, the day before Thanksgiving, Sergeant Detective Maillet strode out of Boston police headquarters with Detective Thomas Cashman and descended the granite stairway under a chill rain.

Behind the wheel of his unmarked vehicle, Maillet gunned west toward Brookline. At last, police had the consent to search that they had not been able to obtain for ten months. Now there was probable cause to suspect David DeWilde had not vanished into thin air or even left the premises on Fisher Avenue.

The new owner had noticed a slight depression in the basement floor, a patch that did not match the rest of the concrete.

Imagining Blaikie in his cell at Charles Street Jail, Maillet shot Cashman a tight grin. "We just might have the sonofabitch now, Tommy. I just wish he could be with us to do the digging."

A police chemist was to meet them at the house.

Half an hour later the detectives were driving up curved Fisher Avenue, flanked by soaring trees and tall shrubbery with vestiges of brown foliage. Outside Blaikie's old house were two unmarked police vehicles. Maillet pulled up behind one of them and led Cashman down the driveway alongside the house.

The bulkhead was open in back and they descended into the dank basement.

Smoking a cigarette, Brighton Detective Moran was near the front with Brookline Detective McDermott and a troubled-looking homeowner.

Nodding greetings, Maillet approached him and flashed a dour smile. "Thank you for getting in touch," Maillet said and he saw the vague yard-square outline nearby on the floor. Lowering beside it, he could see the coat of gray paint was newer than its surroundings. The square had subsided a fraction of an inch along one corner.

"I never noticed it," the owner said, "until I happened to see it from an angle in the light. There was a slight shadow."

He said it must originally have been a so-called dry well.

Moran nodded toward the dim rear of the basement. "There's two more like it, John, only empty. They're three feet on a side, also, and a yard deep."

The ranking officer, Maillet nodded and turned to Detective McDermott. "Billy, we've got a man from Boston missing and possibly his grave in your city. If DeWilde's down there, we've got our missing man and

Brookline's got a murder. In that case, you and Norfolk County step in, all right?''

The taciturn McDermott nodded. ''Sounds good,
Sergeant,'' he said.

''Let's get started then,'' Maillet said, hanging
his tweed jacket on the railing of the stairs to the
kitchen.

Maillet fetched a small sledgehammer and a chisel
from a tool bench and handed them to Maillet.

''I think I'll go upstairs,'' the owner said.

''Good idea,'' Maillet said, crouching. He tapped
the concrete square with the hammer and got a hollow
sound. The floor next to it was solid.

''Here goes nothing,'' he said and brought the hammer down hard on the chisel. It had been fourteen
months since James Blaikie and the Bacon case had
entered his life, ten months since David DeWilde vanished. With a few ringing blows he produced a crack
near a corner of the square.

Removing the triangle of concrete five inches on a
side and about three inches thick, Maillet looked down
at chunks of coal the size of baseballs. The surface of
the concrete fragment was smooth. Its rough under-
side conformed to the pieces of coal on which it had
been poured as fresh cement.

Maillet broke off nearly half of the slab in small
fragments and piled them beside the hole.

''Tom,'' Maillet said, getting to his feet and handing the implements to Moran. ''You probably want a
crack at this.''

''Yes, John, I do,'' Moran said, his jaw firmly set.
The Brighton detective who had been on Blaikie's trail
in the DeWilde case nearly a year firmly pounded the
remainder of the concrete slab to pieces. Within a
quarter of an hour, police were looking down on a
level bed of coal perhaps four inches below the surface
of the floor.

Standing at the edge of the hole, Brookline Detective William McDermott recalled the fearful look on
Kathy Blaikie's face the last time he had seen her outside the house in April. Within five minutes he care-

fully shoveled out a good ten-inch layer of coal, heaping it next to the concrete fragments.

Below the level of the concrete floor, the square hole was brick lined.

Silently, each of the detectives involved in the Blaikie case was taking turns at the task. Next to handle the shovel was Maillet's partner, who had seen Alma Blaikie's death photos at the Waltham police department more than a year earlier. Detective Thomas Cashman reached coal mingled with sand and soon had removed an eight-inch layer of the mixture.

He had also uncovered what looked like a partially buried watermelon and paused in his digging. Boston Police chemist David Brody had arrived and Maillet asked him to inspect the mound. Gently brushing it off with his hand, Brody looked up.

"Trash bag," he reported.

Brody carefully made a six-inch incision in the green plastic with a scalpel. Inside was a layer of white powdery substance, which he delicately brushed away. "It's lime, Sergeant," the chemist said, rising to his feet, "and there's blue fabric underneath."

"That's what he was wearing," Moran said quietly. "A blue work shirt."

Maillet's watch showed 2:25 P.M. and he wrote down the time in his notebook. "Let's stop right here," he said evenly. "We're going to want a medical examiner, and a photographer." He turned to Detective McDermott. "Billy, it looks pretty much like our missing man is your murder victim."

"Yeah," McDermott said. "I'll radio the station. We'll get a state police photographer and an ME over here."

Outside in a pelting rain, Moran felt a storm brewing in his mind as he headed for his vehicle to radio the development to the Brighton station. A small crowd had gathered about the police vehicles. He wondered how he was going to break the news to Dave's mother.

By four o'clock the medical examiner had arrived

and the state police photographer was arranging several lights on tripods about the open pit.

Shooting with color film, he snapped the pile of coal, the concrete fragments, and the green plastic protruding from the remaining fill some two feet down inside the square hole.

The medical examiner scraped more sand and coal away from the trash bag and flayed back the green plastic, revealing what appeared to be a mound of lime.

"The coal must have filtered out gases from decomposition," the chemist said. "That helps explain why there was no telltale odor down here. The white powder looks like ordinary lime. If so, it would have slowed decomposition."

Brookline firefighters, requested for their expertise in handling human remains, slowly raised the lime-coated form. The outlines of a body in a face-down fetal posture emerged from the pit. Over its head was a white freezer bag, tied around the neck.

The corpse was gently placed on a plastic sheet and the chemist took samples of the lime shell from the body, which was clothed in denim. The right hand was missing. Over the right breast of the shirt was an oval cloth patch with the name *Dave* in script letters. The plastic bag was removed by the medical examiner, revealing a bearded face and long dark hair.

Clenching and unclenching his fist, Moran had to stifle a roar. *Mother of God,* he said to himself, *the kid has been mummified.*

In the gathering dusk Assistant Suffolk District Attorney Alice Richmond and Detective John O'Malley sped from Pemberton Square in his car. Informed of the potential find in Brookline, they blasted through rush-hour traffic with blue light flashing. Over and over Richmond thought to herself, *This could be it.* When they reached James Blaikie's former house, reporters and cameras were jamming the driveway entrance. The spinning lights of half a dozen official vehicles shimmered in the raw evening air.

O'Malley had barely stopped the car when Richmond was out and climbing the stairs to the front entrance. Inside the house, uniformed police and detectives from Boston, Brookline, and the state were everywhere. Identifying herself, she was permitted entry to the kitchen and when she approached the door to the cellar, no one had to tell her a body had been discovered down there.

She descended the wooden steps and took in the eerie scene. In the glare of the photographer's lights, people milled around. A camera was clicking. A man with rubber gloves was examining a body stretched on its back as though at rest. Detective Moran was watching with his hands clasped behind him, rocking on his feet like a cop of old on a street corner.

Medical Examiner Nolton Bigelow found a depression between the eyebrows that suggested a blow from a blunt instrument. At the rear of the head, just to the right of the midline, there was a bullet entry wound. However, Dr. Bigelow suspended his judgment about the cause of death until an autopsy could be performed. His primary objective at the scene was officially to pronounce death and supervise the removal of the body as quickly as possible consistent with gathering of evidence.

Relatively well preserved, the left hand still bore fingerprint ridges and Dr. Bigelow decided to remove it for possible fingerprint identification. He did so with a scalpel.

The state police photographer continued taking color shots of the quiet, methodical procedure, careful not to include any of the authorities in the photos. As potential court exhibits for viewing by jurors, they could not contain prejudicing images of the quick attending to the dead.

With the help of the chemist, the medical examiner removed the decedent's clothing, which was to be held as evidence.

Although extensively decomposed, the corpse was not skeletal. If DeWilde had died ten months before, the preserved condition of his body was remarkable to the doctor. He speculated the powdery white substance that had encased the body was the reason. It appeared to be ordinary lime, or powdered limestone, and as such would have absorbed moisture and impeded deterioration.

Detective Moran was walking past Richmond, and their eyes met. "Tom," she said, "how awful."

"Yes," Moran said, looking down into her eyes. "It would take a sadist to do this."

And live over it for three months before fleeing to Phoenix, Richmond thought with a sense of deep revulsion.

She learned from one of the detectives that an empty cigarette packet had been found in the grave. The brand was Pall Mall and her mind raced back to her interview with James Blaikie at her office in March. He had been chain-smoking without benefit of ashtray. Chain-smoking Pall Malls.

Detective Moran excused himself and climbed the stairs to the kitchen. He wanted to reach David's mother before she heard or saw the news on television.

In the kitchen an unhappy host told him to make whatever use of the telephone he needed. "Detective," he said sheepishly, "you were right. I should have let you break up that basement in June."

"It would have been too late for David anyway," Moran said.

"Anyway, Detective, I owe you a can of beer," he said. "Can I get you one?"

Moran forced a grin and shook his head no. "Some other time."

"Oh, right. On duty."

Moran soon had Patricia Wynn on the line.

"Mrs. Wynn, this is Detective Moran," he said gently.

"Hello, Detective."

He kneaded the telephone cord between his thumb and forefinger.

It wasn't necessary to tell her. She sensed why he was calling.

"You've found David," she said evenly.

"Yes, m'am, we have."

Following a silence, she said, "Tom, I want to call Ruth before she hears from anyone else. Can you call me back in fifteen minutes?"

"Sure," he said, "but, please tell me, are you okay?"

"Yes, Tom, I am. Thank you."

Hanging up the phone, he thought, *Some Thanksgiving we're all going to have tomorrow.*

In his second call to Pat Wynn, Moran heard that David's former wife had learned of the discovery on a newscast. Pat thanked him for his efforts in a quietly composed voice. "Jim is behind bars now, because of you, Tom," she said.

He felt the dignity and the strength of the woman. "Pat, how I wish I could've had better news for you."

"Tom, ten months ago I asked you not to forget my son, and you didn't." After a pause, she said, "You will let me know what will be happening next, won't you?"

"I will," he said.

Following their conversation, a towering rage seized Brighton Detective Thomas Moran and he picked the phone up again. He reached Charles Street Jail and a friend who was a guard there. After telling him about the day's discovery, Moran said, "Do me a *fav-uh would-ja?* You know inmate James Blaikie over there? I'd like you to tell the fat little fuck something for me."

Minutes later the guard strolled up to James Blaikie's cell in the century-old lockup.

"Mr. Blaikie," he said, "I've got a message for you."

Jim looked up from his bunk.

"Detective Moran just called and he asked me to

give you this message: 'Enjoy your turkey tomorrow. We found the body.' ''

Blaikie's mouth opened but he said nothing. He stared down at concrete, like the floor from which David DeWilde had just been exhumed.

II

JUDGMENTS

Justice, sir, is the great interest of man on earth.
Daniel Webster

Chapter 20

A true-life version of "The Tell-Tale Heart" by Edgar Allan Poe, the DeWilde story rocked Boston on a forbidding Thanksgiving Day. As in Poe's macabre nineteenth-century tale, a slain man had lain beneath the very feet of his killer.

Months of speculation on the disappearance of David DeWilde ended with a front-page headline in the *Boston Globe:* BODY UNEARTHED IN CELLAR OF MAN LINKED TO BACON CASE. The *Boston Herald's* headline read, HUB MAN BURIED IN CELLAR, SUSPECT CHARGED. Radio and television newscasts led with the story and it was carried by wire services beyond New England.

This murder was elevated above other killings by the circumstances and the names. A body is found in the basement of a house once owned by a former McGovern campaign aide. He is in jail awaiting trial for forgery in connection with his late business associate's company. Moreover, he is under suspicion in the poisoning death of the associate, a scion of the Bacon publishing family, a name known to textbook readers across the country. All of this in Boston, the Athens of America.

In the mortuary of a Brookline funeral home the exhumed body was identified as that of David DeWilde by a close male friend.

Norfolk County medical examiner Nolton Bigelow had a fingerprint analysis made by the state police laboratory overnight. The prints taken from the well preserved left hand of the decedent matched known fingerprints of David DeWilde.

Present during the autopsy were Brookline Detective William McDermott and a state police ballistics expert.

Dr. Bigelow turned his attention to the hole in the back of DeWilde's head, slightly to the right of the midline and halfway up the cranium. The opening measured 1.2 centimeters, or nearly half an inch, in diameter. It was consistent with the entry wound of a .38-caliber bullet fired at close range. The compression and thus widening of such a projectile on impact accounted for a wound slightly larger than the caliber.

The bullet had not exited but lodged in the bone between the brows, just above and slightly right of the nasal bone, causing a comminuted skull fracture, or shattering of the bone. It was the wound that Dr. Bigelow had initially thought the result of a hammer blow.

The trajectory of the bullet had been almost perpendicular from the rear of the skull through the brain and into the frontal bone.

David DeWilde had been shot just between the eyes, from behind.

After removing the deformed lead slug with forceps, Dr. Bigelow placed it on a tray and to the police it was obviously a .38. Detective McDermott recalled that was the bore of the revolver James Blaikie had used in his Phoenix holdups the previous May. Returned to Boston by Sergeant Detective Maillet, the Smith & Wesson was in state police custody.

Dr. Bigelow turned to the fleshless bones of the disintegrated right hand, which had been found with a gold ring at the bottom of the basement grave. He concluded the hand had experienced normal decomposition and fallen off because it had not been lime-coated like much of the body. He expected the state police laboratory would conclude the powdery white substance was calcium carbonate, which had acted as a drying agent and profoundly slowed decomposition.

But for the lime coating, Dr. Bigelow believed, investigators would have found nothing but skeletal remains, like the bones of the right hand, in the basement tomb. He estimated David DeWilde had been dead at least six months.

Finding no other projectiles in the body, Dr. Bigelow concluded that David DeWilde had been killed by a single gunshot fired at nearly point-blank range into the back of his head.

Two miles west of the funeral mortuary that raw Thanksgiving morning an odd scene unfolded on Strathmore Road in Brookline. A man and a younger woman were alternately walking and crouching over something on the ground as they progressed southward from the Chestnut Hill Reservoir transit station.

No residents along the street and yards telephoned authorities to investigate the odd couple. It would not have been necessary to call far. The male was a detective and the pretty blonde in her late twenties was Suffolk assistant district attorney Alice Richmond.

They were measuring the distance from the Suffolk–Norfolk county line to the house on Fisher Avenue where David DeWilde's body had been uncovered the previous day. The reason for their many ups and downs was the length of their measure: twelve inches.

According to an obscure Massachusetts law, Richmond might be able to prosecute the case if the scene of the crime in Norfolk County were within a hundred rods of Suffolk County.

The distance they measured was nearly a hundred feet within the 1,650-foot limit.

Out of respect for the place, she whispered, "We've got the case."

The following morning, District Attorney Garrett Byrne was highly amused by Richmond's tale of duck-walking in Brookline with a ruler on a soggy Thanksgiving morning. As it was, the attorney general of the commonwealth was the ultimate arbiter of jurisdiction. Byrne admired her spirit and volunteered to recommend her.

Also on the morning of November 28th, James Blaikie was arraigned in Brookline Municipal Court, where he was charged with the murder of C. David DeWilde. Bail was set at $100,000, and he was returned to Charles Street Jail.

The morning papers reported an additional problem for James Blaikie. A front-page *Boston Globe* headline read, ''Mrs. Blaikie's death probed . . . Investigation into 1973 suicide reopened.'' ''Burial find may spur new suicide probe'' was the *Boston Herald* headline. Waltham authorities had decided to reinvestigate the death of Blaikie's mother by a gunshot wound behind her right ear in the basement of her home two years before.

In Phoenix, Kathy Blaikie learned of her husband's situation by telephone from his Boston attorney and by coverage in the Arizona news media. Richard Connolly of the *Boston Globe* reached Kathy by telephone, and in an exclusive story on December 5 he reported her professing shock. ''I couldn't believe it, and I still can't believe it,'' she said of the body in the basement, which she had lived over for three months. ''There must be a mistake somewhere. My gŏd, doesn't the bad news ever end?''

She told Connolly she had no plans to come east but said she was working and saving money for her husband's defense. ''But does anyone care?'' Connolly reported her asking. ''Do you think anyone cares?''

Eight days into 1976, Alice Richmond got her wish. Massachusetts attorney general Francis X. Bellotti named her a special assistant attorney general for the purposes of prosecuting the *Commonwealth* vs *James F. Blaikie, Jr.* in the death of David DeWilde.

Richmond became the first woman in Massachusetts history to receive the appointment.

She sought an indictment against James Blaikie for the murder of David DeWilde ''with intent,'' and on January 19, a Norfolk County grand jury returned a true bill charging him with the crime—murder in the first degree.

Frank and Smoki understood perfectly and approved of the strategic decision to shelve the Bacon case and move against Blaikie on the DeWilde death. There was no suicide ruling there to stymie officialdom. Frank could not see the district attorney ever allowing Alice Richmond to seek a murder indictment in connection with Ed's death. Smoki clung to the hope that a conviction of Blaikie for the murder of David DeWilde would be followed by prosecution in the Bacon case.

She was getting relief from personal preoccupations in the nation's bicentennial celebration. It was more than a protracted Fourth of July for her. Named by Deputy Mayor Katharine Kane as functions director for Boston 200, Smoki found herself coordinating everything and everyone from champagne to Secret Service agents for a score of gala events that would mark a year-long observance of the nation's founding. The vaunted Back Bay hostess drew on three decades of experience in cultural and civic organizing and became known as the party-thrower for a city.

On the Fourth of July she was looking forward with special interest to the visit of Queen Elizabeth, scheduled for the following week. Smoki was slated merely to shepherd Her Royal Majesty and entourage into a reception at the Old State House, hard by the site of the Boston Massacre. *Not exactly receiving the Order of the British Empire,* Smoki thought, *but not bad for the hired help.* She was thinking whimsically of the honor bestowed by the Queen upon Pauline Conant Bacon twenty years before in recognition of her work with the English Speaking Union.

Smoki and her daughters carried on a family July Fourth tradition without Ed for the second year. Brooks, eager for her first year at Barnard College, and Hilary, between her sophomore and junior years at the Winsor School, joined Smoki on a friend's balcony overlooking the Charles River for the Boston Pops concert. Below them half a million souls colorfully carpeted the curving two-mile Esplanade. After the glorious finale of *The 1812 Overture* with blasts from U.S. Army howitzers and peals of bells atop Beacon Hill and Back Bay churches, the sky was consumed by the city's grandest fireworks display ever. Bursting rainbows crossed and vaulted ever higher for a thunder-clapping hour and pure white explosions turned night into a day of lightning. Smoki and the girls were left teary-eyed with troubled exhilaration.

The pyrotechnics in the Blaikie case were just beginning.

Scheduled to start early in August, the trial of James Blaikie was eagerly awaited by Boston crime journalists and their audiences. It was seen as the most bizarre case in recent memory and certainly the most notorious ever to be prosecuted by a woman in the commonwealth and perhaps in the country. Veteran reporters warmly anticipated a fascinating duel between the alluring, purposeful Alice E. Richmond and Blaikie's charmingly flinty attorney, Daniel G. Harrington. If hers was an iron fist stretching a velvet glove, a brawler dwelled not far behind his bespectacled congeniality.

Harrington had twelve years on the thirty-year-old Richmond and ten years of legal experience compared to her three years as an assistant district attorney. However, she had prosecuted more than a hundred criminal cases, half a dozen first-degree murders among them, and Harrington had never defended a client in a homicide case.

Recommended by a mutual political acquaintance, Dan Harrington had initially been retained by Blaikie for the sale of his Brookline house shortly before the May 1975 Phoenix holdup spree. In September, when Blaikie was indicted for embezzlement and forgery in the Bacon case, he again telephoned Harrington for legal representation. Following the discovery of DeWilde's body, Harrington got yet another call from Blaikie and became his attorney once more.

As his cocounsel, Harrington called upon attorney Edward F. "Ted" Harrington, a former gangbuster. A Boston College Law School graduate with ties to the Kennedy family, Ted had once headed the Justice Department's Organized Crime Strike Force in New England. The Harringtons were not related, but their

County Cork ancestries were as good as blood between them.

The anticipated bare-knuckles contest between the prosecution and the defense began before a trial could start.

On July 20th, Alice Richmond and Dan Harrington met in Norfolk Superior Court in Dedham on pretrial motions. James Blaikie and Brighton detective Moran were in attendance, ignoring each other in the judicial decorum.

During a recess, an assistant Norfolk County district attorney approached Richmond and advised her to talk about a possible plea bargain with Blaikie's counsel. He was by no means convinced Richmond had a solid case for first-degree murder. Blaikie might be found guilty of a lesser crime. Or a jury might believe he shot David DeWilde in self defense and acquit him. On the other hand, if he were to plead guilty to second-degree murder, he faced life imprisonment with eligibility for parole after fifteen years. He might well go for murder-two, since conviction for murder-one meant life without parole.

Richmond was taken aback. She believed a jury would find Blaikie guilty of killing David DeWilde in cold blood. However, she was prosecuting in Norfolk County under the district attorney there. It was her show, but not completely.

She relayed the offer to Dan Harrington, who quickly got a negative response from his client. However, the attorney said he would be open to further discussion.

Detective Moran learned of the plea bargaining and he was furious. "Alice," he said, clenching his jaw, "we've got a solid case. We can get a conviction for murder-one."

"I agree, Tom," said the grim-faced prosecutor as they were leaving the courtroom. "But those are my instructions. Blaikie hasn't gone for it so far, but I'll be surprised if he doesn't."

"Me, too," Moran said. "We've got a body in the basement of his house, the gun, the money motive, the works."

But the Norfolk DA persisted and a plea discussion did ensue, along with a raging controversy.

Harrington agreed to run the plea idea past Blaikie again at Charles Street Jail and on July 26, a week before the scheduled trial, his client bought it.

However, Harrington and Richmond were reading out of different books. His understanding of the agreement was that Blaikie would plead guilty to second-degree murder and also the Suffolk County forgery and embezzlement charges pending in the Bacon case. He would then serve all sentences concurrently. Richmond's interpretation was that the sentences would be served consecutively, fifteen years for murder and whatever the Suffolk indictments brought.

Word of the deal got to the Bacons and Patricia Wynn, who became instant allies in an effort to derail it. The idea of James Blaikie escaping trial and becoming eligible for parole in fifteen or fewer years was scandalous to them.

Richmond was rafting on the Salmon River in Idaho and out of touch when hell broke loose in Boston.

In a firestorm of meetings and telephone calls with Suffolk and Norfolk county officials, the Bacons and DeWilde's mother vigorously objected to any plea agreement. On July 28, five days before the trial was scheduled to begin, *Boston Herald* crime reporter Ed Corsetti got wind of the deal and pressed Norfolk County officials for information. The judge assigned to the trial issued a so-called gag order, forbidding the defense and prosecution from discussing the plea issue with the news media.

But reporters were all over their sources and the story was on the verge of breaking.

When Richmond returned from the wilds of Idaho three days before the scheduled trial date, she landed in a legal jungle.

Blaikie's attorneys firmly insisted the plea bargain was a done deal. However, Suffolk County district attorney Garrett H. Byrne adamantly refused to include the forgery and embezzlement indictments in any arraignment.

The trial was postponed for a week as a superior court judge heard the bitter dispute. He denied a defense petition that would have enabled Blaikie to serve sentences on all the charges concurrently.

To the deep satisfaction of DeWilde's people and the Bacons, the plea bargain was dead and Blaikie would be tried for first-degree murder in David's death. The forgery indictment and other charges in the Bacon case would wait.

Alice Richmond and the Harringtons had already been as close to a scrap as a courtroom permits, and the trial had yet to begin.

Dedham, Massachusetts, a leafy suburb of some 20,000 residents southwest of Boston, was the site of the oldest frame house in the country and the location of the notorious Sacco–Vanzetti murder trial. The 1921 conviction of two Italian immigrants in the stately Norfolk County Courthouse had ignited an international cause celebre that did not end with their electrocutions in 1927. Whether Nicola Sacco and Bartolomeo Vanzetti were vicious holdup men or radical leftists punished for their politics, the case bearing their name was forever connected with the town.

When jury selection began on Tuesday, August 10, every wooden pew in an oak-paneled court room on the first floor was filled. Spectators gathered outside in vain hope of seeing the baby-faced young defendant. Kathy Blaikie, believed to be living in Phoenix, was nowhere to be seen in the oppressive courtroom.

The following afternoon, besieged by the annual invasion of tropical air, the last of twelve jurors and four alternates was sworn in. They were to be sequestered. The session ended, they left for a chartered bus tour of sites involved in the case, including the basement in Blaikie's former Brookline house.

The next morning a well-groomed James Blaikie sat impassively behind the defense table as the jury of eleven men and five women filed into their pews to the right of Judge James P. McGuire.

In her opening statement, Special Assistant Attorney General Richmond asked the jurors to recall the basement on Fisher Avenue and the open dry well in the floor.

She dwelled on the discovery of the body. In order to convict Blaikie of first-degree murder, the jury would have to believe the crime had been premeditated and she aimed to show the planning and execution had been elaborate. She spoke of the concrete cover on the hole, the layers of coal and sand, and the green plastic sheet over the body.

"They pulled the body out of the hole," she said unemotionally. "The body being in a kind of fetal condition with the back and the rump side facing up, and there was a covering of some kind over that body. It appeared to be lined with concrete. They removed the lining of concrete and there was also a white plastic bag around the head and the bag was tied around the neck with wire and with rope.

"They pulled this body out and put it on a tarp in the basement. They took the bag off the head and started to remove the clothing and they started to remove this substance which was adhering to the skin, and when they removed the white plastic bag they saw a man who appeared to be with a beard, and when they removed his clothes they found nothing at all in his pockets, no money, no kind of identification, nothing at all."

Richmond referred to the name patch "Dave" on the cadaver's shirt, laundry markings on the shirt and trousers indicating DeWilde, the empty Pall Mall cigarette packet, bones of a right hand, and a gold ring.

Turning to the autopsy report, she said it showed "a bullet had entered the head of David DeWilde on the right side in the back" and she placed her forefinger on her blonde hair over the occipital bone. "It entered and had gone in what appeared to the medical examiner to be a straight line right through and absolutely shattered this bone right here." She touched a point between her eyebrows slightly to the right of center.

The packed courtroom was utterly still. Near the

front, Brighton detective Moran was seated next to Patricia Wynn and Ruth DeWilde.

Alice Richmond told the jury they would hear a friend of David's testify that before he left his auto repair shop on January 14, 1975, he exuberantly said, "Jimmy's got it."

Objections started early with Dan Harrington taking exception to the alleged quote. "It is on the face of it hearsay."

"Wait a minute," Judge McGuire said. He explained to the jury that Richmond's remarks were "merely a blueprint of what is anticipated to be offered in evidence." The admissibility of the evidence would later be decided. He instructed Richmond to proceed.

"If it please the Court," Harrington persisted. "I would ask the Court to direct the jury to wipe that remark from their minds."

"I will not do that," Judge McGuire intoned and Richmond resumed her opening remarks.

Moments later, when she spoke of David's friends telling Detective Moran that DeWilde had spoken of large loans owed him by Blaikie, Harrington again objected. Judge McGuire again permitted Richmond's commentary.

Five minutes passed and Richmond told the jury of "a certain document" that Blaikie was using as "collateral" for a bank loan, and Harrington was on his feet again. This time he requested a conference and Richmond joined him at the bench.

"I want this discussion carried on in such a tone that it doesn't reach the jury," Judge McGuire firmly warned the counselors.

Harrington argued that Richmond was getting into the area of the Bacon case, involving the disputed insurance policy, which Blaikie had pledged as loan collateral.

Richmond responded that the document to which she referred was not the allegedly forged beneficiary-change form but a proof of partnership in the Bacon agency, which Blaikie had never produced for the bank.

Judge McGuire ruled she could refer to a partnership agreement but not to the name Bacon, and she agreed.

In the afternoon session Richmond resumed her opening remarks and touched on Blaikie's financial difficulties, his purchase of a .38-caliber gun from a friend, ballistics reports on the slug removed from DeWilde's body, and Brighton detective Moran's interrogations of the defendant. When she spoke of a discussion between Moran and Blaikie concerning a possible lie-detector test, she said Blaikie told Moran, "I will think about it."

Again Dan Harrington was up, this time asking for a mistrial.

Judge McGuire excused the jury and summoned the counselors to the bench. "I will hear you on your motion, Mr. Harrington," he said.

"May it please the court, your honor, this morning you told the jury that the district attorney would give a blueprint of her case. What I heard is more of a scenario of the whole case that would duplicate *Gone With the Wind.*" Glaring at Richmond, he said, "She realizes that she has no evidence to prove premeditated murder. Therefore, she is trying to prejudice the jury through this opening statement."

Judge McGuire denied Harrington's motion for a mistrial and when the jurors returned, he instructed them not to infer that by declining to take a polygraph test the defendant was attempting to hide anything.

Richmond completed her opening statement with a preview of expected testimony from *Globe* reporter Richard J. Connolly, who had interviewed James Blaikie in Phoenix the previous summer. Blaikie, she said, had told Connolly of having a cup of coffee in the kitchen of his house with David and later seeing him off on Harvard Street with the admonition to "be careful" as he was "involved in some deal."

The first government witness was the son of the previous owner of the house on Fisher Avenue. Referring to a diagram of the basement, he testified that the square, brick-lined dry well in the concrete floor near the front of the house was empty and covered with boards when the house was sold to the Blaikies in April 1974. He also told of coal that had been laid in for an older furnace during the early 1940s in the event oil for the newer furnace became unavailable in World War II. However, he said, his family had never had to use the coal and it had remained in a cellar bin.

Taking the witness stand, the current owner described the basement as littered with debris when he bought the house from the Blaikies in June 1975, five months after DeWilde's disappearance.

Next on the stand was Brookline Detective William McDermott. In Richmond's view, as smart a cop as he was tough, he had conducted what she considered an excellent investigation. Spearheading the probe after DeWilde officially became a Brookline murder victim, he had uncannily tracked down and questioned witnesses both obvious and obscure. His reports provided Richmond with detailed accounts of Blaikie's movements before and after DeWilde's disappearance.

McDermott identified police color photographs of the exhumation as each was handed up to him by Richmond.

Asked by Richmond about the white plastic bag, Detective McDermott said, "It was similar to a freezer bag which came to just the top of the Adam's apple area of the neck and it was tied with pieces of rope and a piece of wire." He identified the plastic bag and also pieces of rope in which the body had been trussed.

After testifying to the discovery of right hand bones and a gold ring in the pit, McDermott ended the first day of the trial. He described how he had held the left arm of the deceased while the medical examiner had removed the well-preserved left hand with a scalpel for fingerprinting.

Gathering her papers, Richmond exchanged glances with Patricia Wynn and thought she knew why there was particular hurt in the mother's eyes. The detail of the gold ring had added the painful memory of another untimely death. It had been Pat's wedding ring, which David had treasured as a keepsake of his late father and worn to his own early grave.

Chapter 21

Blaikie insisted to his attorneys that he had killed David DeWilde in self-defense when his creditor-friend became violent in an argument over a $6,000 loan. The Harringtons thought a jury more likely to believe this story than the notion a debt had impelled him to lure a man into his house, execute him, and bury him in the basement. As far as the Harringtons were concerned, nothing in the evidence provided to them by the prosecution supported such premeditation. Rather, Blaikie's attorneys saw the picture of a man who shot his stronger assailant in self-defense, panicked, and foolishly concealed the body in the worst possible hiding place. The very inevitability of the body's discovery argued against premeditation.

The Harringtons settled on a strategy of forcefully attacking the commonwealth's case, which they considered weak in the extreme. The burden of proof was upon Alice Richmond, and they did not think she had the evidence to support it.

Second-degree murder was the best she could get, they believed, and the jury might even find justifiable homicide and acquit Blaikie entirely.

They also decided not to put him on the witness stand. Articulate and presentable as he was, his attorneys were wary of the inherent danger in a defendant's testimony. None had ever spoken more eloquently in his defense than Sir Thomas More, and he had lost his head. Anyone less saintly could expect to look like a cornered rat under the slings and arrows of a prosecutor.

There was also the problem of a defendant live and well on the witness stand and gruesome photos of the deceased in the hands of the jury.

The morning of the second day of the trial, Judge McGuire heard arguments on Dan Harrington's request to suppress a photograph of the exhumation.

In the absence of the jury, the judge inspected the photo of the rope-trussed corpse with a white plastic bag over its head, taken immediately after its removal from the pit.

Harrington insisted the photo would be prejudicial.

"In what respect?" Judge McGuire asked.

"Just that it is grotesque," Harrington said.

Referring to judicial precedents, Richmond contended that "photographs which have some probative value and which are relevant to the case are not excluded merely because they are gruesome."

"My objection is it doesn't show a body," Harrington said. "I don't see a body. I don't know what it is."

"That is what it is," Judge McGuire asserted. Referring to Brookline detective McDermott's testimony, he added, "This is what a witness said it is." He ruled the photo could be admitted as an exhibit for viewing by the jury.

Relieved that the jurors would see the homicide victim, Richmond set about making her case for his cold-blooded murder.

Medical Examiner Nolton Bigelow, M.D. testified to his participation in the removal of the body from its basement grave. He said the yard-square concrete slab and approximately eighteen inches of sand and coal had been removed from the hole by police by the time of his arrival.

The 1940 Yale alumnus and Cornell medical school graduate identified the photo of the disinterred trussed body with a bag over its head and its handless right arm visible. The picture was delivered to the jury by a court officer.

It passed from one silent juror to another. After inspecting it, several of the men and women glanced at an expressionless James Blaikie, who did not look toward the jury box but stared straight ahead.

Richmond asked Dr. Bigelow to describe the gunshot entrance wound.

He stood up on the witness stand and used himself as a model, turning his back to the jury. "It was a trifle to the right of the midline and it was in what is known as the right occipital bone in a region right about here," he said, pointing almost halfway up the back of his own head.

When Richmond presented a photo of the rear of the skull, with the scalp lifted to display the entry bullet wound, Dan Harrington objected to its admission. Judge McGuire overruled him, saying it was necessary to the jury's understanding of the wound's location.

Demonstrating the location of the frontal wound, where the bullet had lodged, Dr. Bigelow faced the jury and pointed between his eyebrows, slightly to the right of his nose.

Harrington objected to two photos showing the body's facial skin flayed back to reveal the shattered brow bone. Sustaining Harrington's objection, Judge McGuire withheld them from the jury.

"It is my opinion," Dr. Bigelow said, "that such a gunshot wound would render an individual unconscious and helpless almost instantly upon the entrance of the bullet into the head." He said the victim of such a wound might have died within five minutes or survived for several hours. In his view, DeWilde had probably been dead between six months and a year.

His criterion, he said, was the decomposition of the parts of the body that were not preserved. "When a person dies, there are ways of preserving the body, such as Egyptian mummies for millennia, thousands of years. This body showed evidences of excellent preservation and also a great deal of decomposition."

"What portion of this body, Doctor, are you describing as extremely well preserved?" Richmond asked.

"The skin."

Richmond knew her next question would go to the heart of her case for premeditated murder and she asked it calmly. "Do you have an opinion as to what caused that skin to be as well preserved as you saw it?"

"Yes, I do have an opinion," Dr. Bigelow replied evenly. "The skin had been covered in large part by cement lime. Cement lime is the substance that one mixes with sand to form concrete. The cement lime is a drying agent, and one of the factors that produces decomposition or rapid decomposition in a body is heat and wetness. Bacteria thrive in a wet-hot environment and that is why decomposition often occurs so rapidly in a corpse in hot weather. But the cement lime dries out the skin and, as a consequence, preserves it as it did in this case extraordinarily well."

For these reasons, Dr. Bigelow said, the body's right hand, which had not been covered with cement lime, had disintegrated naturally. "If the body had not been covered by cement lime, it is my opinion that the entire corpse would have been simply bones."

"On what do you base that opinion, Doctor?" Richmond asked.

"The ground or sand in the cellar was quite damp. The right hand had not been covered with cement lime and, therefore, had decomposed completely into bones. The remainder of the body was covered in this eggshell-like coating which acted in this extraordinary fashion to preserve the skin. The inner organs were also not in contact with cement lime, and they—the brain, the heart, the lungs, the liver, all the internal organs—were virtually completely decomposed and just a kind of an unrecognizable goo on which this body skeleton and skin was draped around."

A low murmuring subsided in the filled courtroom when Richmond asked her next question. "Doctor, concerning the entrance wound which you have described in the right rear portion of the skull and the comminuted fracture in the forehead where you removed the deformed slug, do you have an opinion as to the path of the bullet once it entered the head of this corpse?''

"Yes, I do.''

"And what is that opinion?''

"It is my opinion that the bullet passed directly from behind through the brain and hit the front part, the bones of the frontal region, the front part of the skull, causing the shattering fracture. And so much energy was dissipated in this shattering of the bones that the bullet remained present in place and did not further pass through the skull. And it came directly through, at the time I examined it, the nonexistent brain.''

"I have no further questions, your honor,'' Richmond said. Returning to her seat, she was satisfied that testimony on the cement lime and bullet trajectory would support her scenario of what happened in the menacing calm of James Blaikie's house that brutally cold January afternoon. She believed that while DeWilde was seated at the kitchen table, Blaikie walked up behind him and shot him in the back of the head. Her theory was that Blaikie covered him with cement lime, mistakenly thinking it would render the body unidentifiable, as *quick* lime would have.

In his cross-examination, Dan Harrington wanted to shake Dr. Bigelow's testimony on the probable date of death and raise doubts that DeWilde had been slain on the day of his disappearance.

"Doctor,'' Harrington said, "your testimony this morning was that with the body completely encased in cement, the date of death would be six months to a year.''

"Yes.''

Harrington showed Dr. Bigelow two preautopsy photos. "Doctor, do these exhibits reflect the opinion held by you that the features were in excellent condition?''

The medical examiner viewed the photos of a gaunt face. "Excellent is perhaps an unusual word in the sense that the hair is present, there is a mustache present, the features are such as to be almost identifiable. It is a little grim, yes, but—''

"All right, Doctor. That's fine," Harrington interjected. "Based on all the evidence and what you observed, do you have an opinion whether the deceased could have been dead for a period of *less* than six months?"

"Yes, I have an opinion."

"And what is that, Doctor?"

"That he could not have been dead for a period of less than six months."

"Doctor, on what basis do you make that opinion?"

"All the information that was made available to me at the time I made my examination."

"And from whom did you receive that information, Doctor?"

"I received the information from a variety of sources, most of which were the police."

Harrington cocked his head and asked if he had an estimate of the period in which death had occurred based solely on his own observations without police information, and Dr. Bigelow replied: "No, I do not."

Under redirect by Richmond, the medical examiner said that he would have arrived at the same estimate without knowing when DeWilde had disappeared. However, Harrington thought to himself that doubt had been cast on the ME's opinion.

The vault keeper of David DeWilde's Brookline bank was called as the next witness. Stanley B. Barber testified that he saw DeWilde in the vault area soon after it opened on January 10th.

Barber said someone was with DeWilde and described the companion. "He was a young fellow of medium height, stocky build, very neatly dressed, a black coat, dark coat, and reddish-blonde hair, and the hair was combed back quite neatly, medium height."

A moment later he pointed out an impassive James Blaikie as that man.

Barber testified that Blaikie followed DeWilde with his safe-deposit box into a double booth, where they remained for three or four minutes.

The Friday incident was important in Richmond's mind, for it occurred the day after on which the Harbor National Bank in Boston gave James Blaikie an ultimatum to bring loans totaling $21,000 up to date. The following Tuesday, DeWilde disappeared, and next day James Blaikie payed $800 in cash on his overdue loans.

It was Richmond's belief that the sequence of banking events pointed to motive and premeditation. Blaikie receives money from DeWilde at his bank on Friday for the mysterious deal, actually a Blaikie ruse in her opinion. Blaikie murders DeWilde the following Tuesday, and on Wednesday waltzes into his own bank with cash for his critically overdue loan payments.

In his cross-examination, Dan Harrington tried to impeach the vault keeper's memory. Referring to Barber's interview with Brookline detective William McDermott, Harrington said, "Did you make the following statement: 'I believe or I guess that Mr. DeWilde came to the bank with a second party and it must have been on the tenth as the card shows that DeWilde was assigned to cubicle number 8, which is designed for two people'?"

Richmond objected, but before Judge McGuire could rule, Harrington let loose, "Did you make that statement?" The judge overruled Richmond and Barber responded, "I can't recollect for sure."

Harrington grumbled, "You can't recollect what you said on December—"

Coloring, Richmond was on her feet, addressing the judge. A harried witness answered, "I can't remember."

"Now wait a minute," Judge McGuire declared angrily. "One at a time."

But Harrington pressed on. "Is that correct, sir?"

"Please," the judge said in a commanding tone, gaveling for order.

"I'm sorry," Harrington said contritely.

"There are three people talking all at once," a bristling Judge McGuire observed. Looking at the penitent witness, he ordered, "Don't answer until the question is finished, and, if there is an objection, until I rule.

Then you may answer, if I rule it admissible. Go ahead.''

Harrington asked Barber to consult his access slip of January 3rd for DeWilde's safe-deposit box, which was a record of his use of the box that day. Barber explained it was the same kind of slip as one he had for DeWilde's January 10th visit. Harrington asked if either slip indicated DeWilde was accompanied and Barber replied no.

''So it is not beyond the realm of possibility or probability that Mr. DeWilde and Mr. Blaikie were together on January 3rd, is it?''

''Objection to the form of that question,'' Richmond asserted.

''This is cross-examination,'' Harrington announced.

Judge McGuire frowned at the counselors. ''If I need assistance, I will ask either one of you for it. Objection sustained in that form.''

''I have no further questions of this witness,'' Harrington said with a look of distaste. He had brought out the possibility that Blaikie had not been to DeWilde's bank four days before his disappearance, which could weaken the case for premeditated murder.

Brookline taxi driver Albert Mazin approached the witness stand. Alice Richmond bore in mind his expected testimony would place James Blaikie within 300 paces of the Brighton address where a Boston meter maid found the missing DeWilde's abandoned Volvo. It was Richmond's belief that Blaikie left his own car in a nearby supermarket parking lot on the morning of January 14 and took a one-and-a-half-mile cab ride home. After luring DeWilde to the Blaikie house and murdering him, she figured Jim drove David's Volvo to Royce Road in Brighton, left it there, and walked to his own car. Then, her theory went, he drove to Framingham and met Kathy for lunch.

The cab driver testified that at about eleven-thirty on the morning of January 14, a fare entered his vehicle, which was parked at a cabstand in Brookline near the border of Boston's Brighton section. The cabstand was located on Harvard Street, across from a Purity Supreme supermarket.

Mazin described the male fare as "very, very stocky, very meticulously and well dressed" and wearing "a large fur-collared black coat." After identifying the defendant as that man, the cabbie said Blaikie told him he had dropped his car off for repairs. Richmond recalled to herself that Blaikie had told Detective Moran that he had accidentally locked his keys in his car that morning, the reason he gave for asking DeWilde to the house.

The cabbie said he took Blaikie to his Fisher Avenue house.

Under cross-examination, Dan Harrington elicited answers from the cab driver that characterized Blaikie as friendly, talkative, and neither nervous nor upset. Again the strategy was to portray his client as a man who had no intention of murdering his friend within the hour.

Although cameras were barred from court, media coverage of the trial was extensive and drew even greater overflow crowds to the Norfolk Superior Courthouse the following week.

On Monday, August 16th, the fifth day of the trial, New England remained in thrall of an oppressive air mass pumped from the Gulf of Mexico. Only a staggering caseload had forced the court to remain in session this perennially stifling month.

Through the testimony of DeWilde's friends, mother, and ex-wife, Richmond provided the stolid jurors with a detailed version of the days preceding David's disappearance. The picture emerged of a spirited young man exuberant and then anxiety-ridden about his unexplained deal, purportedly involving more than $10,000 of his money, with James Blaikie.

Matthew Chaet, a friend from whom David had rented a garage bay for his Brighton auto repair business, told of David receiving a telephone call at the shop on January 14 and leaving in good spirits around twelve-thirty.

"Did you ever see David DeWilde after he left the shop that afternoon?" Richmond asked.

"No," the witness replied.

On Tuesday, Dan Harrington intensified his counterattack by vehemently pressing his second and third motions for mistrial.

In the morning, he argued in the absence of the jury that the prosecution had failed to provide the defense with the criminal record of a state witness. The friend of DeWilde's had not yet testified.

Richmond acknowledged her failure to provide the criminal record, calling it an oversight. However, she added, the ten-year limit on the use of the larceny conviction for impeachment purposes had expired. In any event, she did not intend to call the witness.

Judge McGuire nevertheless agreed with Harrington. "I ordered *all* records to be produced," the judge firmly told Richmond, "and they should have been produced." However, Judge McGuire did not find the omission prejudicial against Blaikie and ruled against Harrington's motion for a mistrial.

Harrington's third call for a mistrial came later in the morning. A visibly overwrought Judith Fillippo was testifying to her telephone conversation with DeWilde shortly before his January 14th appointment with Blaikie, the last time she heard David's voice. The court limited testimony to DeWilde's state of mind and instructed her not to say what he allegedly told her.

Richmond hoped to get out word of a luncheon date allegedly planned between Blaikie and DeWilde. In Richmond's mind it was the setup for the kill.

"And what was Mr. DeWilde's tone during this conversation?" Richmond asked.

"He seemed a little calmer but he was still nervous," Judith replied.

"Did he indicate to you whether or not he had any lunch plans?" Richmond asked, igniting a fierce point–counterpoint exchange with the defense.

Dan Harrington: "I object."

Judge McGuire: "Sustained."

Alice Richmond: "Did he say anything at all about lunch?"

Dan Harrington: "I object."

Judge McGuire: "Sustained."

Alice Richmond: "Did you have a conversation with him?"

Dan Harrington: "I object."

Judge McGuire: "She said she had a conversation. That is already in."

Alice Richmond: "Did he say anything about the defendant James Blaikie?"

Dan Harrington: "I object."

"Yes," Fillippo said.

"That may be stricken," the judge said of her answer. "The jury will disregard it."

However, after nervously testifying that David's telephone voice was hesitant and quavering, Fillippo blurted, "He made reference to not returning from his luncheon engagement."

Red-faced, Harrington shot to his feet, demanding a mistrial.

Judge McGuire ordered the jury to disregard Judith Fillippo's paraphrase of DeWilde and instructed her not to convey the alleged content of the telephone conversation.

"Your honor," Harrington implored, "she has already talked about it."

"I will ask you, when I want to hear from you," Judge McGuire snapped. He told Richmond to resume.

But she had no more gotten out the question of whether that was Fillippo's last conversation with DeWilde than Harrington was again heatedly asking for a ruling on his motion for a mistrial.

"At the proper time, I will rule on it," the judge sternly announced, and he asked Fillippo: "Did you ever talk to DeWilde again?"

"No," she said, struggling, "I did not."

Richmond asked, "Did you ever see him again?"

"No, I did not."

In his cross-examination, Harrington bore down on

Fillippo's relationship with David, asking if she stayed with him at night.

"Yes," she said, appearing about to sag in the witness chair.

"Do you feel all right?" Judge McGuire asked gently.

"Yes," she said, almost inaudibly.

"All right," the judge said. "If you have any message, give it to the matron."

Harrington had no further questions and a shaken Judith Fillippo slowly left the witness stand.

Following the emotional scene, Judge McGuire spoke to the jury about "the adversary process" between the commonwealth and the defense. "At times, unfortunately, it becomes somewhat perhaps acrimonious or acerbic but that wouldn't have any effect upon you. You disregard it, disregard it because everyone is trying to do a good, professional job. And because sometimes voices are raised, sometimes the voice of the Court is raised, it has no importance. What is important is what is said as judged by you, and so you will accept my limitations without any question and you will completely disregard anything I order stricken."

He excused the jury and told counselors he would hear the defense motion for a mistrial.

Richmond and Harrington appeared as sociable as two boxers being instructed by a referee.

"I submit to your honor," Harrington said, "that answer was inadmissible as being hearsay, prejudicial, conclusionary, and an opinion. It was shot in there by the witness to convince the jury that Jimmy Blaikie killed David DeWilde at lunch."

"Your honor," Richmond said, "this witness was attempting to do the best she could in a situation that was highly emotional for her and in which she really didn't understand what was required of her."

Judge McGuire took the motion under advisement and after the morning recess informed the counselors in the absence of the jury that the third defense motion for a mistrial was denied. ''The defendant's rights are saved,'' he said.

Next on Richmond's agenda was James Blaikie's woeful financial condition, a key element in her case for money as the murder motive.

Bank and credit company officials testified throughout the afternoon to the hopeless debt into which Blaikie had sunk by January 1975. According to a bank mortgage officer, Blaikie's payment for that month was the last he made on his house loan, which was retired after his sale of the Brookline house in June. Although not permitted to refer to the sailboat, a credit company manager testified that Blaikie had been several months in arrears on a $15,000 loan. Richmond could not and did not allude to Blaikie's 1974 sale of the mortgaged boat to an unsuspecting buyer. The doctor had wound up being changed twice for the sloop, once by Blaikie and, after Blaikie stopped making payments, again by the credit company. The doctor's hopes of recovering his loss from the murder defendant were slim, even if Blaikie were to be acquitted.

According to the combined testimony of creditors, Blaikie's indebtedness amounted to nearly $100,000 on the day he allegedly murdered David DeWilde. His monthly loan payments were more than $1,000.

As the sixth day of the trial ended on the sultry late afternoon of August 17, Alice Richmond believed that motive and opportunity for dispatching David DeWilde had been well established. Next on her agenda were the planning, execution, and coverup.

Several law-enforcement officers were scheduled to testify the following day, among them Brighton detective Moran. His three interrogations of Blaikie were critical to her case.

Detective Moran was anticipating a donnybrook and he was up for one. Moran was used to close-quarters contests in the sanctity of the court and held no animosity toward attorneys. They tried to do their job, and he tried to do his.

The morning before the seventh day of the trial, he

met with Alice Richmond in the district attorney's office on the second floor of the Dedham courthouse.

He wanted to see the notes of Sergeant Detective John Doris, his superior officer, on the crucial February 6 meeting with Blaikie. It was in that interview, Moran's second with Blaikie, that the detective had told Blaikie he was a suspect in DeWilde's disappearance. Jim denied owing DeWilde money, but after Moran told him of the loan note found in DeWilde's safe-deposit box, Blaikie admitted he had been lying. Attending at Moran's request, Sergeant Doris had taken comprehensive notes while Moran had vigorously questioned Blaikie and kept sketchy notes. Moran had not seen the Doris notes recently and wanted to refresh his memory. He asked Richmond for them.

She told him the Doris notes had not been given to the defense and he should limit his testimony to his own reports, concise versions of the interrogations.

Moran was astonished. "Alice," he said, "my reports don't have Blaikie's exact words for the February 6th meeting. That's the one where he says the most incriminating things. They're in Doris's notes."

"Tom," she said, "your reports contain the substance and gist of everything Blaikie said."

"Alice," he said, steaming. "I've got to refer to the Doris notes to give detailed answers. The Harringtons are going to see the exact words aren't in my reports and the shit is going to hit the fan. They're going to call for a mistrial."

"Stay within your three reports," she said.

Moran angrily left the meeting. He felt like the proverbial boxer with one hand tied behind his back.

Alice Richmond was not concerned as she entered the courtroom that morning. She believed her decision to exclude the Doris notes was both legally and tactically correct. In her view they were not necessary to her prosecution and she was not going to use them. As far as judicial rules were concerned, she reasoned she had not been obligated to provide the defense with the Doris notes. They were not exculpatory. Indeed, with their specific language, she saw them as more damaging to Blaikie than Moran's reports.

For that very reason Detective Moran could not understand why she was not using the Doris notes. The answer was that Richmond had relied on Moran's testimony in the probable cause and grand jury proceedings. She had later presented his reports to the Harringtons as the scope of Blaikie's statements to be used in the trial. With the issue settled, she had not wanted to reopen it with the Doris material and left it out of evidence.

She thought she was on firm ground. Moran did not think so.

The first witness of the day was the former college friend of Blaikie's who had paid off a hundred-dollar loan by giving him the weapon used in the 1975 Phoenix holdups. A buyer for a Boston computer firm, he recalled turning the .38 over to Blaikie in late 1972 or early 1973. He said he had thrown eight rounds of ammunition into the deal.

Sergeant Detective Maillet established the continuity of the gun's whereabouts. Maillet told of receiving it from Phoenix police the previous October and placing it in the custody of a Massachusetts state police ballistician.

State police officer George Windisch, a graduate of the Smith & Wesson Armor School in Springfield, Massachusetts, related the findings of his ballistics analysis of the revolver and the .38 slug removed from David DeWilde. Because the copper coating was gone, he was unable to compare the slug fully with one test-fired from the revolver. It was on the copper that spiral grooves from the rifling inside the gun barrel were most evident. However, he said, microscopic analysis indicated that "the projectile removed from the victim and the test projectiles had the same general characteristics." But, he added, "There was an insufficient amount of striations for me to make a positive identification."

Richmond asked, "Trooper Windisch, were you able to determine any characteristics of the bullet which was removed from the victim to indicate that that bullet was *not* fired from this weapon?"

"No, I could not determine that."

Dan Harrington objected.

"Negative evidence," Judge McGuire declared. "Admissible."

In cross-examination Harrington asked, "Now, officer, after test-firing, your ultimate conclusion is that the bullet could have been—but you don't know—could have been fired from that gun?"

"That's correct," Trooper Windisch responded.

In the afternoon session, Boston detective John O'Malley of the Suffolk district attorney's office testified to the March 1975 meeting with Blaikie and his attorney at Alice Richmond's office. DeWilde had been missing for two months.

Richmond did not bring up the Bacon case but asked, "Did you make any observations of Mr. Blaikie?"

"Yes, I did," O'Malley replied.

"With specific reference, Detective, to his hands, did you make any observations about what the defendant was doing with his hands, if anything?"

"He was holding a pack of cigarettes and chain-smoking."

"And can you tell the Court and the jury what brand of cigarettes you observed him smoking, chain-smoking, on March 5, 1975?"

"Pall Malls."

After the witness was excused, Richmond silently thanked Blaikie for burying an empty Pall Mall packet in DeWilde's grave.

Later on, a state police chemist testified the white powdery substance on the body was a calcium carbonate, or limestone. It was exactly what the medical examiner had described as the preservative that had virtually mummified the body—ordinary cement lime.

A state police sergeant from the Firearms Records Bureau took the stand next. Detective Moran was scheduled to follow him. He heard the sergeant report that Blaikie was not licensed to carry a firearm in Massachusetts for at least the previous four years. Taking less than five minutes, the testimony seemed over in a matter of seconds, and shortly after three o'clock Moran found himself being sworn in. Feeling vulnerable without the Doris notes in evidence, Moran nevertheless sat up foursquare in the witness chair and looked down on James Blaikie. The defendant stared back at him like a choir boy.

Under questioning by Alice Richmond, Moran recited his background as a Boston police officer of twenty-five years, with the rank of detective the previous nine. The direct examination went smoothly; it was uninterrupted by objections as Moran concisely answered Richmond's questions about the early days of the DeWilde case, starting with Patricia Wynn reporting her son missing.

Moran's testimony retraced his contacts with David's mother, attorney, former wife, and friends among the scores of persons he interviewed in the case.

He told of finding DeWilde's abandoned car in Brighton eight days after his disappearance, and Richmond asked when he first met the defendant James Blaikie.

Moran replied that he had met Blaikie on January 24th, and he carefully proceeded to describe his first interrogation of Blaikie. In it, Blaikie had told of locking his keys in his car on Brookline's Harvard Street, near the Brighton line, taking a cab home, and telephoning DeWilde, asking him to come to the house.

"What did you say at that time?" Richmond asked.

"I said, 'Why didn't you go down to Dave's?' He is just down the block." Moran was referring to DeWilde's auto repair shop.

"What did the defendant say?"

"He said he wanted to get his own keys to the car and he took the cab home."

Richmond asked what the distance was from the point where Blaikie said he had left his car to DeWilde's shop.

"Eight-tenths of a mile," Moran said, "down Harvard and left on Cambridge."

Richmond nodded, intending later to bring out testimony that the distance to Blaikie's house was twice as long.

Moran said Blaikie next told him DeWilde had come to the house to pick up a fifty-dollar bet he had won on the Super Bowl the previous Sunday. After DeWilde had dropped him off near his car on Harvard Street, Blaikie had driven to Framingham and met his wife for lunch at the Sea & Surf Restaurant.

Moran told of asking Blaikie if he had ever borrowed money from DeWilde. "He said early in the summer he had borrowed $2,000 from him and paid him back. He said at this time that Dave owed him money." Blaikie, Moran said, spoke of discussions between him and DeWilde of going into the insurance business, plans that had fallen through.

Asked if he had any further conversation with Blaikie, Det. Moran testified, "Yes, he told me that Dave had a girlfriend behind Ken's Pub, and I said, 'Do you know where she lives?' He said she was married and had a couple of kids and was living on Royce Road. And then he said, 'Where did you find the car?' I said, 'On Royce Road.' "

Believing she had begun unraveling Blaikie's coverup, Richmond directed Moran through his investigation of DeWilde's safe-deposit box on January 28 and asked what he found in it.

He described a note as reading: " 'Six thousand dollars to J. Blaikie, December 12, 1974, payable on February 12, 1975.' And just to the right of that it said, 'Nine thousand dollars left.' And there was another notation that said, 'Thirty-five hundred dollars, not from J. Blaikie.' "

Both Moran and Richmond believed that the missing $12,500 by that accounting represented the money, on top of the $6,000 loan, that DeWilde had apprehensively been telling friends he had given to Blaikie.

The direct examination reached the point of Moran's crucial second meeting with Blaikie, in which Jim changed his story. On February 6, the detective testified, Blaikie arrived at the Brighton police station without the attorney he had talked about.

"I asked him where his lawyer was, and he said he didn't think he needed one. He said he didn't have anything to hide."

Moran stated that he read Blaikie his rights under the Miranda doctrine in the presence of Sergeant Detective John Doris, who joined in the meeting.

"Would you relate to the jury, please, and the Court what that conversation was?" said Richmond.

"I asked him that day if he had borrowed money from David DeWilde and he again said no, he didn't." Moran told of informing Blaikie about the note in DeWilde's safe-deposit box. "He then said yes, he did borrow $6,000," the detective said.

"And did he indicate whether or not he had paid Mr. DeWilde back?"

"He said he had not paid him back. I then asked Blaikie about an additional $12,000, and he said no, he didn't borrow $12,000."

Blaikie also denied being in the safe-deposit section of the bank with DeWilde on January 10th, Moran said, but when the suspect was informed that he had been placed there by the vaultkeeper, Blaikie recanted. According to Detective Moran, Blaikie also admitted he had gone into a cubicle with DeWilde but did not know what he had done with the safe-deposit box.

"I said, 'The cubicle is so small you had to know what he was doing.' He said, 'I don't know what he did.' "

Moran had sailed through the first hour of his testimony without as much as an objection from Harrington. But, the detective knew, the part most damaging to Blaikie would come in the morning. The Harringtons' hawklike scrutiny would come with it.

On Thursday, August 19, the eighth day of the trial, Detective Moran resumed testimony and described James Blaikie as "cool, calm" in their first meeting. But the February 6th meeting was different, he said. "It started out cool but it ended up with him chain-smoking. He was shaking. He perspired tremendously, had his handkerchief in his hand almost throughout the last part of the interrogation.''

Moran said that after learning he knew about the contents of DeWilde's safe-deposit box, Blaikie stated that ''he was afraid that we would suspect him, and I said, 'Of what?' and he said, 'Of the disappearance of Dave.' ''

Richmond turned to Moran's third and final meeting with Blaikie, on February 25th, also attended by Sergeant Detective Doris at the Brighton police station. Blaikie, Moran said, posed a hypothetical question. ''If he was the middleman in a deal between two parties and he didn't know what the commodity being dealt was, would he be criminally responsible?''

''Did he explain how he had been the middleman?'' Richmond asked, aiming at what she and Moran believed to be a cover story.

''Taking phone calls and relaying messages,'' Moran said. ''He then told me about a man named Ned Woodman. He told me that he was the go-between between David DeWilde and Woodman, that he didn't know what the commodity was and that when he left David on Harvard Street, Brookline, David was going to Brandy's pub to meet Ned Woodman.''

''And did you ask him why he hadn't come forward with this information before?''

''Yes,'' Moran said. ''He said he was afraid to say anything about it.''

''And did he say anything else when he said he was afraid?''

''He didn't want to be suspected of killing David DeWilde.''

Dan Harrington looked up from Moran's reports, which he had been reading as the detective testified. Previously there had been no essential difference between the typed and spoken word, but he could not find the phrase *killing David DeWilde* in any of the reports. In one, Blaikie allegedly said he was afraid police would ''suspect him of *something.*''

Dan thought the distinction important and leaned over to Ted Harrington, pointing to the phrase.

Noticing their huddle, Moran braced himself. He was quoting Blaikie from memory but the words were not in his report. They were in the Doris notes, which Alice Richmond had not included in the evidence. Moran expected to hear the word *mistrial* loud and clear at any instant.

But the Harringtons believed the trial was going their way and no longer wanted a mistrial. Confident that Richmond could not get more than a second-degree conviction, they wanted the trial to finish. If the jury came in with a guilty verdict on murder-one, they thought they could win a reversal on appeal.

Richmond asked, "And did he say anything else?"

"No, I said, 'Who said he was dead?' "

Again Dan Harrington made note of Moran's answer and again the attorney did not speak up.

Moran told of charging Blaikie with frustrating the investigation. "I said, 'Why didn't you tell me this right in the beginning?' He said, 'I was too frightened to do it, and look what happened to David.' "

Of Blaikie's departure from the police station, Moran stated, "He said, 'I just want you to know if I am killed.' I said, 'Please don't get killed until we find David.' " Moran's sarcasm, even toned down in court, caused a stir of nervous laughter and he detected the flicker of a grudging smile on the face of the defendant.

When Richmond had finished, Dan Harrington approached the witness stand. "Detective Moran, after you had these meetings with Mr. Blaikie, did you make memorandums of your conversations with him for your records?"

Thinking, *Here we go*, Moran said, "I made notes here and there."

One by one, Harrington handed Moran his three reports, asking him to show where Blaikie supposedly said he feared being suspected in DeWilde's death. Moran handed each report back, acknowledging the words were not in any of them.

But Harrington did not call for a mistrial, he turned instead to the topic of Blaikie as "a cooperative witness." Harrington insisted that Blaikie in a February 26th meeting with Detective Moran and Sergeant Detective Doris had offered to let them search his house.

"It wasn't the twenty-sixth," Moran said sharply. "It was the twenty-fifth, and he certainly did not. He wouldn't let me in that house at any time."

"Did you ask?"

"You're *damn* right I did," Moran said, coloring. "Excuse me," he said to Judge McGuire. Then he answered the question, "Yes, sir."

Harrington stared at the witness a moment and said, "I have no further questions."

Moran could hardly believe it was over.

But it was not.

The judge asked Alice Richmond if she had any questions to ask under redirect, and she answered yes.

Moran was incredulous. *Alice*, he thought, *leave well enough alone, for chrissakes.*

"Detective Moran," she said, approaching the witness stand, "I show you these three documents, which are what Mr. Daniel Harrington, defense counsel, was using or showed you during cross-examination, I believe, and ask you if all of the statements that the defendant made to you over that period from January twenty-fourth until February twenty-fifth are contained on those three pieces of paper?"

Moran felt his blood drain. He could not believe *Richmond* was asking the very question that *Harrington* had not asked. Moran looked over the pages, but he already knew the answer: The Doris notes were not among them because Richmond had not given them to the defense. Unclenching his jaw, he looked directly at her as though across a wide gulf and said, "No, they are not."

Alice Richmond stared blankly at him from her great distance.

A slight smile formed on James Blaikie's face.

Dan whispered to Ted Harrington, "She must *want* a mistrial." The attorneys agreed that in the face of the revelation they had no choice but to call for one. Dan stood up and announced: "Your honor, if that answer is accepted, I ask for a mistrial. I accepted those statements of the officer on pretrial and therefore I have been misled." Brandishing the three reports, he said, "I was led to understand this contained all of the statements. I ask for a mistrial."

Judge McGuire excused the jury, and when they had filed out of the courtroom, he told Harrington he would hear his motion at the bench.

Scowling, Moran remained seated in the witness stand, furious that Richmond had not included the Doris notes in evidence. Richmond, believing the substance of all Blaikie statements were in Moran's reports, felt let down by the detective as she approached the bench.

Following nearly four hours of hearing and deliberation, Judge McGuire returned to the bench and spoke to the anxious counselors in the absence of the jury. Focusing on Detective Moran's testimony that Blaikie said he "didn't want to be suspected of killing David DeWilde," Judge McGuire found it significantly different from language in the reports in evidence. In one, Blaikie allegedly said he was afraid police would "suspect him of something."

The judge called for the jurors and shortly after three o'clock they filed in.

"Mr. Foreman, ladies and gentlemen, I regret what I have to tell you," he said gravely. "I have declared a mistrial in this matter."

With a look of disbelief, Ruth DeWilde trembled at Patricia Wynn's side. David's mother gazed stoically at Judge McGuire.

He commended the jury for its forbearance through nearly two weeks of August heat, sequestered nightly in a local hotel. "You have done everything a good jury should do," he said, and, regarding his decision, added, "There is no fault I am ascribing to anybody, no fault whatsoever."

With that he thanked them and said, "I bid you good day. You are excused."

The clerk read the declaration of mistrial in the case of *Commonwealth* vs *James F. Blaikie, Jr.*, and informed the defendant that he was to be returned to Charles Street Jail.

Judge McGuire declared, ''Counsel will be advised of the time and place of the next trial. We stand in recess.''

As the judge left and the jury rose to leave, Ruth DeWilde cried out and tearfully collapsed in Patricia Wynn's arms.

Betraying no emotion, a natty James Blaikie was led out by court officers, nineteen months and five days after David DeWilde had left for an early-afternoon meeting with him.

By the time Richmond and Moran met upstairs in the district attorney's office, they were mutually apologetic.

''I'm sorry as hell, Alice,'' a downcast Moran said.

''I am, too, Tom,'' she said, shoving papers into her briefcase.

The prosecutor and detective swallowed their disappointment. Moran wished he could have answered yes to her question whether all the statements were in evidence but felt he could not truthfully. Richmond still believed a yes answer would have been honest, but she realized she had made a mistake in asking the question. The defense had not laid a glove on Moran.

Standing at a window, Brookline detective Billy McDermott whistled. ''Look at this,'' he said.

Richmond and Moran joined him and looked down on the crush of humanity at the foot of the courthouse steps. Photographers and television cameras were at the forefront.

''No way I'm going to sneak out of here wearing *this,*'' Richmond said, referring to her conspicuous yellow dress. ''Well, are you guys with me or do I face the lions alone?''

''I'm with you, Alice,'' Moran said.

McDermott nodded and the lady prosecutor led the gentleman detectives out the office door.

Outside, they descended the steps to a press corps arrayed like a firing squad. Television and still cameras and microphones pointed at them like weapons.

With a detective towering at her either shoulder, Richmond fielded questions from reporters.

Asked for her reaction to the mistrial, Richmond replied she thought the evidence supported Detective Moran's testimony. But Judge McGuire saw it differently, she added, and the decision was his to make.

Another reporter asked what she expected to happen next and Richmond said she would immediately start preparing for the second trial.

One of the television reporters virtually accused her of causing the mistrial and she coldly responded that was not what Judge McGuire had said.

Preferring not to conduct a seminar on the courthouse steps, she followed the detectives as they plowed through the crowd. They would have to start all over again.

Chapter 22

The stone was also back at the bottom of the mountain for the defense, but the Harringtons decided to roll it up another mountain.

Pointing to the massive reporting of the first trial, they filed a motion for a change of venue out of Norfolk County. Superior Court Judge James P. McGuire, who in any event was again going to preside, chose Fall River as the site of the second trial, and it was scheduled for November. The Bristol County town near Buzzards Bay was forty-five miles south of Boston and outside the main area of its news media. Prospective jurors there were presumed less likely than a Norfolk County venire to have been inundated by reporting of the DeWilde case.

In late September, Richmond provided defense counsel with all police reports in her possession, including the report of Brighton sergeant detective John Doris.

In October the election campaigns of President Gerald Ford and Jimmy Carter were in the home stretch when the defense tried to suppress the Doris report. Pulling out all the stops in a pretrial motion, Dan Harrington referred to the report's history as "the evolution of a lie." He quoted Richmond from the transcript of the mistrial hearing at the first trial, "Mr. Harrington certainly did get all the statements of the defendant." If that were true, he argued, the Doris report did not exist then, and if it did not exist then, it was a fabrication.

Harrington focused on an alleged statement of Blaikie's as it appeared in Moran's written report in the first trial. Blaikie "stated that he was deeply in debt from numerous financial problems and was afraid to tell the truth for fear we would *suspect him of something.*"

In the Doris report, Blaikie was alleged to have said, "I thought if I told you the truth I would be *suspected of killing David DeWilde.*"

Harrington took umbrage at another Doris claim, that in the key February 6th meeting at the Brighton police station Blaikie told Doris and Moran he knew he had "a motive to kill" DeWilde but insisted he had not taken his life.

Bristling with indignation, Harrington asserted the Doris report constituted a virtual admission of guilt by Blaikie. "Now suddenly we have got a confession, full blown, prepared to harvest at the next trial in Fall River on November fourth," he declared.

The irony was not lost on Richmond. Here was Harrington arguing to keep out a report that she had omitted from the first trial. "The argument Mr. Harrington has made is superfluous," she said. Referring to the first trial, she added, "What I agreed to give Mr. Harrington were statements that the commonwealth intended to introduce at trial. In so doing, I never represented to Mr. Harrington in any way that there were not additional statements which the commonwealth did not intend to introduce at trial."

A week later, on October 13th, Judge McGuire ruled against the defense motion and the Doris report was admitted into evidence. The position of the court was that defense counsel would have every opportunity to question both Sergeant Detective Doris and Detective Moran under cross-examination in the trial.

When the prosecutor and defense counsel met two weeks later for the start of the second trial, their veneer of civility looked about as thin as their hides.

Like Norfolk County with its Sacco-Vanzetti case, Bristol County had a notorious chapter in its history.

According to an enduring nineteenth-century rhyme, "Lizzie Borden took an ax and gave her mother forty whacks; when she saw what she had done, she gave her father forty-one." However, a jury disagreed, and after a sensational trial in 1893 the much-reviled Fall River spinster was acquitted of murdering her father and stepmother the year before.

Dan Harrington was fortunate with Judge McGuire's choice of drowsy venue on Mount Hope Bay along the southeast coast of Massachusetts. The numbers of journalists and spectators at the Fall River courthouse for the start of the trial were fractions of the crowds at Dedham three months before. Again, Blaikie's wife made no appearance.

Neatly dressed, the defendant looked as incapable of violence as he had in the Dedham courtroom.

Following the impanelment of the jury, ten men and six women, the state opened its case on Monday, November 8, 1976. The twelve jurors and four alternates heard a presentation from Special Assistant Attorney General Richmond that was essentially the same as her opening statement in the first trial, with one major exception. She spoke of Blaikie telling Detective Moran on February 6th, three weeks after DeWilde's disappearance, that he had lied for fear he would be suspected of "killing David." It was the very phrase involved in the collapse of the first trial.

She ended her opening half an hour later with a reference to Blaikie's claim to police of ignorance in the disappearance of DeWilde. When she asked the Court's permission to call her first witness, Dan Harrington rose with a surprise announcement.

"With the Court's permission, the defendant would like an opportunity to make an opening statement at this time."

"You may do that," Judge McGuire said.

Harrington embarked on a radical departure from the first trial. With the Doris report in evidence, he considered Richmond's case stronger by far. He could not simply count on his cross-examination of state's witnesses to weaken the case for premeditated murder.

He would have to argue self-defense explicitly and thereby take the high-risk chance of putting Blaikie on the witness stand, exposing him to cross-examination.

"Mr. Foreman and ladies and gentlemen of the jury," Dan Harrington said graciously. "In the indictment Mr. Blaikie is charged with murder and with intent to murder." After a silence, he continued, "Mr. Blaikie was not charged with the mere taking of another human being's life, for you may take another person's life under certain circumstances and not commit a criminal act, such as in self-defense or by accident. The charge of murder requires a significant fact, upon which the jury must find premeditation with malice aforethought and unjustified killing.

"Now, you have heard Miss Richmond speak to you for well over an hour," he said, glancing at the government table. "Did you hear anything concerning premeditated, unjustified killing with malice aforethought?"

Pacing slowly, Harrington declared, "The fact of the matter is, ladies and gentlemen, that the defense agrees with ninety-nine percent of the facts that Miss Richmond told you. The only fact that we basically disagree with was the killing of DeWilde as a premeditated act with malice aforethought."

Harrington spoke of Blaikie as a college graduate who had purchased a revolver after being appointed treasurer of the Massachusetts campaign committee for George McGovern in the 1972 presidential race. "After being entrusted with large sums of money of the senator, he purchased the revolver to protect his family and himself and that money.

"You will learn more about Mr. DeWilde, the case of this so-called mechanic," Harrington said in a sardonic tone. "You will learn about DeWilde the playboy, the moneylender. You will meet his mistress, a young beautiful girl. You will hear about his luxurious apartment and his sportscar. You will learn about thousands of dollars of money kept in a safe-deposit box to lend at huge interest rates to support his style of life."

Richmond stood up and voiced an objection as emphatic as Harrington's commentary.

Judge McGuire asked her to be seated and instructed the jury not to regard opening statements as evidence but merely as outlines of the testimony or evidence that each side expected to offer later.

"We don't deny Mr. DeWilde had a girlfriend, that he had an ex-wife and a small child," Harrington said in the rhythm of a litany.

"We don't deny that he lent Jim Blaikie six thousand dollars in December of 1974, which money was to be paid the following February 1975.

"We don't deny that Mr. DeWilde on January 14, 1975, did in fact visit the home of James Blaikie to collect that money a month in advance.

"We don't deny the fact, ladies and gentlemen, that Mr. DeWilde went into a rage when Mr. Blaikie was unable to produce that money.

"And we don't deny that in this rage he attacked Mr. Blaikie, and in the position of defending himself from imminent death that he believed he was faced with the fact he did shoot César DeWilde.

"And then in a fit of panic and fear he placed the body in the cellar dry well. We won't deny this.

"What we do deny, ladies and gentlemen, and what we ask you to carefully listen to, is that fact that this was an act of self-defense, not done with premeditation and malice."

Pausing before the jury, Harrington firmly added, "We will show you, ladies and gentlemen, and ask you to listen to the facts that will prove our case, that this was an act of justified self-defense. Thank you very much."

At the government table, Richmond thought Harrington's presentation of justifiable homicide meant he would put Blaikie on the witness stand. That is exactly where she had wanted for nearly two years to see him. In fact, if Harrington did not eventually call him as a witness, she intended to demand that the jury be instructed to disregard the claim that

Blaikie killed in self-defense. Harrington could not have it both ways.

A virtual reenactment of the first trial unfolded before the new jury. One difference was quaint. In keeping with the old English tradition in the antique Fall River courtroom, the witness stand was exactly that— an oaken platform and rail without a chair.

An equally apparent distinction was more significant. Through the testimony of a previous owner of the Fisher Avenue house and the current owner, Harrington raised not a single objection. However, in Brookline detective William McDermott's testimony, Harrington did again object to the admissibility of a photograph depicting DeWilde's trussed body immediately after its removal from the grave. Judge McGuire again agreed to allow the jury to view the photo.

In the second day of testimony, the medical examiner spoke of the preservative effect of the cement lime coating found on the body. Harrington objected to Richmond's effort to elicit testimony on quicklime. At a bench conference he argued that only cement lime, ordinary cement, had been found on the body. Richmond countered that common sense dictated Blaikie had mistakenly used cement lime instead of quicklime, which, she said, would have rendered the body unidentifiable.

Judge McGuire stated there was no established fact pertaining to quicklime and none of the substance had been found in the grave. "We won't go into that matter," he ruled, and Richmond lost a point that in her view supported premeditation, inept premeditation at that.

Next morning, in line with Harrington's opening references to DeWilde as a "playboy" and "moneylender," Blaikie's attorney bore down hard on state's witnesses in cross-examination.

Questioning DeWilde's landlady, he tried to portray DeWilde as more than a humble mechanic by focusing on the five rooms and a sundeck David had rented in her house. Under re-direct by Richmond, the witness said the apartment was modestly furnished. Referring to the room where his visiting daughter would stay, she said, "Paris's room was, I guess, the room that was decorated the most."

The garage owner who had rented a bay to DeWilde for his auto-repair business spoke of money DeWilde allegedly said he had given Blaikie as an "investment." Matthew Chaet said the conversation took place on January 13, the day before DeWilde vanished.

"Did he tell you how much money was involved?" Richmond asked.

Harrington's objection was denied and Chaet answered, "Ten thousand dollars."

"Did he tell you anything else about this investment?" Richmond asked.

Chaet answered that David had expected to be paid the previous day, a Sunday.

"Did he tell you that he had been paid?"

"No, he wasn't paid." Chaet testified DeWilde was concerned about the money but still thought Blaikie would repay him.

Questioned further by Richmond, Chaet told of the last time he had seen David. He repeated his testimony from the first trial, that after a telephone conversation around twelve-fifteen on the afternoon of January 14th, David had excitedly announced, "He's got it. Jimmy's got it."

Chaet said that about twelve-twenty, DeWilde got another call. Over Harrington's objection, the witness was allowed to testify to what he remembered DeWilde as saying, "Oh, you want me to come over there? Okay." Chaet described DeWilde's tone of voice as "surprised," the judge struck the answer, and the witness instead replied, "It was a questioning tone of voice."

According to Chaet, DeWilde won a hand of poker and stuffed the winnings of two or three dollars in change into his pants pocket. DeWilde then got into a friend's car and drove away shortly before twelve-thirty.

"Did you ever see DeWilde after he left?" Richmond asked.

"No, I never saw him again," Chaet said.

In his cross-examination, Harrington drew from Chaet a description of DeWilde as bearded with long hair, six-feet tall and weighing about 170 pounds.

"Would you call him a powerful man?"

"He was strong," Chaet replied.

"Would you say he was very strong?"

"He was."

Harrington asked if DeWilde had shown a violent temper.

"He had a sharp tongue."

"He had a sharp temper as well, didn't he?"

"Not with me he didn't."

"But he had with other people?"

"I never witnessed it," Chaet replied evenly.

"It was a violent temper, wasn't it?"

"I wouldn't say that."

Richmond observed James Blaikie shaking his head and smiling derisively. She saw several jurors turn toward him.

"Now," Harrington said, "did you testify at one time that you personally observed Mr. DeWilde in possession of large sums of money?"

"Yes."

"Can you recall testifying that you knew he loaned large sums of money?"

"No," Chaet said.

In the first trial he had said he was aware only of David's "investments," with the exception of a $2,000 loan to a businessman next door to the garage. Harrington asked him if he remembered that testimony and Chaet said he did not consider the amount a large loan.

Hearing Blaikie groan, Richmond again saw members of the jury look at him.

Following Chaet's testimony, Richmond approached the bench and reported her observation of Blaikie's displays and the jury's attention to them. "I ask from the Court at such time as the jury is excused a direction to the defendant as to the inappropriateness of that conduct during the trial.''

Judge McGuire said he had not observed the actions. ''But I will ask his counsel to discuss this matter with him, and if I do henceforth on the part of anybody see conduct that I consider inappropriate I will feel free to comment on it in the presence of the jury.''

A downcast Ruth DeWilde was sworn in as the last witness of the day and Judge McGuire leaned toward her. ''I observe you seem somewhat distraught,'' he said.

''I'm nervous,'' she said, looking up at him.

''Do you feel you can testify at this particular moment?''

Gripping the rail of the witness stand, she said, ''It's as good as any. Yes.''

''I want you to listen carefully to the questions that are asked,'' the judge said, ''and I don't want you to answer anything except that particular question. If you feel you cannot continue, you will let me know immediately.''

She nodded and Alice Richmond began direct examination. Answering the prosecutor's questions, Ruth said that at the beginning of their marriage, David had been selling foreign cars. Within two years he had started his own business, repairing and selling foreign autos. He worked day and night to get the enterprise going, she said, and she often worked alongside him.

''Mrs. DeWilde,'' Richmond asked, ''did you know a man named James F. Blaikie, Jr.?''

''Yes, I did.''

''How did you know him?''

''I met him about eight years ago when we were both in school,'' Ruth DeWilde said, referring to Northeastern University.

''And, if you know, did your husband know James F. Blaikie, Jr.?''

''After a while he got to know him.''

"How did your husband meet James F. Blaikie, Jr., if you know?"

"I introduced him," Ruth said, looking down at her hands on the railing. Lifting her chin, she said, "They got along real well."

Richmond showed her a snapshot and Ruth identified the two men in the cockpit of a sailboat as Jim and Dave. "It was taken," she said, "one day when we went out on the boat in June of 1973."

With the court's permission, the photo was shown to the jury, their first look at a live David DeWilde.

Ruth testified to the anxiety she observed in her former husband over the weekend preceding his disappearance. When he brought Paris home on the evening of Sunday, January 12th, Ruth said, "He was still a little tense, talked rapidly."

Alice Richmond directed Ruth's attention to January 14, 1975. "Did he call that evening?"

"No."

"As a result of his not calling, what did you do?"

"I tried to find out where he was, immediately after I woke up on January fifteenth."

When she called his mother and the garage, she said, no one knew where he was, but friends thought he had gone to see James Blaikie the previous afternoon. She testified to telephoning him repeatedly and getting the same evasive answer every time.

"When was the last time that you called the defendant?" Richmond asked.

"In March."

"What were the circumstances of your calling him?"

"By then I was frantic," she said, her voice cracking. "I called to ask him to tell me where David was."

"What happened when the phone rang?"

"I received a tape message."

"Did you ever talk to the defendant after January fifteenth?"

"No," Ruth said, with sadness and anger flashing in her eyes.

Cross-examining Ruth DeWilde, Dan Harrington sounded respectful but skeptical. "You and David were divorced, were you not?"

"Yes."

"Were the grounds for that divorce cruelty to you?"

"Objection," Richmond said.

"Excluded," said Judge McGuire.

Harrington reframed his question: "Do you know what the grounds of the divorce were?"

"The grounds were cruel and abusive treatment."

"Did you hear Mr. Chaet testify that David at times had a violent temper?" Harrington asked.

"No."

"Wasn't that the basis of your divorce against César David DeWilde?"

"Definitely not."

In response to questioning, Ruth said she did not know David to make large loans and was aware of his efforts to get a pilot's license.

"Did you know about his girlfriend?" Harrington asked evenly.

"I knew David was going out with Judy," Ruth said.

"Were you still married?"

"I was not," she shot back.

"Were you married to him in 1974?"

"I was not living with him," she said emphatically. Their divorce was granted in April, she explained, and became final six months later.

Following her testimony, the last of the day, Judge McGuire reminded the jury that there would be no session the next day, Veterans Day.

After the holiday, the trial resumed on Friday, November twelfth.

Patricia Wynn reiterated her testimony from the first trial, reporting her conversations with James Blaikie in the days immediately after her son's disappearance. On cross-examination, Dan Harrington continued his probe of DeWilde's personality.

Turning to 1974, Harrington asked David's mother

if she had heard Ruth DeWilde testify "she knew about David's girls."

"I heard her say nothing about David's girls except Judy," Pat Wynn sternly corrected.

"That is Judy," Harrington said, "the girl he had taken up with after they separated?"

"*Long* after," she replied firmly.

Through the remainder of Friday's afternoon session, the jury heard reports of Blaikie's enormous financial problems, and Monday morning Detective Moran figured he could be testifying later that day, the fifth of the trial.

Judith Fillippo took the stand, and under direct examination by Richmond, the attractive brunette told of meeting David. Following an automobile accident of hers in January 1974, her insurance company referred her to DeWilde's shop, she said. She did not repeat the testimony that had almost caused a mistrial in the first trial—David's purported anxiety about an alleged luncheon engagement with Blaikie.

Under cross-examination Harrington went immediately to her friendship with David.

"Did you say your personal relationship with Mr. DeWilde started in January 1974?" he asked.

"If you call being involved in an automobile accident having a personal relationship, yes," Judith replied icily.

"I'm saying, seeing him every night," Harrington said, fixing his gaze on her.

"It started sometime the end of January or the first part of February."

"Now, by 'seeing him every night,' what do you mean? Were you living with him?"

"No, I was not."

"Were you going out with him?"

"Yes, I was."

"Where did you go?"

"Movies, theater, dinner, occasionally out for a drink," she replied.

"And this was the period, was it not, during which he was going through his divorce. Isn't that correct?"

"Yes."

"He got his divorce October 1974, isn't that correct? If you know."

"I didn't know."

"You didn't know he was getting a divorce?" Harrington asked in a scornful tone.

"I knew he was getting a divorce," Judith shot back. "I did not know when he was going through the proceedings."

"Were you a witness to his divorce?"

"No."

Saying he had no further questions, Harrington returned to the defense table.

Testimony followed on the alleged murder weapon by several police officers, including Sergeant Detective John Maillet. They repeated what they had told the previous jury. The fatal .38 slug could not be positively linked to the weapon Maillet identified as Blaikie's. However, the ballistics expert stated the bullet could not have been fired from another weapon.

The time came for Brighton detective Thomas Moran to ascend the witness stand again.

Under direct examination, he related the initial stages of his investigation and after nearly two hours of testimony reached the crucial second meeting with Blaikie, which Sergeant Detective Doris had also attended.

As in the first trial, he told of Blaikie denying a debt to DeWilde until he learned Moran had discovered the note about a $6,000 loan in DeWilde's safe-deposit box.

"When you told him about this, did he say anything?" Richmond asked.

As reassured as he felt with the Doris report in evidence, Moran was tense as he reentered the minefield where the first trial had been blown to pieces. He proceeded warily.

"He said yes, he did borrow the money from David DeWilde, admitted he borrowed the money from David DeWilde, but was afraid to tell us for fear we'd suspect him of killing him.''

Harrington said nothing of Moran's damaging assertion, which appeared in so many words in the Doris report.

"Did he say anything else?" Richmond asked.

"He said, 'All right, I lied. I had serious financial difficulties, and I was afraid if I told you I'd be suspected of killing him.' ''

Harrington continued to remain silent at the defense table.

"Then what did you say?"

" 'Who said he was dead?' ''

"Did Sergeant Doris say anything at the time?"

Harrington objected to the inclusion of a third party, but Judge McGuire allowed it.

"Sergeant Doris said, 'As far as we're concerned, he is only a missing person. What are you saying he's dead for?' ''

"What did Blaikie say?" Richmond asked.

"Blaikie said, 'Well, everybody says he's dead, his friends, his mother.' Sergeant Doris said, 'We want to find Mr. DeWilde. Mrs. Wynn wants to bury her son.' ''

Harrington objected. "He's just playing on the jury's sympathy, your honor."

The judge ordered the answer stricken.

It was the next morning, following the completion of Moran's direct testimony, that Harrington began his blistering cross-examination of the detective. The defense counsel again assailed the credibility of the police reports.

He asked Moran if he had spoken with Richmond at the first trial about the reports on which his testimony would be based.

"Yes, I did."

"Now, did you review those statements?"

"Yes, I did."

"Did you say anything to her as to whether those statements were complete or not?"

"Yes, I did."

"What did you tell her?"

Richmond's objection was denied by Judge Mc-Guire.

"I said," Moran continued, " 'Sergeant Doris's notes aren't included.' "

"What did she say to you?"

" 'Stay within these reports,' " Moran answered, referring to his three accounts of as many interrogations of Blaikie.

The detective gazed intently, like a batter waiting for the next pitch.

"You indicated, did you not, that Sergeant Doris had more statements than you had?"

"No, sir," Moran said firmly "his were *Q* and *A*. Mine were a synopsis."

Moran stated that while he questioned Blaikie and took occasional notes, his superior officer took extensive notes of the interrogation.

Harrington came back at him. "You agree your reports were incomplete?"

"As to *Q & A* they certainly were."

"Were your reports incomplete?" Harrington insisted.

"They were not as in depth as Sergeant Doris's."

Half an hour into his relentless attack, Harrington had not dislodged Moran from his position. Nor in the remaining hour of cross-examination did Moran retreat. With his powerful hands gripping the witness rail, the detective absorbed every verbal punch that the pacing Dan Harrington hurled at him.

When Moran stepped down after nearly six hours of testimony, Richmond next put his superior officer, Sgt. Det. John Doris, on the stand.

In direct examination, the prosecutor reached the February 6th meeting at the Brighton police station and asked the sturdy fair-haired officer how the meeting had begun.

As Moran had, Sergeant Detective Doris recalled that when Blaikie was confronted with evidence of a loan from DeWilde, Blaikie admitted he had lied to avoid being "suspected of killing David."

The utterance of the key phrase a second time brought a cool stare from Harrington.

"What was said then?" Richmond asked.

"I said to him, 'How do you know he is dead? Right now he's only a missing person.' "

"What did the defendant say?"

"He replied, 'I know he's dead. I've spoken to his mother. I've spoken to his friends, and I was the last one to see him alive.' "

Asked by Richmond if Blaikie had said anything more, Sergeant Detective Doris replied, "He said, 'I know I was the last one to see him alive. I know I had a motive to kill him but the last time I saw Dave was on Harvard Street.' "

Motive to kill him echoed in Richmond's mind. There in Blaikie's own words, according to Moran and now Doris, was the final evidentiary brick in the case for premeditation.

Harrington smoldered at the defense table. The ascribing of a motive to Blaikie, allegedly in his own words, was a tremendous blow.

When Blaikie's attorney approached Doris for cross-examination, Richmond saw the broad-shouldered detective lift his hands from the rail of the witness stand and resolutely cross his arms. *My God,* she thought, *he looks like Mr. Clean with hair.*

Harrington immediately zeroed in on the detective's report, asking if it reflected all of his testimony in court that morning.

"Yes, sir," Doris replied evenly.

"All of the statements?" Harrington pressed.

"Yes, sir," Doris repeated.

Under questioning, Doris stated that in preparation for possible testimony in the first trial, he had typed his reports from his notes on two interrogations of Blaikie.

"There are no notes, are there?" Harrington jabbed.

"Excuse me?" Doris asked, frowning.

"Are there really any notes in existence today?" Harrington's question was etched with skepticism.

"Yes, sir, there are."

"There are no *original* notes."

"No, sir."

"There are typewritten notes," Harrington said, weighing the police report.

"Yes, sir," Doris said.

When Sergeant Detective Doris moved down from the witness stand and the morning session ended, Richmond believed the detectives had gotten her case over the hump. She felt the testimony of her next and final witness would bring her presentation to a powerful conclusion. He was the person who fourteen months earlier had blown the lid off the Blaikie saga, sky high.

Richard J. Connolly, who had interviewed Blaikie in Phoenix immediately after his release from Arizona State Prison, had been a respected reporter with the *Boston Globe* for thirty-three years. Richmond hoped his independent testimony would corroborate the police reports. In so doing, Richmond believed, Connolly's testimony would show that Blaikie was coldly sticking to his cover-up seven months after DeWilde's disappearance.

She did not think it was the portrait of a man who had shot his friend in self-defense and panicked.

Neither Connolly nor Richmond made any reference to Blaikie's armed robberies in Phoenix.

The reporter testified that Blaikie spoke of having come to Arizona the previous spring in vain hopes of landing a job in the campaign organization of Congressman Morris Udall.

Concerning Blaikie's relationship with DeWilde, Connolly said the defendant spoke of David as a friend who had loaned him money. "He said he owed him six thousand dollars."

"Did you ask him any further questions about Mr. DeWilde?" Richmond asked.

Connolly replied he asked whether David had come to Blaikie's house on the afternoon of January 14, 1975, and Blaikie said he had.

"How long did he indicate that Mr. DeWilde stayed at the house?" Richmond asked.

"Five to ten minutes."

"Did he indicate to you where they had been?"

"In the kitchen."

"Did he indicate to you what they were doing in the kitchen?"

"He said they had a drink and they talked."

Richmond asked if Blaikie had said anything else about the January 14th meeting.

"I asked him if he paid Mr. DeWilde the six thousand dollars that he owed him, and he said no," Connolly stated. "And I said, 'Why?' He said, 'Well, he didn't ask for the money.' And I asked him why, and he said, 'He knew I was involved in a long drawn-out affair, and it was going to cost money for lawyers' fees and so forth.' "

As the Bacon case was excluded from the trial, Connolly did not add, as he had reported in the *Globe*, that Blaikie was speaking of the Kemper lawsuit that had tied up the benefits from Edwin Bacon's $50,000 life insurance policy.

"Did he indicate whether or not he had that six thousand dollars on January 14, 1975?" Richmond asked.

"He said he had more than six thousand dollars."

"Did he indicate to you where Mr. DeWilde had taken him that day?"

"Yes. He said that Mr. DeWilde gave him a ride to his automobile in the Coolidge Corner area."

"Did he say anything about where he thought Mr. DeWilde was?"

"He said he didn't know where he was. He said, 'As far as I'm concerned someone else was the last to see David alive.' "

Allowing Connolly's virtual reiteration of police testimony to sink in, Richmond stood perfectly motionless before the witness. His description of the kitchen scene was crucial, for Richmond believed it was there that Blaikie had walked up behind an unsuspecting DeWilde and shot him in the back of the head. She turned to the bench. "We have no further witnesses, your honor," she said. "We are prepared to rest."

Harrington had no questions and as Judge McGuire was excusing the jury for the day, Richmond watched an impassive James Blaikie being led away by court officers.

See you tomorrow, she thought.

He was scheduled to testify the following morning.

Chapter 23

At 10:05 A.M. on Wednesday, November 17th, the seventh day of testimony in two weeks, the court clerk polled the jury. He found all ten men and six women, twelve jurors and four alternates, in attendance. Then he announced, "May the record show the defendant James F. Blaikie is present in the courtroom."

This was to be his day in court.

Having completed her case the previous afternoon, Alice Richmond stood and formally announced, "At this time the Commonwealth rests."

Judge McGuire excused the jury and denied a defense motion for a directed verdict of not guilty on the count of first-degree murder.

It was Smoki Bacon's first day at the trial. She had shied away from the earlier sessions but was drawn to this one. An opportunity to see Blaikie on the witness stand in her husband's case might not come. She hoped at least to see Blaikie hang himself for the death of David DeWilde.

However, when her eyes met the defendant's, she was amazed by his reaction. From the defense table James Blaikie nodded in recognition and smiled at her, exactly as he had when she had on occasion run into him during Ed's lifetime.

She felt as though she had fallen through a sheet of ice.

Soon after the jurors had returned, James Blaikie left the defense table and stepped onto the witness stand.

Attending the trial for the first time, Frank Bacon sat beside Patricia Wynn. David DeWilde's mother and Edwin Bacon's brother had remained in touch since waging successful battle against the notorious plea bargain the previous summer. Noticing Pat's anxiety as Blaikie was being sworn in, Frank took her hand in his and received a grateful smile.

Blaikie had never looked more respectable and harmless.

Dan Harrington had been questioning witnesses, but his cocounsel rose for the direct examination of their client. Ted Harrington's strong features spoke of tenacity and directness. The eyes under a hooded brow appeared as alert as an eagle's. His reputation for intellect and determination began with his service to the U.S. Justice Department in the 1960s. Attorney General Robert F. Kennedy personally sent Ted to investigate the 1964 murders of three civil rights volunteers in Mississippi. His work helped convict seven men for conspiracy in the slayings.

Speaking in the tone of a sympathetic older brother, Ted Harrington asked the witness to state his name.

"James F. Blaikie, Jr.," came the firm but gentle reply.

"What do they call you?

"Jimmy, mostly," Blaikie said politely.

Responding to questions, he said he was thirty-one years old and married to a woman named Kathleen, who lived in Arizona.

"What is the condition of your wife?" Ted Harrington asked.

"Bad," Blaikie said, lowering his blue eyes. "She had a nervous breakdown."

Ted Harrington's direct examination elicited a biographical sketch taking Blaikie from his native Waltham to Northeastern University.

"Did you participate in politics?" Ted Harrington asked.

"Yes. Sometime after I graduated, I became involved with local and statewide political contests."

"And what statewide political contests where you involved in?"

"I did some early work for Senator Kennedy, and I eventually worked for Senator George McGovern."

Ted Harrington looked impressed. "What campaign was that?"

"In the 1972 presidential campaign."

"And what was your official position with respect to that campaign?"

"I was the state treasurer for the Massachusetts McGovern for President Committee," Blaikie said, giving the official name.

He told of raising, recording, and banking campaign contributions during the campaign, hiring and supervising a staff.

"As a result of your duties as the treasurer, entrusted with this money, what did you do?" Ted Harrington asked.

"During that period, sometime, I acquired a gun just for protection." Blaikie said he recalled purchasing it from a former college friend, as Sergeant Detective Maillet had testified. He added it had been in the autumn of 1972, following McGovern's nomination.

"Now, did you know Mr. DeWilde, César David DeWilde?" Ted Harrington asked.

"Yes, sir." Blaikie told of meeting DeWilde through Ruth Whitney, a college friend of his and Kathy's in the late 1960s.

"And who introduced you to Ruth DeWilde?"

"My wife."

"Was David a student at Northeastern?"

"No, sir."

"During the college years how would you describe in your own words your relationship with David DeWilde?"

"It was a friendly social relationship." Blaikie said the two couples occasionally double-dated but he did not see much of David in that period. After Jim's marriage to Kathy, he maintained his friendship with DeWilde, who later married Ruth.

"How would you describe your relationship between the period that you got married, he got married, and the time that he got divorced?"

"We became, I guess, increasingly more friendly. We saw each other more frequently."

"Now, take the period from the time that David was going through his divorce proceedings and the time he disappeared in January 1975. Describe your and your wife's relationship with David at that time."

"Well, just preceding and during and after the divorce we saw more of David. Well, beginning with Ruth, and then after the divorce we saw David alone or with whoever he was going out with at the time. We became more and more friendly. He was having problems, and I think he just wanted someone to talk to."

"Did he ever talk to you about loaning money?"

"Yes, sir."

"Did you ever observe Mr. DeWilde's demeanor when he discussed with you his activities of loaning money? Yes or no?"

"Yes."

"Describe it to the jury in your own words."

"Whenever David talked about the business it was usually because he had a problem or question either with an individual or in the payment of money back to David. Whenever he talked about money he always— he gets tense. His whole body would just kind of—he was muscular anyway, and you could see the muscles on his neck."

"Wait a minute," Judge McGuire interrupted. "Answer the question. What was his *demeanor?*"

"Very aroused, uptight," Blaikie said.

"What was the demeanor on his face?" Harrington asked.

"He was extremely tense."

"What did he say to you with respect to these individuals who failed to pay the loans he had made to them?"

"He'd mention he was going to kill them or break their legs if they didn't pay the money up."

Harrington paused, letting the words settle in the silent courtroom of aged wood. "When he made such a remark did you observe his face?"

"Yes."

"What was his demeanor then?"

"Again, very tense and angry," Blaikie said.

Harrington directed Blaikie's attention to his financial condition in December 1974, and asked him to describe it.

"Pretty bad," Blaikie said. "I was in total—I mean I was in debt, a gross total over a hundred thousand. I had a lot of current payments due and interest."

"Were you trying to keep up with them?"

"I was trying to, yes."

"Did you in early December enter into a loan transaction with Mr. DeWilde?"

"Yes." Blaikie told of receiving a loan from DeWilde on December twelfth for $6,000, to be paid in February, exactly the information Detective Moran had found on the note in DeWilde's safe-deposit box. However, Blaikie added, "The interest was a thousand dollars a month."

Here was the alleged loan-sharking friend that Ted Harrington's partner had promised in his opening statement to unveil.

Harrington turned to Blaikie's alleged role of taking telephone messages for DeWilde. Blaikie said David preferred not receiving them at home or at his garage.

"And did you receive any such telephone messages on his behalf?"

"Yes, sir."

"How many?"

"Two, as I remember," Blaikie said. "One was shortly after Christmas, and the other was on January tenth. I don't know who I actually spoke to, someone who identified himself as Ned. The first time was something to the effect of, 'Just tell David the meeting is set up.' "

Alice Richmond recalled that Detective Moran's investigation had turned up no person named Ned, Woodman or otherwise, at the Back Bay address on the envelope in David's apartment. Blaikie, she figured, was carrying the charade all the way into the courtroom.

Replying to Harrington's questions about his relationship with DeWilde after receiving the loan, Blaikie said, "Well, I thought it was the same, you know, friendly, saw him frequently. We went out to dinner."

"There was no change?"

"Not during that period, no."

"Now, after the first of the year did you note any change in DeWilde's attitude toward you?"

"Yes, a very definite change."

"Did you have conversations with him?"

"Many."

"And on these many occasions will you tell the members of the jury what he said to you and what you said to him?"

"Well, first, I didn't understand. He just seemed more—"

Judge McGuire interrupted Blaikie's reference to DeWilde's appearance. "Did you hear the question?"

Harrington told his client, "Just the conversation."

Blaikie nodded in the affirmative. "At first, in the middle of a conversation with me, he would make remarks about the money I owed, like, 'I hope I'm going to get that money back.' And then—"

"What would you say?"

"I'd say, 'I'll have it for you in February,' and he'd say, 'I hope so.' And then finally after several conversations over a period of a few days he finally told me what was bothering him. Obviously something was bothering him."

"What did he say to you?"

Blaikie seemed to be plumbing his memory. " 'Look, Jimmy,' he said, 'I want that money and I want it now.' I said, 'David, what's the matter? We agreed on February.' And he said, 'Well, that's what we agreed before, but I found out you're in a lot worse shape than I thought you were. You're just about bankrupt, and I hear it said you are moving to Arizona, and I'm afraid you're going to run out and I'm going to lose everything.' "

"What did you say to him?" Ted Harrington asked the witness.

"I told him no," Blaikie said, "I was going to sell the house and car to try to pay off my debts. And that's where I was going to get the money to pay him, but I told him I'd give him the money."

"What did he say?"

"He said, 'I don't believe you. You're going to run out on me. I'm going to lose this whole loan. I want it right away and I want the whole amount.' I said, 'David, I can't do that.' He said, 'Well, if you pay me right away you only have to pay me seven thousand.' " Blaikie's arithmetic included the $1,000-a-month interest he claimed DeWilde was demanding on the loan.

"What did you say to him?"

"I told him I couldn't do it. He said, 'Well, you better think about doing it.' "

Blaikie said such conversations occurred with increasing frequency from the first of January on.

"Now, directing your attention to January 10, 1975," Ted Harrington said, "will you tell the jurors in your own words what occurred that day?" It was the day Blaikie had appeared with DeWilde in the safe-deposit area of his bank, according to the vault keeper's testimony.

"Well, January tenth, I had a meeting with David about some insurance matters on the car of Allen Leeds," Blaikie said, referring to a friend of DeWilde's. "That particular morning I received a call from that person who identified himself as Ned. So I went over to the garage that morning to give Ned—give David the message."

"What did you say to him with respect to the message?"

"I just said, 'That person called, Ned, and said the meeting is on and the deal is set.' "

"And when you said that to David what did he say?"

"He seemed pleased with that information."

Judge McGuire interrupted and instructed Blaikie. "No. Strike it. What did he *say?*"

Blaikie nodded apologetically. "He said, 'Oh, good,' and he put down his tools and said, 'Are you doing anything urgent this morning?' And I said no. He said, 'Do you mind driving me over to the bank?' I said, 'All right.' " Blaikie said he drove DeWilde to his bank and on the way David pressed him for the money.

"He said, 'I thought you were going to have some money for me today,' because I told him previously I'd have some at the end of the week. I said, 'I haven't got any today.' He said, 'You better get some. I haven't forgotten. I want my money. I don't want you to skip out on me.' And I tried to say, 'I'm not going to skip on you.' "

Blaikie said that in the safe-deposit booth at David's bank he saw him take a manila envelope from his box and put it in his pocket. Shown the "Ned Woodman" envelope taken from DeWilde's apartment, Blaikie said he had not seen enough of the envelope at the bank to say the two were the same.

"What was his demeanor at this time when you were leaving the bank?" Harrington asked.

"He was still kind of tense. On the way, on the ride back he mentioned again that 'You'd better get the money.' And he thought he'd be too mad to go over to see the Super Bowl with me. 'You better concentrate on getting the money.' "

In telephone conversations over the weekend, Blaikie said, DeWilde continued bringing up the money owed him.

"Monday was kind of a hazy day for both of us," Blaikie said calmly. "I figured by now I better give him some money. So I said, 'Well, tentatively we'll get together Tuesday. I'll come by your garage.' "

"Tuesday was January 14, 1975?"

"Yes, sir."

"Mr. Blaikie," Harrington said near the witness stand, "in your own words as best you can recall the early morning of January 14, 1975, tell this jury what happened in chronological order.'' He gestured as though introducing a friend to the jurors.

''That morning my wife had to visit a girlfriend, I think, up in the Framingham area. So she had gone up there ahead of me in her own car, and I had planned to meet her for lunch at the Sea & Surf Restaurant about oneish. I had to go into the Registry of Motor Vehicles that morning to do some paperwork. And after I came from the registry I was coming back toward Brookline, and it was still early. I didn't have to go over to David's garage for awhile, so what I planned to do was just drop in at Coolidge Corner. Kathy wanted me to pick up a couple of things at the store.''

Blaikie said he parked, browsed at a bookstore, looked about a plant shop, and then purchased cigarettes at the Sunnyhurst food store.

''Did you have during this shopping tour the money in your possession for David DeWilde?'' Harrington asked.

''No,'' Blaikie said. ''I had it locked up at home.''

''Now, after you had completed the tour of these several shops, what did you do?''

''I went back to my car.''

''And when you reached your car what did you do?''

''I put the bag down, my little briefcase, and looked for my keys and I couldn't find them.''

''What time was this?''

''Sometime near twelve o'clock, I guess,'' Blaikie said.

''When you found the car was locked what did you do?''

Blaikie told of walking to a nearby cabstand and taking a five- to ten-minute taxi ride home. His description of a pleasantly chatty journey was similar to the testimony of the cab driver.

''During this ride back to your home what was the state of your mind?'' Harrington asked.

''I was relaxed. I figured I could find the keys all right.''

''Where did the cabby drive you?''

''He drove me to Fisher Avenue.''

''Right in front of your house?''

''Yes.''

Harrington nodded approvingly of behavior that hardly sounded deceptive.

''After the taxi went, what did you do?''

''I got out of the cab, said, 'Goodbye' to the cabby, paid him off, went into the house, put the groceries away, took off my coat, and I went to look for the keys and get David's money.'' Blaikie said he could not find the spare keys and ''time was going on by now and—''

''You say 'time was going on.' You had some meeting to attend?''

''Well, I had to give over the money, pick up the insurance papers, and then I wanted—David's shop is right near the Mass. Pike anyway—to get on the Mass. Pike and go up to Framingham to meet my wife.''

''What time were you supposed to meet your wife?''

''One o'clock.''

''What time was this when you were searching for the keys?''

''Sometime after twelve o'clock, twelve-fifteen, something like that. But I couldn't find the keys, so I figured maybe the best thing to do would be to have David come over and meet me. I figured at least he'd know how to get in my car, start it up. So I called him up.''

Blaikie's testimony was similar to that of Mickey Chaet, who had spoken of taking a call for David at the garage.

''Did you have a conversation with David at this time?''

''Yes, sir,'' Blaikie stated. ''I said, 'This is Jimmy.' He said, 'Oh, hi,' and asked me if I had it. And I said, 'Yes, I've got some money for you.' He said, 'Oh, good.' He was excited, and I asked him if he would mind now picking me up because my car was at Coolidge Corner and I had lost the keys or they were locked in the car. He said, 'Yeah, yeah, sure.' I think he was in the middle of a card game when he was talking to me, so we hung up.''

Observing Blaikie intently, Richmond recalled Detective Moran asking Blaikie why he kept referring to Coolidge Corner when the Brookline intersection was a mile southeast of the actual location of his car in Brighton. Dave's shop was less than a mile northwest of the car.

Blaikie had said he thought of the entire stretch as Coolidge Corner, but, like Moran, Richmond thought she knew the real answer. If Blaikie had told DeWilde where the car really was, David would have wondered why on earth Jim had not cabbed less than the mile to DeWilde's shop instead of taking a taxi southwest to Fisher Hills, nearly twice that distance. DeWilde might have become suspicious about Blaikie's curious itinerary, she reasoned, and balked at the idea of driving to Brookline.

"After you hung up on the first conversation what did you do?" Ted Harrington asked.

"I continued to look for the keys. I think I called my wife in Framingham. I didn't get hold of her personally, but I left a message with the girl to tell my wife I'd be a few minutes late. And then I did find the keys."

"Where did you find them?"

"I had a little file cabinet in the study where I kept warranties and guarantees, and the keys were just as they were when I bought the car, in the warranty folder."

"Now, you testified that you told DeWilde that you had some money for him?"

"Yes." He said the money was in a gray metal cash box in a study looking out on the driveway alongside the house. "I took out five hundred dollars, I figured that was the best I could do, maybe keep him happy."

"What did you do with the five hundred dollars?"

"Put it on the desk in an envelope." Then, Blaikie said, when David had not arrived ten to fifteen minutes after their conversation, he telephoned the garage a second time.

"Who did you speak to?"

"Again, I don't know. It might have been Mickey,

might have been one of the workers, but it wasn't David. I said, 'Is David still there?' He said yes, and he handed the phone to David.''

''Now, you had a second conversation with David?'' Harrington asked, driving at the similarity between Blaikie's testimony and that of the state's witness.

''Yes, sir,'' Blaikie said. ''He said hi and I said hi, and I said, 'Aren't you coming over?' And I explained to him what the problem was with the car. I said, 'I need you to drive me down to Coolidge Corner to get my car.' And he said, 'Oh, oh. You want me to come over there?' And I said, 'Yes, if you can.' He said, 'Sure, no problem.' And then I said, 'Don't forget to bring the papers on the car, Allen Leeds's car.' ''

''What did he say?''

'' 'Right, okay,' something like that, and he hung up.''

''What next occurred?''

''Well, about—I don't know, five, six minutes later, I saw a car pull up in my driveway, a gray-toned Volvo. David got out.''

As Blaikie was for the first time about to give his version of how David died, Frank Bacon felt Patricia Wynn's grip tighten on his hand.

''And how was David attired?'' Harrington asked.

''He had on his blue mechanic's clothes.''

''And did he come into the house?''

''He came around the back door. Most people when they park in the driveway, they come in the back door and enter through the kitchen. So he came around, and I went around to meet him. He came in, and I was walking to the door. He said, like this, 'Well, have you got the money for me?' And he threw his—''

''Before you go on,'' Harrington interrupted, ''describe to the jury in your own words what David DeWilde looked like at this time on January 14, 1975.''

''David was big, muscular, very dark, dark eyes, long dark hair, dark beard, and he had on his work uniform.'' Blaikie guessed he was six feet tall and weighed about 170 pounds. Lapsing into the present tense, he added, "He's a strong kid, a big, muscular kid."

"How tall are you, Jimmy?"

"Five-six and a half."

Harrington did not ask the 200-plus-pounder his weight. "David DeWilde came into your kitchen. What did he say when he came in?"

"He came in, excited, and he said, 'Well, have you got the money?' And I said, 'Yes, I've got some money for you.' And he threw the keys down on the little sideboard by the kitchen, the door going out of the kitchen. And I walked into the study. And I took the money off the table, and I said, 'Here's your money.' He looked at it and said, 'How much is here?' And he started to tense up. I said, 'Well, all I can afford to give you now is five hundred dollars.' And he got very angry. His whole complexion changed. His face got flushed, and he had a way when he got angry, all his muscles kind of flexed, and he just got tense."

After a pause, Blaikie continued: "He said, 'What do you mean, five hundred dollars? I told you I wanted the whole thing.' I said, 'David, I told you I'd get you what I could,' and he took the money and threw it down on the desk, and he said—I don't know—'I want the whole thing. I told you to get the whole thing.' And then he came up, and I had a tie on. He grabbed me by the tie, and he said, 'I told you what I'll do to you. I'll break your legs, you fat little bastard, if you don't give me that money.' And then he slapped me and I—"

"What was your state of mind at that time?"

"Petrified. I never, you know—I never thought he'd get this bad over it. I said, 'David, that's all I can afford. That's all I've got to live on.' And he said, 'I don't care if that's all you've got. I want the whole thing. I want all of that. I want more. I'm going to break your leg,' again. He said—I said, 'Come on, David, I'm not trying to lie to you.' I said, 'Look, I'll show you.' I opened up the drawer and opened the cash box, and I took out the rest of the money.

"I think there was another, I don't know, fourteen

hundred-some-odd dollars in there. I said, 'Look, David, this is all I've got to live on,' and he said, 'I don't care. I'll break your other goddam leg too.' "

Ted Harrington asked, "In that cash box was there anything else besides the fourteen hundred dollars?"

"Yes, sir. I kept the .38 in there too."

"When you took out the fourteen hundred dollars what did you do with it?"

"I tried to show him this was all I had, I wasn't trying to lie. I said, 'This is it,' and he wanted the whole thing. He started to come at me again, so I took the gun out again. I said, 'Dave, get out of here. Take the five hundred and I'll try to have more later.' "

"He said, 'I don't want it later.' He looked at the gun. 'You won't shoot me, you asshole,' and knocked it out of my hand, and he punched me, and I fell—"

"First of all, first you took out the gun?"

"Yes, sir."

"And what did you say to him?"

"I told him to 'Get out of here. Get out of my house.' "

"And when you had the gun on DeWilde, describe his demeanor."

"He was like a madman. He was just—his whole face was contorted. I've never seen anybody so angry."

"What was your state of mind at that time?"

"I was afraid; shaking, afraid, terrified."

"When you took the gun out what did he next do in this sequence, if you can? You took the gun out. What did he do?"

He said something like, 'You won't shoot me. You won't use that,' or something like that. 'I'm going to break your neck,' and he knocked it out of my hand."

"Where did the gun go?"

"On the side, off to the side."

"Then what next did he do?"

"He hit me somewhere around here," he said touching his left cheek, "and I fell down."

"You fell on the floor?"

"Yes, sir."

"And tell as best you can recall how you fell on the floor. What was your position on the floor?"

"Kind of on my back, off a little to the side. I don't remember, sir."

"You fell down?"

"Yes, sir."

"Where was the gun in relation to you when you hit the floor?"

"Right off to the side."

"What next did David do?"

"He jumped over me to get the gun, and I got it first and I just . . . I shot him." Blaikie's look appeared penitent.

"You said he jumped over you. If you could, just describe in more detail for us so the jury can understand. You said he jumped over you. You were lying on the floor?"

"Yes."

"How did he jump over you? Did he jump perpendicularly over you? Did he jump up and down or how?"

"I guess kind of perpendicular. I don't remember. Or kind of at an angle. He was going over me to get it, and I just pulled it out before he could get it. I just pulled back and just shot him."

"Were you aiming at all?"

"No."

"After you pulled the trigger what happened?"

"I don't know. I think I blacked out for—I don't know—a minute or two or three. I don't know. The noise and where he hit me, I was just dazed."

"Some period of time elapsed?"

"Yes, sir."

"What did you next do?"

"I don't know. Eventually I sat up and I saw him lying over there. I don't know. I still didn't realize what had happened, I don't think, and I reached over and I shook him.

"I said, 'David, David,' and there was blood all over him. I guess I turned him over, and I listened. I didn't get any heart, couldn't hear his heart or breathing or anything, and I got up. I remember wandering around the house room to room.''

"What was your state of mind at this time?"

"In a daze. I was shaking, and I don't know, I felt sick. My ears were still ringing. I don't know, I was in a daze."

"What did you do?"

"I remember, like I said, walking around, wandering around the house. Next I went back in the room, and he was still there. I don't know, I guess I just panicked. I should have called the police then but I panicked—''

"Wait a minute," Judge McGuire admonished.

"No," Harrington said to his client. "What did you do? You said he was still there. Did you look at him?"

"He was still there. I didn't want to look at him. The blood. I went out, walked around again, and I thought I had to get him out of there. I don't know what I was thinking. I couldn't look at his face. I guess I was crazy. I just wanted to cover up his face.

"I took a little white plastic bag from the kitchen, and I grabbed string or something out of a little junk drawer, and I covered up his face and tied it so the blood would stop. And I sat down for another few minutes.''

Judge McGuire observed several spectators reacting visibly to the testimony and he called a recess, asking the jury to withdraw.

"Mr. Sheriff," he said to the Bristol County officer, "I direct you now, speaking in the absence of the jury, if you see any activity on the part of anybody in this courtroom by way of nodding his head in assent or dissent or smiling or anything else of that type, I want it brought to my attention at once. Bring in the jury.''

Ted Harrington resumed his direct examination of an apparently dejected James Blaikie. "Will you describe to the jury what Mr. DeWilde's face looked like just prior to putting the bag on.''

"It was pale, and there was blood on the back of his neck and running down.''

"After you put the bag over his head what did you do next?"

"I went out again. I just, I don't know, I just figured I have—I can't leave it here. I can't leave David here. I didn't know what to do. I went running from room to room again."

"What was your state of mind?"

"Just cra—I don't know. Like I was going crazy. I didn't know what to do."

"What did you do?"

"I went back up and I tried to lift him up. Because he was so heavy I couldn't lift him. I didn't know what to do. And then, I don't know, I figured maybe I could lift him down somewhere like the basement. So I put my arms underneath his shoulders and I dragged him down the stairs. He was so heavy I almost fell, and everything fell out of his pockets, went all over everything."

"When you say everything fell out of his pockets, what fell out of his pockets?"

"I don't know. Change and some stuff. I don't know. Then I took him down the basement and put him over in the corner by the bar. It was dark and no one went over there. I just laid him down over there."

"How did you take him? Explain to the jury in more detail how you took him down the stairs and took him across the cellar."

"I just put my arms under his shoulders and just walked backwards and dragged him down."

"When you got to the basement tell the jury where you dragged him, to what location in the basement."

"Over in the front part."

Asked to indicate the area on an exhibit, Blaikie stepped down and walked up to a large diagram of the basement resting on an easel. He pointed to the bay front of the basement.

"What did you do with the body when it was lying there by the bar?" Harrington asked.

"I just covered it up with plastic bags and some old rug material that was there, covered him up so I wouldn't have to look at it."

"What did you do next?"

"I just wanted to get out of there. I just wanted to get out of there. And I don't know. I said, 'Oh, my God, *Kathy—*' "

"What did you do?"

"I went up, and sometime I think I called the Sea & Surf again to tell her I wasn't coming. I don't even remember what it was. I went upstairs, and I went out to the driveway. And I had the keys to my station wagon and David's car was there. The Volvo was there, so I went back in and took the keys to the Volvo off the sideboard. I just got in the Volvo and I drove towards Coolidge Corner the back way. And the first street I saw some space, I put the car in there and got out and got my car and drove up to Framingham. I wanted to get away."

"Do you recall where you parked David's car or the Volvo?"

"Yes. It was the first street before you get to Harvard Street as you come down, I guess it is, Brainerd Road, whatever it is. The continuation of Corey Road."

"And after you left the Volvo where did you go?"

"I walked around to where my car was parked."

"How far away was it?"

"A block, block and a half."

"Did you get in your car?"

"Yes."

"What did you do?"

"I got in the car, and I just drove out to Framingham."

"When you say 'Framingham,' where did you go?"

"I went to the Sea & Surf Restaurant."

"And who did you meet there?"

"My wife."

"And what did you do at the Sea & Surf?"

"I think I had a drink, a couple of drinks. Some food was already ordered, and the whole afternoon, I don't remember, I was just in a daze."

"Did you tell your wife what had occurred?"

"No, sir."

"What time did you reach the Sea & Surf?"

"I don't know. Around two o'clock, a little before."

"After you left the Sea & Surf where did you go?"

"I don't remember. I just remember my wife had something to do, and I remember following her around that day. And eventually we came home."

"What time did you return to the house?"

"Suppertime. Really, I don't remember."

"Did you tell your wife when you got home what had occurred?"

"No, sir."

"What was your state of mind at this time?"

"I was still like—like in a daze, like in panic. I didn't know what to do. I was afraid, you know, eventually Kathy might go down to the cellar and I—"

"So after you returned to your home what next did you do with respect to this matter?"

"I did nothing until that night. Kathy went to bed, and I told her I was going to stay up and do some reading or something. After she went to bed I went down in the basement again. And I don't know, I just thought I can't leave—"

Ted Harrington prodded his client. "Don't tell us what you were thinking. What did you do?"

"I think I was going to lift him out and take him out and put him in the car. But he was too heavy. I couldn't move him. I didn't know what to do, and I remember I walked into the back part of the cellar there for awhile where the burner is and walking all around. And I came back, and I knew I couldn't move him very far.

"I remembered when we first bought the house one of the pipes burst, and the water went all over the floor, and the gardener opened up the trap and put the water down there. I remembered that was kind of a big hole, so I took the boards off, and I saw that it was big. And so I managed to drag David over and just put him in the hole. And then I didn't look at him. I put more plastic bags, and at that time I didn't put the boards back on, on the hole, and I left the cellar."

At his seat near the front of the courtroom, Detective Moran made a mental note. Blaikie can't put the body in the hole later that night, because rigor mortis would have set in. Moran thought it important to bring the medical examiner back to go over that point.

"Did you tell your wife what had occurred?"

"No, sir."

"Did you ever tell your wife what had occurred?"

"No, sir."

"What next did you do with respect to the body in the dry well?"

"I still didn't know what to do. The only thing I figured to do—"

"What next did you *do?*"

"About a week—I didn't know, five days, a week, something like that, I thought maybe all I could do was fill in the hole. So I went down to get some cement and sand and stuff."

"Where did you go?"

"I went down to the hardware store at the time I was using, Cleveland Circle Hardware," Blaikie said, referring to a major Brookline crossroads a quarter-mile from his house.

"What did you purchase there?"

"They didn't have that much. I got—I don't know—two or three bags, instant-ready cement and some sand and one bag of mortar mix, all he had. And, in fact, I had to go down to their other store in Coolidge Corner to get another couple of bags."

"What did you purchase at the other store?"

"A couple more bags."

"How many bags of cement in total did you purchase, approximately?"

"I don't know; four, five, six. I don't know, cement and sand."

"What did you do with this material?"

"I brought it home, and Kathy was away. And I took the boards off and started—first, I thought of filling it up with cement, but I didn't have enough bags. So I just put in, I guess, sand in there, just swept garbage in there, filled it up with coal, and then just leveled it off.''

"What did you first put in there, if you recall? What was the first material?''

"May have been cement, sand. I swept some broken plaster I put into it. I don't know.''

"And what other materials did you put in there?''

"Coal, sand, finished it up.''

"When you say 'finished it up,' what did you do?''

"I mixed the cement and just covered up the top of the hole.''

"Did you do any activity with respect to the hole?''

"I don't know. A day or two later when it dried I threw some paint on it, went over it with gray paint.''

"Now, did you clean up the cement bags?''

"No, I left everything there.''

"Now, from the day that you painted the freshly finished cement, did you ever return to that portion of the basement?''

"Never went near that hole again.''

"During the period in February and March of 1975, what did you do with respect to that house?''

"I just wanted to get out of there, get away from the house and Brookline and everything.''

Ending the direct examination of his client, Ted Harrington made his way back to his table as Alice Richmond was standing up at hers.

Chapter 24

Immediately upon beginning her cross-examination, Alice Richmond maintained a distance from the defendant but went straight for his credibility.

"Mr. Blaikie, your financial problems started long before December 1974, didn't they?" she asked in an even voice.

"Yes, ma'am," Blaikie replied softly.

Answering questions concerning his career, he described the brief white-collar jobs he held between his 1968 graduation from college and 1971.

Richmond asked where he went to work then.

"I went to work by myself."

"By yourself?" Richmond asked, aware he had then begun his association with the Bacon insurance agency.

"Self-employed, yes," Blaikie replied.

"Where was your office, Mr. Blaikie?" Richmond asked.

Ted Harrington requested a bench conference.

"Your honor," he said, "she is getting into the fact that he worked with Bacon in the insurance company. And this is highly prejudicial. It has been kept out of this trial, and I think she should be cautioned to stay away from this association with Bacon. We did not bring that out on direct examination."

"Any reference to Bacon in regard to his employment?" Judge McGuire asked.

Richmond stated, "He worked with the Bacon insurance agency for three years, and he is now in the view of the Commonwealth saying he was self-employed when in fact he wasn't self-employed.''

''What is the relevancy of bringing up the Bacon matter?'' Judge McGuire asked her.

''To show, your honor,'' Richmond said, ''that he ceased being employed at a job that had any income in 1971 or 1972 when he went to the Bacon Insurance Agency.'' Richmond handed the judge a deposition taken from Blaikie in connection with his claim to Bacon's insurance policy. ''He said he only took a thousand dollars out of that company in 1974, a thousand dollars in 1973. We are talking about a man who admitted he was over one hundred thousand dollars in debt, and I think the jury is entitled to know. This all goes to motive.''

Judge McGuire took the matter under advisement and called the morning recess.

Detective Moran approached Alice Richmond with his observation about rigor mortis and the time Blaikie claimed to have placed the body in the dry well. Blaikie had said he did not stuff the body in the hole until after Kathy had gone to bed. Depending on when she retired, DeWilde could have been dead as many as eight or more hours since the 12:30 P.M. shooting. Like Moran, Richmond did not think the body would have been pliable enough to be folded into a fetal posture. She made a mental note to recall the medical examiner to the witness stand after Blaikie had left it.

Following recess, Judge McGuire handed the transcript of Blaikie's deposition back down to Richmond. ''I will allow you to show his earnings or lack of earnings during this period that he was in the insurance business, that he did or didn't have a license. And I don't want the name Bacon mentioned.''

Drawing near Blaikie, Richmond asked if he had ever presented himself as a registered insurance broker, and he replied he had spoken of himself as an ''agent.''

Referring to the deposition, she inquired, ''Do you

remember being asked the question, 'You do hold an insurance broker's license?' ''

''I don't remember the question, no.''

She handed a copy of his deposition up to him and said, ''I want you just to read this question on line 44 to yourself.''

He consulted the document, looked up, and returned it to her waiting hand in front of the witness box.

''Mr. Blaikie, were you asked the question, 'You do hold an insurance broker's license?' ''

''Yes, I guess I was.''

''What did you say to that? How did you answer that question?''

''At the time I thought I was licensed. I later learned that I wasn't.''

''How did you answer the question?''

''In the affirmative,'' Blaikie replied casually. He looked like a student bored with the lesson.

''You know perfectly well you had to be registered to sell insurance, didn't you?''

''I just never got around to doing it,'' Blaikie responded.

''You were selling insurance in the state for over three years at that time, isn't that right?''

''Selling was a small part of what I did, yes.''

''Are you self-employed as what?''

''I was in business—''

Ted Harrington interrupted his client with an objection and with a look of annoyance Blaikie snapped: *''Now,* what?''

''Wait a minute,'' Judge McGuire sternly declared, glaring at Blaikie. *''You* be quiet. You've got a lawyer here.''

Satisfied with the hornet's nest she had stirred up, Alice Richmond thought to herself, *Behold our mild-mannered Mr. Blaikie lashing out at his own attorney.*

''I'd like her to define the period of time,'' Ted Harrington said.

"What time?" the judge asked Richmond, looking down forbearingly on the untidy scene.

Richmond referred to the years from 1970 to 1974, and wheeled toward Blaikie, asking, "That is at least four years that you were involved in the insurance business here in Massachusetts?"

"Yes."

"And you never had a license, Mr. Blaikie, did you?"

"No, I learned I didn't."

An hour into her cross-examination, Richmond pressed Blaikie on his finances. Her objective was to convince the jury that he had more than the $1,900 he claimed on the day he killed David DeWilde. She sought to demonstrate that he had not shot DeWilde in a dispute over a loan repayment, but he had murdered him in cold blood to avoid ever paying back his debt of at least $6,000.

From his bank records she listed aloud six checks written by Blaikie after January 14th, including one to Frederick's of Hollywood, for a total of $1,200. Not included were the payment of $800 on bank loans, $700 in mortgage payments, and living expenses. She asked how he could explain expenditures amounting to nearly a thousand dollars more than the $1,900 he supposedly had on January 14th and Blaikie said he borrowed money from other friends.

Through her questioning, Richmond elicited an admission from Blaikie that he had not purchased the sand and cement used to seal DeWilde's grave from the hardware store he ordinarily patronized. Blaikie said the reason was he had an unpaid account at his regular shop.

Richmond responded, "Isn't it true, Mr. Blaikie, that unlike your usual habit of either charging things or paying by check you paid for that sand in cash, didn't you?"

"I didn't charge it. Whether I paid by check or cash I don't recall."

"You didn't have a charge account at the Cleveland

Circle hardware store, and you didn't give them a check, did you, Mr. Blaikie.''

"I don't think I had any money in the checking account."

"Mr. Blaikie, did you ever give them a check?"

"I don't recall," Blaikie firmly replied.

Going over Blaikie's canceled checks, Richmond spotted one for a payment on his wife's new car. "By the way, did you tell us this morning that your wife had a nervous breakdown?"

"Yes," Blaikie said, lowering his eyes.

"When did she have the nervous breakdown, Mr. Blaikie?"

"She just fell apart after I was out here in Boston and charged in this," he replied, referring to the previous autumn.

"She fell apart, just fell apart?" Richmond asked, raising an eyebrow. "Do you know that your wife works at the Saint Paul Insurance Company, 1500 East Thomas Road in Phoenix, Arizona?"

"Yes."

"Do you know that she's been working there since July 15, 1975?"

"Yes."

"And do you know that in the last six months she's missed two days of work due to a heavy cold? Do you know that?"

"Yes."

"And she's missed no other work, Mr. Blaikie?"

"Yes, I realize that."

Richmond focused on payments to a contractor named Peter Janowicz. He had, Blaikie acknowledged, done stucco repair work on the side of the Brookline house in October 1974, three months before the death of David DeWilde.

Richmond drew on Brookline detective McDermott's report of an interview with Janowicz. "Isn't it a fact that sometime shortly after you did the stucco work you told Mr. Janowicz that you intended to do some cement work yourself, and you asked him about mixing cement? Do you remember that?"

"No."

"Do you remember asking him about mixing cement?"

"I remember asking him about doing the brickwork on the front steps."

"Do you remember asking him how to mix cement because there was some work you wanted to do yourself, Mr. Blaikie?"

"No, because I already knew how to mix cement."

Richmond asked Blaikie to read to himself from the McDermott interview with Janowicz, which she handed to him.

"Does that refresh your memory?" she asked, receiving the exhibit back.

"Yes."

"Did you ask Mr. Janowicz how to mix some cement?"

"No, I told Mr. Janowicz I was thinking of doing some brickwork on the front steps."

"You don't remember him saying to you, 'You know, you got to make that a little stiff, and if you don't make it stiff it will fall. It will keep on falling,' when he described putting cement up on a wall. You don't remember that part of the conversation?"

"No. I remember that statement but not from that conversation."

"Do you remember him saying, 'But if you do anything on the floor, you know, on the ground, you can pour it in, just pour it in like water. You know what I mean? It's easy.' Do you remember Mr. Janowicz saying that to you?"

"No, I don't."

"Where did you buy the paint to put over the grave?" Richmond asked.

"I think I had it in the house."

"You didn't go out and buy it specially?"

"I may have. I don't know. I had a lot of paint around there."

"Well, you were buying sand, right? Is that what you told us this morning, that you bought sand?"

"I bought cement and some sand."

"Did you also buy some paint?"

"I don't believe I bought the paint."

"Did you buy some tools then, too, afterwards?" She was alluding to the trowels used to smooth the wet cement on DeWilde's grave.

"No."

"You already had the tools?"

"I had those for years."

Richmond drew his attention to January 10th, four days before DeWilde's death, and asked if that was the day an officer of the Harbor National Bank had called about his loan arrearage.

"I believe so."

"Isn't it true," Richmond said, "that on January 10, 1975, the bank officer told you that pursuant to the rules and regulations of the State of Massachusetts that they were giving you a ten-day notice of demand to pay the entire Harbormaster account of $1,900? Didn't he tell you that?"

"He may have, yes."

"And when you went in there to see him early Monday morning, January 13, 1975, he told you that it was all over, that you had to start paying your bills or they were going to call all your notes at the Harbor National Bank, didn't he?"

"Whatever he testified to I remember he said, yes."

"What did you say Mr. Blaikie?"

"I don't recall specifically what I said."

"That there was no problem, right?"

"Probably tried to."

"You got a little angry with the banker, didn't you?"

"I wouldn't say I got angry."

"Did you get a little defensive?"

"Yes, probably a little defensive."

She recited Blaikie's testimony that he returned from his failed trip to Phoenix with approximately $200 in May 1975.

"That's about right," he said.

"You went to the hotel and stayed there for about a week?"

"Yes."

"Isn't it true that you stayed at the motel to avoid people who were trying to talk to you about David DeWilde?"

"Among other things, yes."

"It wasn't because you knew his body was buried in the basement?" she asked, glaring.

"That was a big part of it, Miss Richmond."

"And you never paid that bill, or did you, at the Newton Motor Lodge?"

"Part of it, no."

"You left them too owing some money?"

"Yes."

"How did you pay for the trip back to Arizona?"

"I wrote a rubber check," Blaikie said.

She asked if he recalled the day his father died in a Veterans Administration Hospital.

"Not the specific day, no."

"I show you this piece of paper and ask you to look at it," she said, handing him his father's death certificate. "See if it refreshes your recollection as to the date your father died."

"Yes."

"What date did your father die?"

"March 9, 1974." He somehow misread the date, which was March 8.

"Mr. Blaikie, when you made this claim for one lump payment on your father's life insurance on April 25, 1974, you gave his date of death as March 21, 1974, didn't you?"

"I did?" Blaikie asked, appearing surprised.

"Just look at the sheet." She handed him a copy of the Veterans Administration claim form he had filed for the benefits on his late father's $5,000 life insurance policy.

"Yes," he said.

Richmond had determined that Blaikie's mother had been maintaining premium payments on the Veterans Administration life insurance policy of her chronically ill husband. The date of her last payment was August 14, 1973, the day of her death by gunshot wound. In December, Jim received notification that his father's insurance policy had lapsed because of nonpayment.

Early in 1974, Blaikie wrote the Veterans Administration, requesting reinstatement of the policy. In March his chronically ill father died at the VA hospital in Bedford, Massachusetts. According to a death certificate, the cause of his death was double pneumonia.

" 'March 21, 1974.' " Richmond repeated the date, which was nearly two weeks after his father's death. "And the reason you did that, Mr. Blaikie, was that the payments were not up to date on this policy until March 15, 1974, isn't that right?"

"No."

"That is a mistake on the date of death of your father?" she said, referring to the form he had filled out.

"What it appears to be, yes."

"You signed this under a line, Mr. Blaikie, that said, 'I certify that the foregoing is true and correct to the best of my knowledge and belief.' Didn't you?"

"I just made an error," he said. "That's all."

Richmond asked him about the thirty-foot sailboat he sold in March 1974. "At the time that you sold the boat you had a loan for it with the General Electric Credit Corporation, is that right?"

Over Ted Harrington's objection, Judge McGuire allowed Richmond to continue.

"Mr. Blaikie," Richmond said, approaching the witness, "in March of 1974, you sold the thirty-foot Pearson sailboat, isn't that right?"

"Yes, ma'am."

"You sold it through the brokerage of Wells Yachts, Incorporated, did you not?"

"Yes, ma'am."

"You sold it to a Dr. Lewis, is that correct?"

"Yes, ma'am."

"Do you recall receiving a letter from Clinton Wells on behalf of Wells Yachts on March 4, 1974?" She showed him a copy of the letter.

"Yes," he said.

"In the letter did Mr. Wells tell you to deliver the boat free and clear to Dr. Lewis?"

"Yes."

"And what he meant by free and clear, Mr. Blaikie, was that there was a chattel mortgage on that boat."

Ted Harrington's objection was sustained.

"Mr. Blaikie," Richmond said, "was there a chattel mortgage on that boat at that time?"

"Yes."

"You at no time told Dr. Lewis about that chattel mortgage on that boat when you sold it to him and received money from him, did you?"

"No."

"And you received how much money from Dr. Lewis for that boat?"

"You have it down there. I don't remember."

"About sixteen thousand dollars, wasn't it, Mr. Blaikie?"

"Approximately."

"You never told the General Electric Credit Corporation that you sold the chattel on which they had the mortgage, did you?"

"No."

"You never told them you sold the sailboat?"

"No."

"Did you ever tell Dr. Lewis about that chattel mortgage?"

"I did eventually, yes."

"When did you tell him, Mr. Blaikie?"

"I don't remember. Eventually."

Judge McGuire asked, "What do you mean by 'eventually'?"

Blaikie looked at him haplessly and said: "At some time after that."

"When?" Richmond demanded.

"I don't recall," Blaikie said.

"Give us your best estimates."

"I have no recollection when I told him."

"Did you tell him in 1974?"

"I don't remember when it was."

''Did you tell him in 1975?''

Ted Harrington vigorously objected. ''He said he doesn't remember.''

''I will allow it,'' Judge McGuire said.

''I don't remember when it was,'' Blaikie said.

''You never told Dr. Lewis at all, did you?'' Richmond said, directly in front of him, her color rising.

''I told him in the end, yes.''

''When was the *end?*'' Richmond asked.

''I don't recall.''

Turning to Blaikie's possession of a .38 revolver, Richmond asked, ''Did you register it?''

''No.''

''And you were using the gun when you carried large sums of money for the McGovern campaign?''

''Yes, on occasion.''

''You were carrying a gun, is that right?''

''Yes.''

''And that was for your protection?''

''Yes.''

''And, Mr. Blaikie, you know that in order to carry a firearm in the State of Massachusetts you need to have a permit, is that right?''

''Sure.''

''You were the treasurer of the McGovern campaign?''

''Right.''

''It certainly would have been embarrassing in the McGovern campaign if you had been found to be carrying a handgun without a permit in your official capacity as the treasurer of the McGovern campaign, would it not?''

Harrington's objection was sustained.

Through Blaikie's answers to her questions, Richmond established that Blaikie received the $6,000 loan from DeWilde at David's auto repair shop.

''He handed you the six thousand dollars and said, 'Jimmy, here's the money'?'' she asked.

''To the best of my recollection I went over there to meet him to get the money.''

Showing him the loan note found in DeWilde's safe-deposit box, she asked Blaikie if there was any reference on the exhibit to the thousand-dollar-a-month interest to which he had testified.''

"No," he said.

"You are lying about that too, aren't you, Mr. Blaikie?"

"No, I'm not, Miss Richmond."

"You asked him for it because you said that you wanted to buy out the widow of the insurance business that you were then in, isn't that what you told him?" she asked, alluding to the Bacon agency.

"No. At that time we never would have mentioned it."

"That wasn't true either, was it, Mr. Blaikie?"

"No."

Ted Harrington objected. "How can it be true? He denied it."

"Wait a minute," Judge McGuire said. "His answer is no. The question is excluded."

"Now, Mr. Blaikie, you said this morning that you went back to your house to get the car keys, right, for your station wagon?"

"On January fourteenth?"

"January fourteenth, right. And you had one set of keys in the house, right?"

"Yes."

"Now, Mr. Blaikie, isn't it a fact that if you had locked your car keys in the car you would have locked your house keys in the car as well?"

Ted Harrington objected.

"I will allow it," the judge ruled.

"No."

"You carry two sets of key rings, one for car keys, and one for house keys?"

"Yes," he said, "because we were switching the cars around. It was easier."

"Now, Mr. Blaikie, you say that Mr. DeWilde hit you in the face, right?"

"Which time?"

"Well, Mr. DeWilde hit you in the face on January 14, 1975?"

"He hit me twice."

"All right, the first time when he knocked you over by hitting you twice, how—"

Ted Harrington objected, stating her question was not consistent with the testimony. "The first time he did not knock him over."

"The first time he did not knock you over," Richmond said.

"He slapped me the first time."

"The time that he hit you, he knocked you over, is that right?"

"He stunned me and I fell over, yes."

"You fell over?"

"I fell down, yes."

"Mr. Blaikie, how much did you weigh on January 14, 1975?"

"About what I weigh now."

"How much is that?"

"Around two hundred pounds."

"Mr. Blaikie, was Mr. DeWilde left-handed or right-handed?"

"I have no idea."

Demonstrating with her hands, Richmond looked as though she might strike the defendant. "Did he hit you with his *left* hand or his *right* hand?"

"I don't even remember. He just hit me. I remember that."

"You don't know from which side of his body it came from, his left hand or his right hand?"

"No."

"Where did he hit you, Mr. Blaikie?"

"In the head."

"Where?"

"The head."

"Where in the head?"

"Well, the first time he slapped me he slapped me across the face like that." He demonstrated a slap to his left cheek.

''Now go to the second time. Did he hit you with his fist or slap you?''

''His fist.''

''You don't remember whether it was his left fist or right fist?''

''No.''

''You did know—''

''He hit me here, though, like this.'' He firmly brought his clenched right hand to his chin.

''Here on the chin,'' Richmond said, miming him. ''Is that what you are saying?''

''Yes.''

She walked away from the witness stand, turned and, facing him, asked if there were gold carpeting on the floor of the study where he supposedly shot DeWilde. Blaikie answered that there was, but it had been covered to protect it from paint while he had been redecorating the room.

''You told us this morning that you left the room after you shot David and walked around the house awhile?''

''Yes.''

''You came back to that room, couldn't bear to look at David's face, right?''

''Yes.''

''How long had you been walking around the house before you came back when you couldn't bear to look at David's face?''

''I don't know. It's hazy in my mind.''

''Give us your best estimate.''

''I have no estimate. I don't remember. It's like there was no sense of time.''

''There was blood all over this floor, wasn't there, Mr. Blaikie?''

''No, there wasn't.''

''Didn't you tell us this morning there was blood coming out of his back, the back of his head, and there was blood all over his clothes and blood down the back, didn't you tell us that this morning?''

''No, I didn't.''

''There was no blood at all, is that right?''

"Yes, there was blood."

"Where was the blood?"

"Here," he said, reaching to the back of his head.

"None of it got on the rug?"

"No."

Richmond asked if he recalled the testimony of the state police chemist.

"Yes," Blaikie said.

"There was blood all over his shirt?"

"Yes."

"And blood on his pants?"

"Yes."

"When you pulled him along didn't you get blood all over the carpet?"

"No."

"No blood at all on the carpeting? That is not the reason you replaced the carpet, is it, Mr. Blaikie?"

"I never replaced the carpet, just tore it up."

"You tore it up because you had bloodstains all over it, didn't you?"

"No," Blaikie said. He had the confident look of a chess player thwarting attacks by the opposing queen no matter her direction. On the witness stand for five hours, three of them under cross-examination, testifying in his own defense seemed to agree with him.

It was nearly four o'clock, the regular time for adjournment, and at the bench Richmond said she was far from finished. Despite Ted Harrington's request that her cross-examination be completed that day whatever the hour, Judge McGuire called for the regular recess until ten o'clock the following morning.

As the courtroom was emptying and Richmond was gathering papers at the government table, a court officer approached her.

"Counselor," he said, "you're doing great, but you want to know what I think for what it's worth?"

"Sure," she said, slipping him a pleasant if harried smile.

"I think you're being too easy on Blaikie."

Intrigued, she asked, "Oh, how's that?"

"Well, he's not taking you seriously. He looks like he's in control."

Richmond felt herself blanch with a shock of recognition. She had been guarding against coming on like a vengeful fury and apparently had come across like a pussycat.

"Officer," she said, "you're a very observant person."

Chapter 25

The following morning, November 18th, Judge Mc-Guire entered the courtroom and James Blaikie returned to the witness stand.

The clerk said, "Mr. Blaikie, you are reminded that you are still under oath."

"Yes," Blaikie said.

Alice Richmond rose for the eighth day of testimony, her second day of cross-examining Blaikie. He had been talking in the abstract about the death scene, claiming little recollection of it. Today, if she had anything to say about it, he would have to recreate that moment vividly and face its results in the full view of the jury. She intended to take the gloves off.

"Now, Mr. Blaikie," Richmond said, "directing your attention back to January 14, 1975, will you describe for us again what happened when David De-Wilde said, 'What do you mean, five hundred dollars?' "

Blaikie repeated his earlier testimony that DeWilde flew into a rage.

"He said again to the effect, 'I expect the whole thing, and I'll break your neck, you fat little bastard.' " Blaikie said with a hurt look.

"Didn't you tell us yesterday, 'He started to come at me again so I took the gun out again' ?"

Ted Harrington firmly objected. "That is out of context."

"I will allow it," Judge McGuire responded.

''Yes,'' Blaikie said. ''When he came at me again that's what I did, yes.''

Moving more briskly than she had the previous day, Richmond closed in on the witness stand. ''Mr. Blaikie, tell us again where he punched you. Show us *how* he did it.''

Appearing startled by her bold approach, Blaikie responded, ''He just hit me. I don't remember how it happened. I went down after that.''

''Do you remember saying anything yesterday about him hitting you on the cheekbone, yesterday, on the left side?''

''When he slapped me, yes.''

His words were barely out and she hurled another question. ''Was Mr. DeWilde *right*-handed or *left*-handed?''

Blaikie appeared flustered. ''I told you I don't know.''

''Would it refresh your memory if I say Mr. De-Wilde was *left*-handed?'' she said, eyes widening.

''It wouldn't refresh my memory, I never knew.''

Because, she thought, *he never hit you.* Surveying the jury, she cocked a brow and silently asked, *Does a left-hander standing in front of him slap him on the left side of the face?*

With her cold gaze back on the witness, she said, ''Mr Blaikie, tell us what happened when you fell on the floor.''

''When I fell on the floor?''

''Yes.''

''Again, I was in a daze. I remember him going over me to get to the gun and just me pulling it out and shooting him.''

''Can you *show* us the position you fell on the floor?''

''Only roughly. I don't remember.''

''With the Court's permission,'' Richmond said, ''may the defendant show the jury how he fell down on the floor?''

Judge McGuire said, ''On the record now he says, 'I don't remember.' If you remember, indicate it to the jury.''

"I just fell down," Blaikie said, refusing to demonstrate. "I really don't remember exactly how or where I fell."

It appeared to Richmond that Blaikie's cool was failing him, just as detectives Moran and Doris had described his loss of composure under questioning. She strode to the evidence table and hoisted the .38 Special. "And this gun flew out of your hand to the side, is that right?"

"Yes," Blaikie said, eyeing the revolver.

"Which side did it slide to?"

"As I recall, if I were standing with the gun, like that," Blaikie said, swinging his right hand to the right.

"How far away from you was he?"

"I don't know."

"At what angle was he?"

"I don't remember."

Weighing the gun, she asked, "Could you see it when you were looking down on the floor?"

"Not immediately when I fell down, no."

"And Mr. DeWilde just did a Superman leap over you to this gun?" she asked sardonically.

"I remember him leaping over me."

"I object," Ted Harrington said, "to the word 'Superman,' and ask that it be stricken."

Judge McGuire ordered it stricken.

Harrington added, "Also, Miss Richmond may find it very funny, but I don't know that the other people in this room do."

"The jury and the Court know how serious it is," the judge said. "Proceed."

"How many feet away from you was that gun?" she asked.

"I don't remember. When I fell all I remember is him going for it and me pulling it away and shooting."

"Did you have to cock the gun?"

"It may have been cocked."

He hadn't but spoken when she demanded, "You kept it in the cash box cocked?"

"I may have cocked it when I took it out."

"You might have cocked it when you pulled it out the first time?"

"I don't remember. It is possible."

"Then you showed it to Mr. DeWilde and said, 'Get out of here'?"

"Yes."

"Mr. Blaikie," Richmond said, approaching him, "I show you this gun which has been marked Exhibit Number 53."

"Let me see it first," Judge McGuire interjected, and after confirming the revolver was unloaded, he returned it to Richmond.

"I ask you if you can identify it," Richmond said, handing the firearm to Blaikie.

"It appears to be the gun I had."

"Now, show us. What did you do with that gun? Pretend I'm Mr. DeWilde. What did you do with that gun?"

In an utterly silent courtroom, she stood directly in front of the witness stand, looking up at Blaikie and his gun.

"I just remember getting ahead of him before he could get it and just shooting," Blaikie said, looking down at her dubiously.

"I'm Mr. DeWilde," she said. "You do what you did to Mr. DeWilde."

"I just pulled it," he said pointing the gun at her, "told him to get out, get out of the house."

"Did you cock the gun at that time?"

"I don't remember."

"Now, show us please how the gun flew out of your hand."

"It was just knocked out."

"How far away from the gun was Mr. DeWilde when you grabbed the gun and shot him?"

"I don't remember."

"What position was Mr. DeWilde in?"

"He was laying over trying to get to it."

"He was trying to get to it?"

"Yes."

"You fired just one shot, didn't you, Mr. Blaikie?"

"Yes, ma'am."

"It entered his head here," she said, turning her back to Blaikie and the gun, placing her right index finger on the back of her head. "Right of the midline, on the right side."

"Yes."

Facing him again, she said, "You heard it went straight through and lodged in his frontal bone." She pointed between her eyebrows to the right of her nose.

"Yes."

"Isn't it a fact, Mr. Blaikie," she said in a firm voice, "that he was sitting at a table, and you came up behind him on his right side and fired one shot into the back of his head?"

"No, that's not true," Blaikie said.

"Your honor," Ted Harrington said, "unless there is evidence to that I ask it be stricken because it is highly prejudicial."

Judge McGuire ruled, "He said it wasn't true. That was his answer."

"I ask that the question be stricken. There is no evidence to that."

"Cross-examination," the judge said evenly. "I will allow it."

Richmond returned the gun to the evidence table.

Referring to the *Boston Globe* reporter who interviewed Blaikie in Phoenix, she said, "Mr. Blaikie, did you tell Mr. Connolly, did you not, that when David came over to your house he sat down at the table in the kitchen and had something to drink? Didn't you tell Mr. Connolly that?"

"Yes. I lied when I told Mr. Connolly that."

Richmond looked up at the admission. "Now, Mr. Blaikie, you said that you ran into the kitchen at some point and got this white freezer bag because you couldn't stand looking at Mr. DeWilde's face, is that right?"

"Yes."

"Did you hear Detective McDermott testify?" she asked, referring to the Brookline police officer.

"I heard the detective testify, yes."

"Did you hear Detective McDermott say there was wire around the white bag?"

"If he said it he must have known what there was."

"You put it there, Mr. Blaikie?"

"I was in a daze at that time, Miss Richmond."

"Now, Mr. Blaikie, you put the bag on first and then checked to see if Mr. DeWilde was still breathing, whatever?"

"No. I did that as soon as I was able to sit up after it happened."

"As soon as you were able to sit up? Have you had any first aid?"

"I've had a little from my father, yes."

"Would you know if somebody was alive, if they were in a coma, if they were unconscious?"

Harrington objected.

"He may answer it if he knows," Judge McGuire said.

"I believe so," Blaikie said.

"How would you know, Mr. Blaikie?"

"They'd still have respiration, heartbeats."

"You didn't check to see if he was dead or alive, did you?"

"Yes, I did."

"If he was alive would you have called the ambulance?"

"I don't know what I would have done, honestly."

"You put the plastic bag over his head and tied the wire around it, is that right?"

"Yes, ma'am."

"Didn't you do that, Mr. Blaikie, so you wouldn't get any more blood in your house?"

"That's why I tied it, yes, so the blood wouldn't go everywhere. It was all over the back lying down."

"You never checked to see whether he was dead or alive before you put that bag on, did you?"

You'll hear, she thought, *what the medical examiner has to say about whether David was dead or alive at the time.*

"Now, Mr. Blaikie," she resumed, "you told us yesterday that you took him downstairs, right?"

"Yes."

"So that when your wife came home the corpse was in the basement?"

"Yes, ma'am."

"And you didn't tell your wife about this, did you?"

"No."

"You never told your wife about this?"

"No."

Richmond drew testimony of his purported two o'clock rendezvous with Kathy at the Framingham restaurant.

"Mr. Blaikie, what time did you go down the basement and begin to think about putting the body in the hole?"

"It was after she went to bed." He guessed after ten o'clock.

"Mr. Blaikie, when you went down there, whatever time, to put the body in the hole after your wife had gone to sleep, what did you do? Tell us exactly what you did."

"I thought for a few moments, thought about trying to take him out of the house. And I tried to lift him. I couldn't lift him, and then again I walked in the back by the oil burner, walked around. I wondered for a long period as to what to do, and then I remembered, as I testified yesterday, about the hole."

"Then what did you do?"

"Then I tried to move David, and evidently—I don't know—the way the bag was tied or something, all the blood had piled up there. And when I moved it, it all released."

"Tell us exactly what you did to get him into the hole."

"I don't remember. It was awfully heavy. Somehow—somehow I got him in the hole."

"Tell us exactly what you did."

"I don't remember, Miss Richmond."

"Do you remember that he was in a semifetal position with his head and legs down?"

"I heard testimony to that, yes."

"Did you ever hear of rigor mortis, Mr. Blaikie?"

"Yes."

"Do you know anything about rigor mortis?"

"A little from school. I remember way back."

"Do you remember that a body with rigor mortis gets absolutely rigid?"

"Yes."

Gotcha, Alice thought. *Wait until you hear what Dr. Bigelow has to say about the timetable of rigor mortis and how long a body is pliable after death.*

"Now, Mr. Blaikie, you left the body there and put the boards back on the hole, is that right?"

"I put some bags or something over him. I don't recall."

"You put bags over him in the hole and then you put the boards back?"

"As best I remember, yes."

"I believe you told us yesterday that you left him there for five days to a week?"

"Approximately."

"Mr. Blaikie, did it start to smell?"

"Yes, after a while it did."

"Didn't that smell permeate the whole house?"

"No."

"No? Your wife never smelled it?"

"No."

"Five to seven days you left the body there?"

"Approximately. I don't remember."

"What did it smell like, Mr. Blaikie?"

"It was bad, again, I guess, as the detective testified, it must have been cool in there because it really didn't get that bad."

"*Five* to *seven* days? Will you describe the smell?"

"It was a strong smell. I can't describe it."

"Did it get worse as time went on?"

"Yes. That's why I decided to fill in the hole."

"Otherwise you weren't going to fill in the hole?" Richmond's tone was incredulous.

"No. It just kind of reminded me it was there. I was trying to forget it."

"Now, about five days to a week later when you decided that the body was beginning to smell, and you went and bought the concrete, what did you do when you got the concrete and the sand home?"

"I remember first I thought I was going to fill the whole hole up, but I didn't have enough concrete. So I just put sand, concrete, and plaster there, that I swept in the hole, and the coal, and filled it up."

"That's why you put the concrete on the body first?"

"I guess so. Yes, I thought it would fill the hole all up. I didn't have enough."

"You spread the bags neatly over the body, did you not?"

"Again, I only remember vaguely how it happened."

"Mr. Blaikie, when did you put the rope around the body?"

"I don't remember if I put it around or it was just there, or I just threw it in over him."

"I show you this photograph marked Exhibit Number 25 and ask you to look at that please." She held it for him to see.

Blaikie ignored the macabre color glossy of De-Wilde's rope-trussed body in rotting clothes with a white bag over the head and the right hand missing. The body was indeed in a fetal position.

"Do you see a rope in that photograph, Mr. Blaikie?"

Following a glance, he said, "It looks like it, yes."

"Is this rope extending down from the neck to the legs as well?"

Without looking, he said, "I think so."

"Look at the photograph, Mr. Blaikie!" she demanded.

Peering at it, he answered, "I still can't tell."

Pointing, she said, "Do you see this piece of rope extending down to the legs?"

He refused to look.

How does it feel, Mr. Blaikie, Richmond thought, *to be confronted with the godawful results of your deeds in a cellar nearly two years ago?*

Distancing herself from the witness stand, Richmond turned to face him. "Isn't it a fact, Mr. Blaikie, that you put that concrete on that body thinking that it was going to disintegrate the body?"

Ted Harrington rose up, objecting.

"He may answer," Judge McGuire said.

"Your honor," Harrington said, "there is no evidence of this and it is highly prejudicial."

The judge responded, "She is asking about his state of mind. He may answer if he knows."

"No," Blaikie said. "I know concrete would never do that."

"What do you know that concrete would do, Mr. Blaikie?"

"Fill that hole."

"Well, with reference to the body, Mr. Blaikie, what would the concrete do?"

"As far as I know, I never thought concrete would do anything."

"Did you think it would preserve the body?"

Judge McGuire interrupted. "Excluded. He has answered, his lack of knowledge."

"When you put the plastic bags over it and you put the sand over it, you still had some empty room, didn't you?" Richmond asked.

"That's where I put the coal in to fill up the hole."

"You filled up that hole all the way to the top, didn't you?"

"I guess so, yes."

"You poured the concrete over the coal, which was all the way up to the top at that time, isn't that right?"

"I poured the concrete to fill up the hole, the cement."

Richmond returned the photo to the evidence table and shifted from the concealment of the body to the coverup of the crime.

"Now, Mr. Blaikie, you told a number of people that Mr. DeWilde dropped you off at Coolidge Corner?"

Blaikie admitted he had spoken of the Brookline intersection to David's mother, former wife, and friends as well as to Detective Moran.

"And he didn't drive you to Coolidge Corner, did he?"

"No."

"In fact, the reason you said Coolidge Corner is that you didn't want the police to get too close to the Purity Supreme, did you?" she said, referring to the supermarket where he had parked his car.

"No. I just told them to make up a story. I lied."

"Now, isn't it true, Mr. Blaikie, that you sent your wife to the Sea & Surf Restaurant that day so she wouldn't be in the house when you killed David?"

"No."

"Isn't it true that you called her at twelve-fifteen, or called the restaurant, and left word you'd be delayed and would be a little late?"

"Yes, ma'am."

"Isn't that because you had just set everything up, Mr. Blaikie, and you had just called Mr. DeWilde to tell him everything was all set, that you *had it?*"

"No. I was late because of the key situation."

Marching toward the witness, Richmond announced, "Isn't it a fact you killed him when he got there, immediately, put the body in that hole and did almost all the work you had to do aside from painting the top of that hole, and then you called your wife and said, 'I'm coming out to see you' ?"

"I object to the form of that question," Ted Harrington declared.

"Sustained," Judge McGuire said. "The jury will disregard the question."

"Now, Mr. Blaikie, you told Detective Moran, did you not, that Mr. DeWilde had a girlfriend who lived behind Ken's Pub?"

"Yes."

"You knew Mr. DeWilde didn't have a girlfriend who lived behind Ken's Pub?"

"Yes."

"And you told him that to explain how the car came

to be there when you knew it would be eventually found on Royce Road?''

"I don't know what my thinking was."

"You knew, furthermore, where Royce Road was, didn't you?''

"Not by name, no. I knew where it was but I didn't know the name.''

"And that's why you asked Detective Moran where Royce Road was after he told you that the car had been found on Royce Road?''

"I remember asking him that. I don't remember why I asked him."

"You knew perfectly well where the car had been found because you had put it there, didn't you, Mr. Blaikie?''

"Yes, I did."

"You still asked Detective Moran where Royce Road was?''

"Yes."

"That was because you had also told Detective Moran about the girlfriend that David DeWilde had who lived behind Ken's Pub, which was the street that you knew the car was going to be found on, isn't that right?''

"Yes."

"You did that to mislead the police, didn't you?''

"Probably, yes."

"Do you recall Detective Moran asking you on January 24, 1975, whether you owed any money to Mr. DeWilde?''

"I remember his asking me."

"You said no, didn't you?''

"Yes, I lied."

"You are telling us the truth now, aren't you, Mr. Blaikie?''

"I'm trying to."

Turning to the February 6th meeting with Detective Moran, Richmond asked, "Do you remember saying, 'All right, I lied. I had an awful lot of financial problems. I was deeply in debt, borrowed six thousand dollars from Dave. I thought if I told the truth I would be suspected of killing Dave.' Do you remember saying that to Detective Moran?''

"I remember saying everything up to the point of suspecting, which I recall saying, 'You'd suspect me of something.' ''

"Is that what you recall, Mr. Blaikie?''

"Yes.''

"Do you recall Sergeant Doris saying, 'How do you know he's dead? Right now he's only a missing person'?''

"I remember him testifying to that. I don't recall him saying that.''

"You don't recall Detective Moran saying, 'Who said he was dead?' ''

"Yes, on the stand.''

"You don't recall saying, 'I know he's dead. I have spoken to his mother and some of his friends, and I was the last one to see him alive'?''

"I remember saying, 'According to his friends I'm the last one who saw him,' yes.''

"But you did know he was dead, didn't you, Mr. Blaikie?''

"Yes, ma'am.''

"You were telling the truth there, weren't you?''

"I didn't say that.''

"Do you remember Sergeant Doris telling you that he thought you were lying?''

Ted Harrington's objection was sustained by Judge McGuire.

Richmond pressed on. "Do you recall saying to Sergeant Doris, 'I know I was the last one to see him alive. I know I had a motive to kill him, but the last time I saw him was on Harvard Street'?''

"I remember parts of that. Other parts I never said.''

"What did you never say?''

"I never said, 'I have a motive for killing him.' ''

"You never said that to Sergeant Doris?''

"No, ma'am.''

"Did you hear him testify?''

"Yes.''

She asked if he had ever said as much to Detective Moran.

"No, ma'am."

"But you did have a motive for killing him, didn't you, Mr. Blaikie?"

"I had no motive other than to protect myself."

"At no time during the two months or two and a half months that you had contact with Detective Moran did you permit him in your house, did you?"

"No, ma'am."

"In fact, every time he suggested to you, Mr. Blaikie, 'If it's convenient to you I will come up to the house,' you told him you'd come to the police station?"

"Yes, ma'am."

"The reason was you didn't want Detective Moran in your house looking around for a body, isn't that true?"

"Yes, ma'am."

Richmond turned to what she and Detective Moran believed was Blaikie's ploy to con DeWilde into thinking his money was going into a drug deal. The prosecution also believed that after killing DeWilde, Blaikie used the fictitious deal as a red herring.

"On February twenty-fourth when you called Detective Moran—and by the way, Mr. Blaikie, he was getting pretty warm on your trail, wasn't he?"

"I object," Ted Harrington said.

Judge McGuire sustained.

Richmond asked Blaikie about his mention in that meeting of a certain Ned Woodman, who had been calling him with messages for David DeWilde about a mysterious deal.

Blaikie said Detective Moran's recollection was essentially correct.

"You didn't say, 'Woodman'?" Richmond asked.

"I don't recall that. I'm pretty sure I didn't at that time. I believe I just said, 'Ned,' yes."

"Did you tell him Woodman had an address at 49 Hereford Street?"

"As I recall, later he read some addresses to me,"

Blaikie said, alluding to the envelope found in De-Wilde's room. "And I recognized one because I had lived there."

"Do you remember telling Detective Moran that you didn't know what the commodity being dealt was even though you were the middleman?"

"Yes, ma'am."

"That was a lie, wasn't it?"

"Most of these conversations—part of the conversation was a lie."

"And isn't it true that you also told him that when DeWilde left you at the Purity Supreme on January 14, 1975, DeWilde was going to Brandy's to meet Woodman?"

"Yes. I told him he was going to meet *Ned*."

"Not *Woodman?*"

"I don't believe so."

"Detective Moran is mistaken about that too?"

"Only about that part, yes."

"But the whole sentence was a lie, wasn't it, Mr. Blaikie?"

"Stating he was going to Brandy's, obviously, yes."

"You were still lying February 25, 1975, isn't that right?" Richmond insisted.

"About what?"

"About where Mr. DeWilde was and what happened."

"Yes."

"You were still lying, weren't you?"

"Yes."

"You were trying to throw suspicion on yet another person weren't you, Mr. Blaikie?"

"All I know is, as you say, he was hot on my trail or warm on my trail," Blaikie said. "I just knew that they knew I did it, were going to connect it up eventually, trying to forestall it to protect my wife and whatever."

His eight hours on the witness stand, two of them that morning, were showing. Blaikie appeared now like a fighter on the ropes, trying simply to stay on his feet.

Richmond seemed to be gaining strength with her every blow.

"They were going to catch you eventually," she said decisively, "the way you buried that body and painted the cement?"

"Yes," Blaikie said with an air of resignation.

"So you were lying to the police in an attempt to mislead them?"

"Yes, ma'am."

"And that attempt to suggest that somebody else, possibly somebody involved with drugs might have killed David DeWilde?"

"I was trying to mislead them."

"You knew David DeWilde wasn't involved in drugs, didn't you, Mr. Blaikie?"

"No."

"You didn't know that?"

"No."

"He was a good friend of yours?"

"Yes."

"You saw him socially a lot?"

"Yes."

"Do you smoke dope?"

"Only the kind that's legal, cigarettes."

Ted Harrington objected, but Judge McGuire allowed the answer to stand.

"Did you ever see DeWilde using drugs?" Richmond asked.

"Yes. Yes, ma'am."

"Where?"

"Numerous places."

"Who was with you?"

"I was with him myself or he was there with other people."

"What other people?"

"Many different people. I've known David for what, ten, eleven years."

"What kind of drugs, Mr. Blaikie?"

Ted Harrington spoke up: "Your honor—"

"No," Judge McGuire said, "I'm going to let her inquire. What kind of drugs?"

"Marijuana," Blaikie said, looking at the judge. "Cocaine."

"Marijuana, cocaine too?" Richmond asked.

"Yes."

"You never used drugs when you were in the party?"

"I have one time smoked marijuana but never had drugs with David, never did cocaine."

"You never did drugs?"

"Never did any cocaine."

"And you told Detective Moran about Ned Woodman and the implications of the drug deal to throw suspicion off you, didn't you?" Richmond asked.

"I told him about Ned, yes, probably to mislead him, yes."

She held up the manila envelope containing a nonexistent flight number and untraceable names.

"Mr. Blaikie, isn't the reason that you knew about this envelope because you gave this information to Mr. DeWilde over the telephone when you talked to him that weekend?"

"No."

"Isn't the reason that you knew about this information because you were setting him up to *kill* him?"

"Of course not."

"You had made all these attempts so the police would believe there was a strong-arm drug dealer involved in the disappearance of David DeWilde?"

"To divert suspicion, yes."

"Didn't you also say David had gotten a phone call on January 16, 1975, from Woodman?"

"Yes."

"And that was a lie too, wasn't it?"

"Yes."

"And you didn't recognize Woodman's voice over the phone?"

"There was no call," Blaikie said with a glimmer of impatience, "so there was nothing to recognize."

"You told Detective Moran you recognized the voice over the phone, did you not?"

"Yes."

"That was a lie too, wasn't it?" Richmond asked, closing the distance on the witness stand.

"Yes. There was never any call."

"You also told Detective Moran, 'You better not mention my name' or you and your wife will both be killed?"

"Yes."

"That was a lie?"

"Yes."

"And didn't you also ask Detective Moran to make a note of your apprehension?"

"Yes."

"What did Detective Moran say to you?"

"I don't remember what he said."

"Didn't Detective Moran say that you shouldn't show up dead until they found DeWilde?"

"Yes," Blaikie said, almost appearing to smile.

"It's funny, isn't it, Mr. Blaikie?" Richmond was glaring at him.

"I don't think it was funny at all."

"You laughed at the time, didn't you?"

"Out of nervousness, maybe. I don't recall."

"You almost laughed now, didn't you?"

"No."

"And all the time you knew where David DeWilde was, didn't you?"

In response to Richmond's questioning, Blaikie also acknowledged lying to *Boston Globe* Reporter Richard Connolly about David's whereabouts.

"Do you remember saying to Pat Wynn on a number of occasions over the course of January, February, March of 1975, that you were really concerned, that you were really worried, 'David's been gone a long time. I wonder where he could be.' Do you remember saying that to Mrs. Wynn four, five, six times?"

"Yes, in substance I did, yes."

"You were lying then, too, weren't you, Mr. Blaikie?"

"Yes, ma'am."

Richmond paused to let the admission sink in. Lies to police, lies to a reporter and, finally, lies to a mother from a man who had shot her son and buried him in a basement.

"I have no further questions, your honor," she said, her voice deepening in contempt. Walking away from Blaikie, she felt in her mind and gut that the prediction she had made twenty months before had come true: James Blaikie had croaked himself on the witness stand.

She hoped her next and final witness, Dr. Nolton Bigelow, would nail down the corners of Blaikie's legal coffin.

Chapter 26

In line with Detective Moran's observations, Richmond believed Blaikie had made four key mistakes in his testimony. All were related to forensic medicine.

First was Blaikie's story that DeWilde knocked the gun out of his hand, a scramble for the weapon ensued, and then he shot DeWilde.

Second was the claim that he thought DeWilde was dead immediately after shooting him.

Third was his insistence that he shot DeWilde early in the afternoon but did not place the body in the dry well until after Kathy had gone to sleep that night.

Fourth was the assertion that he had sealed the grave in concrete nearly a week later.

These were the pillars of Blaikie's defense: justifiable homicide. To shake or topple them, Richmond called the associate Norfolk County medical examiner back to the stand as a rebuttal witness.

Aware that testimony could well end that evening, Frank Bacon had the sense that the close of a bitterly fought contest was unfolding. At their tables, the stern expressions of Alice Richmond and the Harringtons had turned deadly grim, like the faces of combatants answering the final bell.

Dr. Nolton Hunter Bigelow reached the witness stand and the clerk reminded him that he was still under oath. The dignified Yale and Cornell University medical school graduate nodded his understanding.

"Doctor Bigelow," Richmond said, approaching him, "please assume the following facts. Assume one man approximately five-foot-six and a half weighing somewhere between two hundred and two hundred fifteen pounds lying on the floor on his back, reaching for a gun, which is to his right side.''

Continuing with Blaikie's version of events, she asked the doctor to assume there is a taller man ''jumping over'' the man on the floor almost at a right angle and ''then laying over and trying to get the gun.''

''Assume finally that the short man lying on his back grabs the gun and shoots the man on top of him in the back of the head.''

Daniel Harrington objected to the phrase ''on top of him,'' and Judge McGuire ordered it stricken.

Richmond settled for Blaikie's vague description of DeWilde ''laying over and trying to get the gun.'' She asked the medical examiner if in his opinion the hypothetical struggle was consistent with the trajectory of the fatal bullet as he had described it in his earlier testimony.

Dr. Bigelow firmly stated, ''That hypothesis could not have explained the situation that I saw when I examined the path of the bullet in the decedent that I testified to previously.''

As with all the points she was attempting to make, Richmond was laying down evidence that she would interpret in her closing argument.

She then turned to the subject of rigor mortis and asked Dr. Bigelow to explain it.

''Following the death of virtually anybody or any animal, for that matter, the body is limp for a period of time,'' he said. ''Then, at least in human beings, in a period of roughly two to four hours a situation occurs where the muscles of the body go into a spasm or a state of tension which is known as rigor mortis, so that not only the jaw but the extremities, the arms and the legs, are also in a state of complete rigidity. And this then lasts for a period of from twenty-four to forty-eight hours.''

Richmond asked, ''When your body is in this state of complete rigidity, can it be easily moved or folded up, if you know?''

"It is very difficult to change the position of the arms, the legs, or the torso of a body while it is in the state of full rigor mortis."

Directing the medical examiner to assume the hypothetical body had been shot in the back of the head between noon and one o'clock, she asked if it could have been stuffed into a hole one yard square and a yard deep eight to nine hours later.

"It would be extraordinarily difficult, virtually impossible," Dr. Bigelow replied. "After that period of time the body would be in a state of full rigor mortis. It would be then, since the body is completely rigid, not possible to twist the torso over on the extremities, not possible to move the arms so that it could be folded up to place it in that hole."

"You saw the position that the corpse in the basement was in, is that correct?"

"That is correct."

"And would that position have been possible after a minimum of eight hours had elapsed from the time that a bullet was fired into the back of someone's head, assuming they had died?"

"In my opinion, this would be impossible to perform after eight hours."

By that reckoning, Richmond hoped the jury would conclude Blaikie put DeWilde in the hole *before* meeting Kathy at the Framingham restaurant and not *after* she had retired that night. Here was scientific evidence, she believed, that Blaikie's plan to murder David included a place to conceal his body. In her view there was nothing *impromptu* about his actions and everything premeditated about them. The question was whether the jury agreed with her.

Again she asked Dr. Bigelow to assume that the hypothetical man, who happened to be DeWilde's size, had been shot in the back of the head between noon and one o'clock. A freezer bag had been placed over his head and tied around the neck sometime before one-thirty. In the hypothesis, based on Blaikie's version of events, the body was dragged downstairs to the basement. That evening someone lifted the body and the blood trapped in the bag spilled out in an amount described by the state police chemist as sufficient to stain the back and sides of the dead man's shirt and the back of his pants.

"Do you have an opinion whether or not the person was dead or alive when that bag was put over his head?"

The grisly idea triggered a stirring among spectators.

Daniel Harrington objected to the line of questioning on the grounds Blaikie had not said exactly when he had tied the bag around DeWilde's neck. But in fact Blaikie had testified he did so before dragging the body downstairs and calling Kathy at the restaurant a second time, at 1:14 P.M.

Judge McGuire allowed the question.

"It is my opinion," Dr. Bigelow said, "the person who had the bag placed over his head after being shot was alive at the time the bag was placed over the head."

"On what do you base that opinion, Doctor?"

"On the fact that when a person dies," Dr. Bigelow said, "the heart stops beating." Without blood pressure, he added, little blood seeps through wounds and only as the result of gravity.

"But with the amount of blood that you mentioned," he said, "it would be my opinion that the heart kept beating and that blood would gush forth from that hole in the head at the site of the gunshot wound."

Meaning, Richmond thought to herself, Blaikie used the freezer bag to prevent more blood from spilling on the floor and DeWilde might have been buried alive. Next on her agenda was when Blaikie could reasonably have sealed the tomb. Blaikie had said approximately five to seven days after death.

"Directing your attention, please, Doctor, to what happens to a body, a human body which is presumably dead, with regard to the putrefaction process, will you explain to the jury in general terms the decomposition process of the human body?"

"Following death," Dr. Bigelow said, "all vital activities cease, and the process of decomposition begins immediately. The bacteria within the body, any insects around tend to swarm over a corpse.

"The process of bacterial decomposition then begins to occur and the tissues become—the skin becomes tender, becomes discolored. In a period of time one of the outstanding features which anybody can recognize if they have been in the presence of a body that has been dead for two days or more is that a distinctly unpleasant odor occurs. And this odor becomes progressively worse so that within a period of a week it is virtually impossible for a person to be in the same room with such a corpse."

Richmond asked him to assume the hypothetical body had been left in the basement hole with nothing over it but plastic bags and loose boards for seven days. "Do you have an opinion, Doctor, whether or not there would be any odor?"

"Yes, I do," he said. "It is my opinion that the odor by that time would be overwhelming."

"By 'overwhelming' what do you mean?"

"Well, so disagreeable that a person could—an untrained individual unused to the odor of decomposition would find it almost impossible to stay within the house at all. It would permeate the whole house."

Take your pick, Blaikie, Richmond thought. *You either sealed the pit before Kathy could smell death or she smelled it. You can't have it both ways.*

"I have no further questions," she said.

Under cross-examination by Daniel Harrington, Dr. Bigelow said he had no doubts about the means by which David DeWilde met his death.

Referring to the bullet trajectory through the skull from the back to front as described by Dr. Bigelow, Harrington asked, "Is it fair to say there must have been massive hemorrhaging in the brain?"

"In all likelihood."

"Doctor, isn't it fair to say that the massive hemorrhaging of the brain caused bleeding in the head?"

"Yes, bleeding in the head."

"The blood already in the head is there, is it not?"

"Yes, but that blood circulates very rapidly while the heart is beating."

"Didn't you testify that in a person incurring such an injury, that death would be consistent in less than five minutes?"

"It could occur in less than five minutes," Dr. Bigelow said. "A person could live for hours or days."

"Is that *with* medical attention?"

"Usually death is postponed with medical attention."

"Doctor," Harrington said, "how long beyond the less than five minutes you quoted would DeWilde be expected to live if he had no medical attention?"

"Two to four hours."

Several jurors appeared as stunned as Harrington by the implication.

Exuding skepticism, Harrington asked, "With *no* medical attention?"

"Right."

"A bullet passing directly through this man's brain?"

"I'd say that is unlikely, but it could occur in that fashion."

"Doctor, I suggest to you it is impossible."

"You can *suggest* it," Dr. Bigelow fired back.

Recounting the brain damage, Harrington asked, "Now, does the brain control the heart?"

"To some extent."

"And the heart can function without the brain? Without mechanical aids?"

"Well, for a short period of time."

"You mean to say," Harrington said, "that you can take a brain out of a man's body and the heart could continue beating?"

"Provided there wasn't too great a loss of blood."

"How long?" Harrington insisted.

"Well, the situations as you describe do occur."

"How often do they occur, Doctor?"

"Rarely."

Turning to the blood that issued from the bag around

DeWilde's head and onto his clothing, Harrington drew testimony that if the head were lying back, blood could only have come from the bullet wound. He sought to weaken the inference that DeWilde might have been unconscious but alive for minutes or even hours after the shooting.

"This blood flow would be independent of any heart action?" Harrington asked.

"No, it could not," Dr. Bigelow maintained.

"Blood is a liquid, isn't it?"

"Yes. Blood tends to settle but not rapidly."

"I didn't say 'rapidly,' " Dan Harrington fired back. "I'm saying over a period of hours. It does obey the laws of gravity, does it not?"

"Yes."

"If a body is lying on its back and the blood is lying loose, it does follow the law of gravity?"

"It drips out slowly," Dr. Bigelow said, adhering to his earlier testimony. "A small amount of blood would drip out slowly through that bullet hole if, as you suggest, the body was lying on its back."

"And even dripping slowly over a period of eight hours?"

"Yes, a *small* amount of blood would definitely drip out over a period of hours."

Harrington attacked the medical examiner's testimony that the odor of a decaying body in an unsealed dry well would have been conspicuous in the house after several days, contrary to Blaikie's testimony. However, lacking evidence of the temperature in the basement, Harrington could elicit no opinion from Dr. Bigelow that winter temperatures might have impeded decomposition. In any event, the witness maintained the dampness of the brick-lined dry well with its earthen floor would have accelerated decomposition.

Under questioning, Dr. Bigelow acknowledged that if the body had been folded before the presence of rigor mortis, it would have remained in a fetal position.

Testimony in the trial of James Blaikie was drawing to a close with the November day. The remaining issue was the most critical, whether Blaikie had shot David DeWilde in a desperate act of self-defense or coldly fired a bullet into the back of his head.

Harrington picked up on the hypothetical question Richmond had asked Dr. Bigelow concerning the trajectory of the bullet. "Let's say the gun was on the ground, Doctor, and DeWilde leaned over Blaikie, and as he leaned at a perpendicular angle with his back to Blaikie reaching for the gun, Blaikie grabs the gun and shoots. Under those conditions is the path of the bullet inconsistent?"

"The path of the bullet goes from behind the occipital bone right here," Dr. Bigelow said, pointing almost in the middle of the back of his head, "and traveled virtually perpendicular to the long axis of the body." He pointed his right index finger straight up and jabbed his left index finger against it at a ninety-degree angle. "And it is very difficult for me to see any situation where a person lying on the ground on his back could fire at an angle which would be perpendicular to the long axis of another person's body and travel in a straight line from this point in the back of the head.

"A person on the ground would fire up at an angle, and I simply can't understand how a head can be twisted around so that this bullet coming up at that angle could occur."

Harrington contended, "DeWilde had been *over* the body. He was not in flight. He actually had hit the floor reaching for the gun—"

"Objection," Richmond declared.

Judge McGuire told Harrington he could pose a hypothetical question.

"Doctor," Harrington said patiently, "a male, Blaikie, is now on the ground. He had the gun in his hand and is holding the gun in front of him. The other person, namely DeWilde, has gone over him, and he at this time is in the process of actually going over him to get the gun, lands on the ground directly in front of Blaikie. And Blaikie at this moment takes the gun and fires it. The person who he's fired at has his back toward Blaikie. Would the path of the bullet as you found it in DeWilde's head during your examination be inconsistent with those facts?''

''Objection,'' Richmond said, rising. ''Facts not in evidence.''

Judge McGuire stated, ''There is no evidence that I recall that DeWilde was on the floor. If you care to amend it in that respect, I will allow it.''

Dan Harrington nodded and asked Dr. Bigelow, ''DeWilde leans over at a perpendicular angle, across Blaikie at a perpendicular angle and Blaikie shoots. The person now is at the same level as Blaikie's hand.''

Richmond vigorously objected. Blaikie in his vague testimony had not told where the gun hand was in relation to DeWilde's head.

Her objection was sustained.

Dr. Bigelow asserted that his opinion would be the same whether DeWilde was standing or leaning over Blaikie and reaching for a gun on the floor. It was inconceivable, the ME said, that the fatal shot could have been fired by Blaikie in either event.

Richmond was back on her feet for further redirect examination.

''Do you have an opinion, Doctor, whether or not the condition of the skin as you observed it when the concrete was removed on the evening of November 26, 1975, would have been consistent with a body in the hole for five to seven days with just a plastic covering and four boards on it?''

''I have such an opinion.''

''What is your opinion?''

''It is my opinion that this is not the state of preservation that I would have seen if the body had been uncovered by some preservative agents for five to seven days.''

''Thank you,'' Richmond said. ''No further questions.''

Judge McGuire excused Dr. Bigelow, and Ted Harrington called James Blaikie back to the stand.

''Mr. Blaikie,'' the former federal prosecutor said,

"when you shot Mr. DeWilde was he standing over you?"

"No," Blaikie said. "I just—"

Judge McGuire stopped him. "You have answered it," he said.

"Was he flying over you to get the gun?"

"It was on the ground."

Judge McGuire interjected, "Was *he, not* the gun?"

"*No*," Blaikie responded, appearing angry and completely flustered. "I said he was on the floor."

"In other words," Ted Harrington said, "you shot him after he had reached the floor."

"Yes."

"You were both going for the gun."

"Yes."

"And he wasn't standing up perpendicular when you shot him?"

"No, of course not," Blaikie said.

Ted Harrington turned to Alice Richmond and said, "Your witness."

She practically marched up to the witness stand, asking, "Are you sure you remember that? You didn't remember that this morning, did you?"

"I thought I made it clear," Blaikie said forebearingly, "he landed when he flew over me."

"You didn't tell us that this morning."

"No, not that—I thought I made it clear that he landed."

"You couldn't remember where the gun was, is that right?"

"It was on the floor."

"You couldn't remember how far it was away from you?"

"No."

"You couldn't remember anything about what you just said until just now, isn't that right, Mr. Blaikie?"

"No, that is not true."

"You didn't say that this morning, did you?"

Richmond stood squarely in front of him. "You didn't say that this morning, did you?"

"I thought it was inherent when I said he jumped over me, he landed."

"You didn't say it in direct yesterday, did you, Mr. Blaikie?"

"Yesterday?"

"Yesterday."

"I don't think I said it specifically," Blaikie said. "I just assumed that he landed."

His words echoed terrifyingly in Richmond's mind. *I just assumed that he landed* on the floor. It was as though Blaikie were describing a scene he had never witnessed. She looked into his youngster's blue eyes and thought she understood why David DeWilde had gone alone into an execution chamber. Why Edwin Bacon had turned his back in his office. You would think this bright, funny kid capable of anything but murder.

She removed her gaze from his, looked up at Judge McGuire, and said, "I have no further questions."

"The evidence is closed," Judge McGuire announced, and he excused the jury until the following morning. His gavel came down at five minutes to six on the tenth day of trial in two-and-a-half weeks.

Chapter 27

On Friday morning, November 19th, Dan Harrington stood near his client as he began his closing argument to the jury.

He emphasized Blaikie's admission that he had killed David DeWilde, not by design but in self-defense. Dismissing the alleged money motive as absurd, he said, "James Blaikie had total debts of one hundred fifteen thousand dollars, but for some reason he decided to kill this man because he owed him six thousand dollars. Will that make him sleep better?"

Mocking the charge of first-degree murder, Harrington spoke of Blaikie calling DeWilde at his garage that fateful morning, leaving the body in the basement, and parking DeWilde's car near his own.

"Now, *this* is the premeditated plan of a cold-blooded killer," he announced with a thin smile for the government table. Returning his gaze to the jury, he asked, "Does this speak to you of premeditation?"

Approaching the jurors, Harrington said the defense was not afraid of the alleged evidence brought by the commonwealth, but said, "What we are afraid of is an emotional reaction to the pictures of a man dead for ten months."

He dwelled on the lifestyle of the man who loaned Blaikie $6,000 at an alleged interest rate of $1,000 a month. "He had an expensive way of life," Harrington said. "Judy Fillippo and he were out four, five nights a week. Six even. It was a good life. It was a swinging life, the life of dinners, theaters, the dog track. *All this* on this man's pay.''

Unspokenly referring to Blaikie's testimony, he added, ''The prosecution for some reason brought out in testimony that once in a while David DeWilde even had a little cocaine, enjoyed cocaine.''

Harrington quoted witnesses as testifying, ''De-Wilde had a sharp temper. He'd get angry. He'd swear. He was strong.''

Then, describing the death scene through his client's testimony, he said, ''DeWilde, violent, goes to him and knocks the gun out of his hand, and he swore at him. He testified up there eight hours, giving different versions because he was truthful. There was a violent act, and he suddenly found himself on the floor. He didn't tell you he fell at twenty-five degrees, at sixty-nine degrees, but just that he fell and the gun fell—was knocked out of his hand. And all he remembers is a body leaping over him going for the gun, and he grabs the gun in the nick of time. And what if David DeWilde had gotten the gun? Would he be on the stand today instead of Jimmy Blaikie?''

Addressing the question of why Blaikie did not report the allegedly justified shooting, Harrington asserted, ''Because he couldn't face the fact that he had killed a man. He couldn't live with it. He lied, cast suspicion on others. He talked with Moran. Why did he do it? His whole life now was gone.''

His hand swept toward his impassive client. ''This is a man in panic. When he was gripped by fear, what did he tell us? 'Why did you do it?' He said, 'I wanted to protect Kathy. I knew I was going to get caught.' He knew he was going to get caught. *Everybody* knew it. 'We know he left the garage, went to your house, and we know he was never seen again.' He knew the body was going to be found downstairs. He knew it, and that's why he collapsed. But he said, 'I wanted to protect my wife, to try to get her away from that and bring her to Phoenix, to face the music alone.' If she heard about it—you know what happened to her—to this wonderful man that loved her, and she collapsed, mentally collapsed.''

Scanning the jurors, Harrington said: "The question is for you to decide, was he guilty of a crime? And if he was, what is it? Murder-one, premeditation, murder-two without premeditation, with malice aforethought, or was it Jimmy Blaikie had provocation, a young man in fear? And it is up to you to make that decision. Under all the circumstances was he justified in doing the act which he committed? And if he was, will you find him not guilty of murder, and that it was justified by reason of self-defense?''

Returning to the defense table, Dan Harrington nodded to Alice Richmond. If a lion was leaving the arena to a bird, she was a hawk by the glint in her eyes.

"You may proceed," Judge McGuire said, and Alice Richmond stood up.

Speaking in a firm, even tone, she surveyed the jury. "I ask you to remember as you review the evidence to keep in mind two things. Mr. DeWilde is not on trial here, nor is Detective Moran, nor any other people. The only one on trial is James F. Blaikie, and you must look at the evidence and determine whether or not Mr. Blaikie had a plan.''

She acknowledged that the burden of proof was upon the prosecution and James Blaikie had been under no obligation to testify. "Now, in this particular case Mr. Blaikie waived that privilege and took the stand. He is not to be given a gold medal for testifying. Merely, that was his choice. That was his defense.''

Passing slowly before the jurors, she spoke of Blaikie's earlier refusal to tell DeWilde's family, police, and a news reporter that he had killed David.

With a glance at the defense table, she intoned, "This is not the mind of somebody who is panicky. This is the mind of somebody who thinks he committed the perfect crime and he is confounded with new problems. The police are not so willing to believe him just because he was the treasurer of the McGovern campaign. The press are not so ready to believe him just because he lives in a big house in the Fisher Hill area of Brookline.''

Speaking of DeWilde's grave, she picked up a jagged three-inch-thick concrete fragment from the evidence table and weighed it as she passed before the jury. ''He filled that right up to the top, and he poured the concrete on top of it,'' she said. ''As Mr. De-Wilde's body began to decompose inside and shrink up, the sand began to settle and get moist and damp. As Dr. Bigelow and witnesses have told you, that hole was there and it began settling, and the coal on top began to settle. It was that settling factor which Mr. Blaikie never expected would happen. He didn't anticipate that.''

She spoke of the autopsy and said, ''There is no question the cause of death listed on this medical certificate is a gunshot wound to the head. If Mr. De-Wilde died of anything else it would be impossible to tell anyway because Doctor Bigelow told you in his initial testimony that his insides were undifferentiated mush. 'Goo,' I think, is the word he used. And that wasn't introduced to shock you. It is horrible, I agree, but each and every one of you looked at those pictures because you are deciding a very important matter. And you saw the defendant yesterday when I showed him those pictures push it away. He couldn't look. That was the way he buried the body. *You* didn't bury it. *I* didn't bury it. That's the way *he* buried it,'' she proclaimed, jabbing a finger in Blaikie's direction on her slow course to the evidence table.

She picked up the .38 lead slug taken from De-Wilde's cranium and displayed it in the palm of her hand near the jurors. Slightly squashed, it was less than half an inch in length and diameter. ''It's interesting about bullets,'' she said. ''When they are not in a body they don't look like much. This bullet was fired into the back of Mr. DeWilde's head. You saw Dr. Bigelow on the stand yesterday. You saw the contortions that he got into to show you how it would be impossible for the path of the bullet as he observed it, which was straight through, ladies and gentlemen, straight through, to *curve,* given the facts Mr. Blaikie testified to.''

Whether DeWilde was standing or lying down at the time he was shot, Richmond said, Dr. Bigelow's opinion was the same.

''There are people on this jury, I believe,'' she said, ''who would feel that somebody like Mr. DeWilde, a man who worked with his hands and by all accounts was a strong fellow, would do some damage to somebody like this if in fact there was a struggle. David DeWilde is not going to die with a bullet in the back of his head without doing some damage if he *knew* he was fighting for his life. And he *didn't* know that because he never saw where it came from.''

In a deepening voice, she stated, ''It came from behind him and he never saw it.''

Pointing her finger like a weapon at the defendant, she went on, ''Mr. Blaikie lifts the gun to his head. And this man didn't even have the decency to leave the plastic bag off the head until he died. He put it on the head so that the job was finished and put that body in that hole before rigor mortis set in and covered it up. And he never wanted anybody to find him.''

Nearing the jurors she exhorted, ''Keep in mind what this man did. I ask you to bring in a verdict of guilty.''

Sitting beside Patricia Wynn, Frank Bacon thought Alice Richmond had delivered her knockout punch. He was filled with admiration for the chic and scrappy prosecutor returning to her chair. She had come off the deck after the first trial and fought back like hell. Whatever was to happen in the case of his brother's death, Frank knew James Blaikie had met his Waterloo in this venerable old building on the Massachusetts coast.

Now, he thought, *we'll see what a jury of his peers has to say about it.*

He exchanged hopeful glances with Patricia Wynn, and after court recessed at noon, David DeWilde's mother approached Alice Richmond with a look of profound gratitude.

In his instructions to the jury that afternoon, Judge McGuire focused on the legal concept of proof beyond a reasonable doubt.

"It has been described as being proof to a moral certainty but not proof to a mathematical certainty," he said. "Proof beyond a reasonable doubt does not mean proof beyond all doubt nor proof beyond a whimsical or fanciful doubt nor proof beyond the possibility of innocence. A reasonable doubt does not mean such doubt as may exist in the mind of a man who is earnestly seeking for doubt or for an excuse to acquit a defendant. But it does mean such doubt as remains in the mind of a reasonable man who is earnestly seeking the truth."

Turning to the varieties of homicide, Judge McGuire said, "Murder committed with deliberately premeditated malice aforethought is murder in the first degree. Murder which does not appear to be in the first degree is murder in the second degree. The degree of murder shall be found by the jury."

Deliberately premeditated, he said, referred to prior formation of purpose to kill rather than to any definite length of time. Coming down from English common law, *malice* did not necessarily imply ill will toward the person killed, he stated.

"Any intentional killing of a human being without legal justification or excuse with no extenuating circumstances sufficient to reduce the crime to manslaughter is malicious within the meaning of that expression. And there cannot be a conviction of murder either in the first or second degree unless the jury finds malice. That is an essential element, and that is what distinguishes murder from manslaughter, where malice is not an element."

Of the term *aforethought,* Judge McGuire said, "If the killing was intentional or the act followed the thought immediately without time for deliberation or reflection and there was no justification, excuse, or extenuation, the killing was with malice aforethought."

Manslaughter, he said, is "the least blameworthy of unlawful homicide," adding that it required an absence of malice.

As to justifiable homicide in self-defense, Judge McGuire stated, "The right to use deadly force by way of self-defense is not available to one threatened until he has availed himself of all reasonable and proper means in the circumstances to avoid combat."

The rule applied to a person assaulted in his own domicile, he said, and furthermore, "The rule does not impose an absolute duty to retreat regardless of consideration to personal safety. The proper application of this doctrine does not require an innocent victim to increase his own peril out of regard for the safety of his assailant."

On the question of reasonable force used in purported self-defense, Judge McGuire said, "The jury should consider evidence of the relative physical capability of the combatant, the characteristics of the weapon used, the availability of maneuver room in or means to escape from the area in which the incident occurred."

When he had finished, Alice Richmond asked to be heard and was joined at the bench by the Harringtons. She asked Judge McGuire to read to the jury from a case that explicitly stated that deliberate premeditation could be found occurring within minutes or even seconds of a homicide. The judge responded, "I said that the word 'deliberately' in the expression 'deliberately premeditated malice aforethought' has reference to prior formation of purpose to kill rather than any definite length of time."

He denied her request and spoke to the jury. Twelve of them would seek a verdict, which must be unanimous, he said. The clerk was to draw the names of eleven jurors by lot, and they would join the foreman in deliberation. The four alternates were to remain under the separate watch of a court officer.

"I conclude by telling you, Mr. Foreman and ladies and gentlemen, that the obligation you have as jurors is an onerous one, a difficult one," Judge McGuire said. "If this is to be a government of laws and not a government of men, we depend essentially upon jurors such as you. May your verdict speak the truth."

The jurors filed out of the courtroom at three-thirty in the afternoon, and a haggard James Blaikie was escorted out moments later.

In the first-floor office provided her for the trial, Alice Richmond's eyes were filled with anger. Frank Bacon got the impression from her look that yet another disaster could be brewing in this torturous saga.

"Frank, I'm really afraid the jury will get hung up on premeditation," she said. "If they're not convinced Blaikie planned to kill David days or hours in advance, they might not see it as premeditated. They could come back with a conviction for murder-two or manslaughter. Or acquittal."

"Look, Alice," Bacon said firmly, looking down into her eyes. "You've done all you can, more than I ever expected anyone would do. Pat Wynn feels the same. You did great."

The man and woman who might never have met but for two deaths looked at each other.

"Thank you," she said, cracking a nervous smile. "I just hope my 'great' was great enough."

With a hint of a grin, Frank said, "From where I sat it was."

Less than an hour after the start of the jury's deliberations, a court officer summoned the defense and prosecution back into the courtroom.

Visibly tense, Alice glanced at Frank and preceded him out of the office.

Juries were not known to convict in so short a time.

Soon after counselors had returned to their tables and spectators reassembled in the courtroom, Judge McGuire emerged from his chambers.

"Let the record show it is twenty-five minutes past four o'clock," he said, "and the Court is in receipt of a question from the jury, sealed, not opened." He asked that the defendant return, and moments later James Blaikie was ushered to the defense table.

In the jury's absence, Judge McGuire unsealed the envelope and read, " 'Your honor, the jury would appreciate a written definition of the three guilty charges—murder in the first degree, murder in the second degree, and manslaughter.' "

He invited comments at the bench and both Richmond and the Haringtons stood tensely before him.

Richmond again asked the judge to read the jury language indicating premeditation could occur in seconds.

Ted Harrington strenuously objected on the grounds that the state had produced evidence of Blaikie deciding to kill DeWilde weeks in advance of the homicide. "To put in at this stage the definition of deliberate premeditation before the jury, saying it could be formed in a few seconds, in light of the evidence would be highly prejudicial."

The judge called for the jury and when they had filed in he informed them he could not fulfill their request. "I'm going to send you back to the jury room," he said, "and if you have occasion to send me any question other than this, you may do so. You are excused."

It seemed to Frank Bacon that Alice Richmond's fears about the issue of premeditation were well-founded.

Half an hour later the jurors had another request.

At 5:10 P.M., with Blaikie but not the jury in attendance, the judge announced he had received a second note from the jury foreman.

This time the jurors did not ask for written definitions but for a reiteration of the judge's statements concerning the differences between the three possible guilty verdicts—murder in the first degree, second-degree murder, and voluntary manslaughter. Judge McGuire declared the request legitimate and summoned the twelve jurors and four alternates.

In their presence he asked the court reporter to read pertinent sections of the charge he had delivered that morning. Among them, she recited, "The word 'deliberately' in the expression 'deliberately premeditated malice aforethought' has reference to prior formation of purpose to kill rather than to any definite length of time.''

Richmond gained slight relief from the restatement of the crucial time factor.

At 5:28 P.M. Judge McGuire instructed the jury to resume its deliberation.

Four hours passed. Richmond, Frank Bacon and Pat Wynn were having soft drinks in Alice's temporary office when they got word the jury was returning.

Minutes later, at 9:40 P.M., all parties were in the courtroom when Judge McGuire arrived.

A verdict had not been reached.

Speaking to the entire jury, the judge said, ''I have in mind it now being close to quarter of ten that you have had a long day. You have been here all day and night, and so I'm going to ask you to retire for the night and to resume your deliberations tomorrow morning.''

As he was instructing them not to discuss the case, Alice Richmond thought six hours had surely been enough time to reach a guilty verdict. The Harringtons figured the jurors could have brought in an acquittal by then.

The sixteen men and women filed out of their pews utterly without expression.

Chapter 28

The next morning, a nearly freezing Saturday the 20th, clouds concealed most of the violet November sky.

Frank Bacon chose to wait out the jury at home instead of in Fall River. If a verdict was to be reached on the second day of deliberation, Alice Richmond would let him know the outcome by telephone. At his Dover estate, the sweet pungency of fallen leaves took him back once more to football afternoons at Groton two decades before. Ed and their parents had come to cheer him on as varsity captain. The further along Frank went in life, especially over the past two years, the more he treasured the bracing clarity of those earlier Saturdays. Now and then a referee missed a call, but by and large you were rewarded for accomplishment and penalized for infractions. Right then and there.

He did not see how Alice Richmond could lose, but he had given up hoping for justice. Anything less than a conviction for first-degree murder would be a defeat, as far as he was concerned. Richmond could have had murder-two in the notorious plea-bargain four months before, without the monumental exertions of two trials. If Blaikie were to be acquitted on grounds of self-defense, Frank knew he would never feel anything more than bitterness and contempt for the so-called criminal justice system.

Brighton Detective Tom Moran was at his second home on a New Hampshire lake. He had an adequate supply of Budweiser to celebrate or forget the outcome of his most difficult and intriguing case in a quarter-century of police work. But Tom Moran gave little thought to losing. To his way of thinking, the greater part of luck was confidence.

Sergeant Detective John Maillet was at home with his three daughters in the Roslindale section of Boston. He also was not one to hang around for verdicts. He certainly hoped the jury put Blaikie away, but it was not Maillet's case and to him winning it would be a vicarious pleasure.

The Bacon case was his, and Maillet doubted it would ever be prosecuted. If Blaikie went to the slammer on DeWilde, that would pretty much be that. District attorneys weren't keen on putting someone away a second time when there were so many other worthy candidates for the commonwealth's care and attention. He figured if Blaikie walks on DeWilde, the Harringtons win combat ribbons. Then, what DA is going after them and their client with the body of a man officially ruled a suicide?

Smoki Bacon heard newscasts over the radio at her Back Bay townhouse. The lead story of the hour was the jury's first, inconclusive day of deliberation. She tensely read the *Globe* and *Herald* accounts over coffee in the dining room. Never before had she called herself a pessimist, but she realized she expected James Blaikie to get off scot-free before the day was done. Not the least casualty of the past two and a half years had been her faith.

Nearly forty minutes after resuming deliberation, twelve jurors filed into the courtroom at 10:40 A.M.

Seated with Brookline Detective William McDermott at the government table, Alice Richmond could see the foreman from nearby coastal Dartmouth was carrying the verdict card.

This was it.

In a pew behind the oak rail separating spectators from the court, Pat Wynn and Ruth DeWilde sat beside each other. Fond of each other despite divorce, David's mother and former wife had helped get each other this far in one piece. Neither knew how she would react to anything other than a guilty verdict.

Thirty-one-year-old James Blaikie rose with the others when Judge McGuire entered. The defendant appeared calm with his hands at his side.

From the bench the judge nodded to the clerk, who stated, "Jurors, please rise." When all were standing, the clerk asked, "Mr. Foreman, have you agreed upon a verdict?"

"Yes," came the reply.

"Mr. Foreman," the clerk said, "on indictment, Norfolk County, 64865, Commonwealth versus James F. Blaikie, Jr., how do you find the defendant, guilty or not guilty?"

"Guilty," the foreman answered.

Cries were followed by a silence, and the clerk asked the ultimate question.

"Guilty of what?"

"Murder in the first degree."

Turning around, Alice Richmond caught sight of James Blaikie betraying emotion for the first time since she had met him. Head bowed, he was weeping.

Then she found the relieved faces of Patricia Wynn and Ruth DeWilde and breathed easily for the first time in two years.

"Guilty," Alice Richmond said from the upstairs office as soon as Frank Bacon's voice came on the phone. "Murder in the first degree."

Exchanging grim smiles with Billy McDermott, who was placing calls to fellow detectives John Maillet and Tom Moran, she waited for Frank's response.

It was a Yankee cheer. *"Su-pa!"* After a pause, attention to detail followed. "He's been sentenced?"

"Yes, life in prison, without eligibility for parole. He's on his way to Walpole now," she said, referring to the state's maximum-security penitentiary.

Frank knew that meant Blaikie could, after fifteen years, try for commutation of sentence to second-degree murder and, given so-called good behavior, could seek parole. But, this day anyway, that bridge seemed far off.

"You've done it, Alice," he said, inwardly exulting at the news. When she described James Blaikie's tearful reaction to the verdict, he thought, *This one's for David and for Eddie.*

Following their conversation, Frank pondered his own simple concept of justice. It came from Gilbert and Sullivan, who a century before had written, "Let the punishment fit the crime."

However, Frank was fairly satisfied. He knew he would be, as long as James Blaikie never reentered the society that refused to shoot him in the back of the head.

Chapter 29

By the summer of 1977, the fatal shooting of Alma Blaikie and the poisoning death of Edwin Bacon were dead issues.

Waltham authorities had reinvestigated the 1973 death of James Blaikie's mother and reported finding no evidence to change the original ruling of suicide.

Suffolk County officials had no intention of prosecuting Walpole inmate James Blaikie on the forgery and embezzlement indictments in the Bacon case. The matter of Edwin Bacon's death was no more likely to go before a grand jury.

His survivors understood the reality but did not accept it. They were still left with the conviction that a family member had been murdered and his death had been wrongly termed a suicide.

In an effort to revive the case, Smoki turned for help to elected officials who had welcomed her vigorous support and that of Ed Bacon over the years.

Of the half-dozen political figures, only one could or would volunteer assistance. State Representative Barney Frank, a longstanding Bacon family friend and future congressman, urged the Suffolk County medical examiner's office to reevaluate Bacon's death.

On the legal front, Frank Bacon put Smoki in touch with a professionally and literally towering Boston attorney with a reputation for virtuoso lawyering.

The six-foot five-inch Edward Masterman recommended a strategy as ingenious as the case was bizarre. If the state was not going to prosecute Blaikie in criminal court, Masterman could do so, in effect, in civil court.

The attorney advised Smoki to bring a lawsuit against the Federal Kemper Life Assurance Company, charging negligence that caused the death of Edwin Bacon. In the process of deciding the case, a jury would first have to conclude whether or not James Blaikie had murdered Edwin Bacon. There at last would be an official verdict. It would carry no sentence for Blaikie, but Smoki and her daughters might win damages from Kemper.

In July, their attorney initiated one of the most remarkable lawsuits in American legal history.

In a complaint filed by Masterman in Suffolk Superior Court, Smoki Bacon went public with her family's private beliefs of three years. The news media reported her allegations that the beneficiary-change application was "forged," and Kemper approved it "without the knowledge and consent of Bacon."

In the lawsuit, her first formal charge against James Blaikie followed:

> On or about July 29, 1974, after being notified of the change of beneficiary to himself, James F. Blaikie, Jr. killed Edwin C. Bacon to obtain the proceeds of life insurance policy number 613600.

Further, Smoki claimed that Kemper was "so negligent and careless in approving the forged and fraudulent application" that the company "caused the reasonably foreseeable death of Edwin C. Bacon."

Her suit demanded a damage award of four million dollars for Bacon's alleged conscious pain and suffering and wrongful death and for her loss of consortium.

It would be a landmark case nationally if Masterman were to win it. Researchers were unable to find another exactly like it. One came close. In an Alabama case two decades before, a jury had found an insurer responsible for the murder of a young woman. Her aunt had secretly taken out a life policy on her niece and was later found guilty of murdering her. A civil court jury awarded damages to the victim's father, and in 1957 the Alabama high court upheld the action. However, the lawsuit differed from *Bacon* versus *Kemper* in a critical aspect. Unlike the Alabama woman, Blaikie had not been convicted of murder. Indeed, he had never been indicted in connection with Bacon's death.

Masterman would have to pull off a hat trick. In hockey parlance it meant a player scoring three goals in a game. In *Bacon* vs *Kemper* it would mean proving Blaikie murdered Bacon, Kemper caused the death, and Smoki with her daughters deserved financial compensation.

Later in 1977, the Bacons got partial satisfaction from the Suffolk County medical examiner's office. At Barney Frank's urging, the ME requested a report from John Maillet. The sergeant detective stated it was his investigative judgment that Edwin Bacon had been murdered and James Blaikie was a suspect in the case. In November, the ME revised Bacon's 1974 death certificate, changing the category of poisoning from "suicide" to "unknown."

It was clear to the Bacons that their only remaining hope of resolving the mystery of Edwin Bacon was the lawsuit.

Although far from certain of the outcome, Smoki took grim satisfaction in naming Kemper as a defendant in court. After all, the company had gotten a court order in 1975 to prevent her from demanding the insurance benefits. She had been forced to battle Blaikie for the $50,000 in court, at her own expense.

Kemper's first line of defense was that very two-year-old injunction. Attorneys for the company argued in their pretrial motion that it prevented Smoki from taking any legal action in connection with the insurance policy. Furthermore, Kemper counsel insisted, the proceeds of the policy had ultimately gone to her and the company had thereby met all of its contractual obligations.

Masterman countered that the injunction did not insulate Kemper from a negligence suit and the court ruled in his favor, but not until June 1979. By then Frank Bacon and his wife had separated. In October, Smoki wed a Harvard classmate of Ed's by the name of Richard Concannon. She only half-jokingly told friends she was grateful his name was not Cannon. With her second husband, she continued residing at her Back Bay townhouse and put her social prowess to practical use. The couple formed a public relations firm, specializing in cultural, civic, and other nonprofit activities.

Divorced by Kathy, James Blaikie was regarded as a cooperative inmate by authorities at Walpole state prison, where he had been incarcerated for three years. At the maximum-security facility, he was a participant in a program intended to dissuade visiting youths from leading lives of crime. Interviewed by a local television station, he displayed one obvious result of prison life—weight loss. He had slimmed down considerably from his standard two hundred pounds. A former acquaintance saw the broadcast and she thought the trim James Blaikie handsome. In January 1980, his good behavior earned him a transfer to a medium-security state penitentiary.

With three years of Barnard College behind her, Brooks Bacon was working for a New York publisher that year, and Hilary was in her third year at Harvard University when Jimmy Carter lost his bid for reelection to Ronald Reagan. A trial date was still nowhere in sight.

Kemper and Bacon attorneys continued to gather evidence and take depositions for another year and a half. A June 1982 trial was set, but Kemper requested a postponement until the fall. One of the reasons cited by the company's Boston attorney was a masterpiece of understatement. "It is expected that the case will involve novel questions of law and fact.'' The judge agreed and granted the continuance.

In September, both sides were bogged down in discovery proceedings and agreed to a postponement until January 1983. That date was also pushed back at the request of both parties.

Hoping to get Blaikie on the witness stand, Masterman arranged to take a deposition from the inmate in prison.

Blaikie's role in the case was as eccentric as his association with Edwin Bacon had been.

Although accused of murder in the lawsuit, Blaikie was not a codefendant with Kemper. He was rather the human equivalent of an object that had allegedly killed someone because of another party's alleged negligence. By analogy, if a lawsuit claims a person was killed by a falling hammer left carelessly on the edge of a scaffold by a carpenter, it is the carpenter who is charged with causing the death. In that regard, Kemper was the carpenter and Blaikie was the hammer.

In his February 1983 deposition at the Norfolk state penitentiary, the veteran of six years in prison responded defiantly to questioning by Bacon and Kemper attorneys. Blaikie said he would not answer Masterman's questions concerning Edwin Bacon.

''Your counsel advised you,'' Masterman said, ''and you intend to take the Fifth Amendment to any questions dealing with the death of Edwin Bacon?''

''That would probably be one area I would stay away from.''

''Let me put a very direct question to you then, *sir,*'' Masterman said harshly. ''Whether or not you in fact administered the cyanide which killed Edwin Bacon, whether or not you did that? Did you do that?''

''I did not do that,'' Blaikie said without hesitation or emotion.

''So you don't take the Fifth on that,'' Masterman said.

"On that, no," Blaikie said. "I am referring to the matters of the insurance."

Masterman asked where he had been around noon on July 29, 1974, the day of Bacon's death.

"Again," Blaikie said, "I am not going to answer any questions in this area."

Masterman named every hour between six in the evening until midnight and each time Blaikie invoked the Fifth Amendment.

Staring at Blaikie, Masterman asked if on that day he had tied Bacon's dog up in the office.

"Again, I am going to decline to answer," Blaikie said impassively.

"It is a fact, *sir,*" Masterman said gruffly, "that you did put cyanide into the coffee which Mr. Bacon drank sometime during the day of July 29, 1974."

"That I denied before and I will deny again," Blaikie said firmly. "That is the only area I will comment on."

He insisted that his first knowledge of Bacon's death came on the morning of July 30, when he arrived at Commercial Wharf and saw official vehicles there.

The deposition ended as inconclusively as it had begun.

Late in 1984, as Ronald Reagan was well on his way to a second term in the White House, *Bacon* versus *Kemper* was again scheduled for trial the following January. Eight years of legal wrangling had gone by since the filing of the lawsuit.

This time the court date was for real.

At Suffolk County Courthouse in Boston's Pemberton Square, the trial began in the civil division on January 21, 1985. It was the building where Blaikie would have been tried in the criminal division had he been indicted for murder in the Bacon case ten years before.

Alice Richmond was no longer there. After the DeWilde murder trial, she had left the district attorney's office to teach and was currently a partner in a major Boston law firm.

Unlike a criminal trial, in which guilt has to be proven to a certainty beyond a reasonable doubt, a civil suit calls for the less rigorous proof by a fair preponderance of evidence. The jury would have to decide whether Smoki Bacon had proved through evidence that her assertions were *more likely* to be true than not. If the jury were to find the evidence more or equally supportive of Kemper, Bacon would lose her case.

The trial judge, William Glover Young, was as scholarly as he appeared and sounded. A Harvard Law School graduate who taught courses at his alma mater, he was regarded at the age of forty-four as a younger Mr. Chips, an educator driven by a deep sense of humanity. His courtroom persona was no different. He had received national attention the year before with his adroit handling of an explosive sexual assault case in southeastern Massachusetts. It was the "Big Dan's" case, named after the New Bedford barroom where a local woman had allegedly been gang-raped on a pool table. Young silenced his court with resolute calm as angry outbursts from spectators threatened to disrupt proceedings, which ended with four guilty verdicts and two acquittals.

Judge Young's first step in the Kemper trial was to order a *voir dire* examination of James Blaikie. The judge wanted to determine in the jury's absence whether the testimony of the accused murderer would serve a fair purpose.

Wearing drab prison clothing but no handcuffs, James Blaikie was escorted into the courtroom by officers. From the witness box his blank gaze met Smoki's cold stare as though they were strangers.

Judge Young explained he had ordered Blaikie's manacles removed. "I think that no one should testify and give evidence in a court of law shackled," the judge said to Blaikie. "But have in mind that my primary concern is for the litigants and all the people in the courtroom. It is a privilege, given the fact that you are under sentence, that I let you testify without the cuffs.''

"Thank you, your honor," Blaikie replied, sounding genuinely grateful.

Under direct examination by Masterman, Blaikie gave his name and prison address. But when asked to state why he was in prison, he invoked the Fifth Amendment on advice of attorney and refused to supply the answer. He listened intently to Masterman's question if he had been associated with the Bacon agency, and he responded, "Again I refuse to answer for the same reasons."

In the next few minutes, Masterman asked more than a dozen questions, some in the form of accusations: Blaikie had forged the insurance form, removed the Kemper policy from Bacon's office, acquired cyanide, tied up the sled dog Kayak, placed the poison in Bacon's coffee sometime after six on the night of Bacon's death, returned to his office some days later and placed the can of cyanide in Bacon's file cabinet.

To each statement, Blaikie succinctly responded, "I refuse to answer."

With his wavy gray hair swept back, Masterman rose up to his full height and cocked a derisive smile. "Let me shift to other matters before the death of Bacon," he said, moving toward the witness. "Your mother was named Alma Blaikie and allegedly committed suicide on August 14, 1973. And I put it to you, *sir*, that she did not commit suicide but that you, in fact, shot her."

Expressionless, Blaikie said, "Again, I decline to answer."

He had barely answered when Masterman asserted, "And I put it to you, *sir*, that you shot her at a time when you were in need of money, isn't that true, *sir*?"

"Again, I decline to answer."

"And I put it to you that you killed César David DeWilde when you were in need of money, didn't you?" Masterman said with increasing volume.

"Again, I decline to answer."

"And I put it to you, *sir,* that you placed a note under your mother's body essentially saying, 'I can't take it any more,' didn't you?"

"Again, I decline to answer."

"And the note that was found under Mr. Bacon's body, 'I can't take it any more,' was put there by you, wasn't it?"

"Again, I decline to answer."

"And that your father's death was not accidental and that, in fact, you killed your father as well, didn't you?"

"Again, I decline to answer."

The following morning Judge Young ruled in the absence of the jury that Masterman could not call James Blaikie as a witness. Blaikie's unwavering invocation of the Fifth Amendment would tend to prejudice the jury, the judge concluded.

The decision was a serious blow to Bacon's case. The jury would hear of James Blaikie but never see the man accused of murder.

With the agreement of counselors, Judge Young shifted the trial to Harvard Law School in Cambridge, where his students would have the opportunity to observe it. The courtroom was located in Austin Hall, a weathered Romanesque building a short stroll from Harvard Yard, where Ed Bacon had graduated three decades before.

Heading Bacon's legal team, Masterman opened his case with Edwin Bacon's prominent history and a chronicle of the life insurance policy, from its purchase in 1971 to 1974 and Kemper's issuing a check for the benefits to one James Blaikie. Terming Blaikie's claim to the insurance proceeds a fraud, Masterman accused him of murdering Bacon for the $50,000.

Kemper's lead counsel, Boston attorney Edward S. Rooney, made it clear in his opening statement that the defense considered James Blaikie's guilt or innocence irrelevant to the case. Contrasting with Masterman's urbanity, the shorter Rooney was a six-footer with the girth and stance of a heavyweight boxer. "Kemper did not cause the death of Mr. Bacon," he stated emphatically. Without suggesting whether Bacon had died by his own hand or Blaikie's, he added, "It had no duty to protect Mr. Bacon from any homicide act of his longtime business partner, Mr. Blaikie."

Rooney allowed that the beneficiary change had not been signed by Bacon, but insisted that Kemper had taken every reasonable precaution to assure the form was genuine. The service department had compared Bacon's putative signature with the exemplar in its files and found them identical to the naked eye.

"You will see the signature," Rooney told the jury. "You will hear the experts say it is not the legitimate handwriting of Mr. Bacon. But they came to this conclusion only after hours of study of that signature against legitimate standards. Kemper says it was not negligent, it did not cause the death, it was not responsible for the death of Mr. Bacon. It did not have anything to do with any sodium cyanide poisoning."

After Smoki had testified to her discovery of her husband's body, Rooney demonstrated in his cross-examination that Edwin Bacon's dismal finances and his marital relationship would be the key elements in the Kemper defense. The implication, that Bacon had committed suicide in despondency, became clear. Rooney elicited an account of Smoki's legendary social activities and suggested her husband had not been involved in all of them.

"About sixty percent of them," she fired back.

She was required to read aloud before the court family fiscal records going back to the early 1970s. It was a virtual catalogue of chronically overdue bills and mortgage arrearage. What emerged after her two days on the witness stand was a bleak picture. Hounded for more than $100,000 by some thirty creditors, Ed Bacon had $38 in cash to his name on the day he died.

More than one of the twelve jurors and four alternates blinked at the spoken bottom line.

On the fifth day, twenty-four-year-old Hilary Bacon strode up to the witness box. The Harvard graduate was a first-year law student at Notre Dame University. Her long strawberry-blonde hair was as curly as ever, but the reed-thin girl had grown into a willowy and pretty young woman. Her sensitivity about her father's death, however, had not diminished. She testified to her educational background, but at Masterman's mere mention of her father's death she began weeping in silence.

In an even voice, Judge Young suggested she stand down if she liked and resume her testimony later.

She nodded yes and Masterman was not disappointed as his witness withdrew from the courtroom with her mother. Hilary had displayed a genuine emotional reaction, which, he sensed, had been received sympathetically by the jury. Masterman was concerned that in Blaikie's unexplained absence, it was the Bacon family and their difficulties on trial. In view of Smoki's flamboyant social life and Ed's decrepit finances, Masterman worried the key question on the minds of jurors could well be whether or not Smoki Bacon beat her husband.

In that respect, Frank Bacon's upcoming testimony was crucial.

He had not attended the first week of court. As in the DeWilde trial, the only witness he wanted to observe was James Blaikie. Absent Blaikie, Frank intended only to testify.

He ascended the witness stand with head held high. Just turned fifty, he was completely white haired as his father had been at that age. Also as trim as ever in his father's image, Frank retained his boyish good looks.

Following his divorce, he had remarried the previous year but remained close to the daughter and sons of his first marriage. He was putting Chip and Geoff through medical schools and Avril was on the management team of his computer systems firm.

After Frank had described the closeness of his relationship with Ed, Masterman asked him to characterize his brother's marriage.

"I think Ed and Smoki had a stable marriage," Frank replied matter of factly. "I saw it go through ups and downs, but I think it was a good marriage. Smoki was very active in Boston and I think Ed very much enjoyed that activity."

Asked by Masterman to describe the marriage in a word, Frank replied, "I think it was a *solid* marriage. That is an adjective that comes to mind quite readily. I felt Ed and Smoki had some different interests that sometimes drew them a bit apart. There were times, I think, when business was not as good as it might be with Ed, where there was pressure on the family, which I don't think is abnormal. But I think it was a solid marriage."

Considering it the plain truth, Smoki appreciated his saying it. Following his testimony, the last of the day, she told him so in the lobby, and he nodded cordially.

"How do you think it's going, Smoke?"

"Actually, not great," she replied nervously. "I think that without Blaikie here, our chances of convincing a jury he's a murderer are practically nil. Ed Masterman is hopeful, but he's concerned."

Frank Bacon wished her good luck and left the gloomy antique law school building for the slashing cold of a late January dusk. Walking to his car, he glanced at the frosted scenes of his golden days at Harvard, Ed's before him, and they evoked bittersweet memories. How well it had all started out for Eddie and how wretchedly it had all ended. As on the morning of his brother's death a decade earlier, Frank Bacon's eyes brimmed. They often had, every time he had thought of his brother since that disastrous morning. Frank knew he would not return to the trial. It only rekindled an anger about which he could do nothing.

The following day, Edwin Bacon's younger daughter took the witness stand in her second effort to testify.

In a halting voice, Hilary recalled her girlhood and her father helping her with French, Latin, and math, building a model of an Alaskan village with her. "I made little sled dogs," she said with a grin, "and he spent hours making a little sled."

She spoke of dog sledding with him in New Hampshire, boating with him and the rest of the family, and she appeared to be having little difficulty.

When Masterman asked whether she had spoken to him on the night of July 29, she closed her eyes at the mention of the date and appeared to summon her spirit. "It was after sunset. And I called him all the time, as it were. And that evening I called him up and I was in his office at home. It was after sunset and I tried pulling on the light and it didn't go on."

She took a breath and resumed, "I said, 'Dad, this is Hilary. The lightbulb is out in your office.' And he said, 'Oh.' And I said, "Can you bring some light bulbs on your way?' And he said, 'Sure.' And I said, 'See you later, see you later. Love you. Bye bye.' "

Her head lowered, and Masterman looked down.

At last lifting his eyes to her pained gaze, he said, "If you can, tell us what sort of person your dad was."

"I guess he was amazing in that he was really kind," she said softly. "He was incredibly giving. He had a way of talking to people about anything. Every now and then he'd take me horseback riding. And I remember he'd be out there talking with my riding instructor about horses." The recollection brought a wan smile to her face.

"Can you tell us now," Masterman gently asked, "how your father's death affected you in the following weeks and months?"

Squeezing her hands, she struggled to say, "I guess it started when my mother first told me. I told her that she was lying and I didn't believe her. And I cried a lot. And for about a year afterwards. We had a closed-casket funeral, so I never saw him. And then for about a year afterward . . ."

She broke into tears and her slight shoulders began to tremble.

"All right," Masterman said. "That is all, your honor. I have no further questions. Thank you, Hilary."

The inscrutable jurors next heard from a pathologist who had reviewed the Edwin Bacon autopsy report.

Dr. Luke G. Tedeschi of Boston University Medical School described the effects of cyanide poisoning. He explained that the ingested cyanide salt reacted with stomach acid and formed cyanide gas. The agent was a means of extermination used by Nazis in World War II. The gas eroded and inflamed Bacon's stomach lining and caused "excruciating pain," he said. The cyanide entered the bloodstream, shutting down respiration. Frantic and futile efforts at breathing would have been accompanied by severe chest pains. After a period of dizziness and wracking convulsions, Bacon became comatose and died from "asphyxiation of oxygen to the brain, secondary to cyanide toxicity."

Asked by Masterman how long Bacon might have lived after the onset of poisoning, Dr. Tedeschi estimated from one to ten minutes.

Following his testimony, a female juror handed a note to a court officer who delivered it to Judge Young. It read that she was feeling sick. Without explaining the reason, the judge called for a recess.

Hilary returned to law school at South Bend, Indiana, and Brooks came up to Boston from New York, prepared to testify in the second week of the trial. She understood, talking to her mother, that Ed Masterman was concerned the jury could be developing a perception that her father had indeed taken his own life. James Blaikie was the little man who wasn't there, and the jury had not been told, would not be told, where the accused was, whether he was even alive. No statement before jurors about his conviction for the murder of David DeWilde was permissible. Brooks simply had to tell the truth about her relationship with her father. Aside from the admission by Kemper that Ed had not signed the pivotal insurance form, they needed a picture of Ed Bacon the man—the husband and father—troubled by business difficulties but essentially hopeful and incapable of suicide.

On the eighth day of the trial, now in its second week, Brooks was the last Bacon who would face the jurors and alternates, twelve men and four women.

With her mother's firmness and her father's brown eyes, the attractive twenty-six-year-old brunette projected a vulnerable composure as she was sworn in to testify.

Masterman took her through school at Winsor in Boston and her studies at Barnard College in New York, where she presently worked in sales for a British publishing company. Answering questions under direct examination, she spoke of her family as "very close" and recalled that her father bought her a tennis racket when she was six years old. "We used to go out and hit the ball every Saturday morning," she said with a faint smile. "He wanted to make sure my form was really good. We used to play tennis a lot together."

She also waited up for Ed to return from his office and help her with her math. After her mother left early for work, Brooks would have breakfast with her sister and father, and he often would drive them to nearby Winsor school, chit-chatting all the way. There were regular Sunday family luncheons with their Grandmother Bacon at her Back Bay house. Her father also would drive to Weymouth on the South Shore of Boston and bring Grandmother Ginepra back to the townhouse for dinner.

At the age of six, with her parents, she campaigned door-to-door in the Back Bay for Edward W. Brooke, who in 1966 became the first black in the U.S. Senate in nearly nine decades.

On the subject of family difficulties, she said, "Mother and Dad would have disagreements sometimes and I knew that there were some problems with bills. And everyone I knew, their families had arguments. Things don't work out perfectly all the time, but we loved each other, we cared about each other very much."

Asked by Masterman how she was affected by her father's death in its immediate aftermath, Brooks told about staying in town that summer, working as an usher at the Charles Playhouse, while Hilary was in New Hampshire with their Uncle Frank and his family. Her mother worked during the day. "Most of my friends were out of town," she said. "We have a big house and I spent a whole month just sort of going from empty room to empty room. We had a dog and I used to watch him looking for dad and I felt the same way about it."

"Let me take you to today," Masterman said. "Now, it is eleven years later. Have you come to terms with this loss?"

"It is still very difficult for me," she said, frowning in thought. "There is a lot that is unresolved."

Rooney did not cross-examine and Masterman believed the Bacon women had brought their father to life in that courtroom.

The following morning, a tall gray-haired John Maillet, three years in retirement, went under oath. The face of the sixty-year-old former homicide sergeant detective had hollowed since his days on the Bacon case. The mirthful creases about his mouth and eyes had deepened but they were locked in a deadpan expression.

Masterman took him back to the start of his investigation of Bacon's death in the summer of 1974, and asked if at some time he had been given "certain pieces of paper" by Patricia Haskell, the Bacon agency secretary at the time.

"Yes, sir, I was," Maillet said.

Without saying so, Masterman was getting to the scratch pad with "Edwin C. Bacon" hand-written in it several times. The FBI had concluded the penman probably forged Bacon's signature on the insurance form.

Because FBI laboratory findings are inadmissible in civil cases, Masterman could not introduce the report. However, he was able through Maillet's testimony to establish the fact that there had been a police investigation of James Blaikie in connection with Bacon's death. The attorney intended to ask if he had formed a judgment about the case even though he knew Judge Young would not allow the question.

"Now, as a result of your investigation, sir," Masterman said, "my question is whether or not you arrived at an opinion—"

Instantly Judge Young called counselors to the side bar and asked Masterman to state the question as he intended to ask it.

Masterman replied, "Whether or not he has an opinion as to the cause of death and as to who caused the death. He'll say, 'Yes.' And then if permitted to answer he would say, 'Cyanide. James Blaikie.' "

"I object," Rooney grumbled.

"Sustained," Judge Young said, and the bench conference ended.

Permitted only to identify the invoice for cyanide he had obtained at the chemical company, Maillet stepped down from his brief time on the witness stand.

Smoki met up with him in the lobby, where his amiable persona could emerge.

"Thank you, John," she said, shaking his hand like an old friend.

"Well," he said, "they didn't let me say much in there."

"John," she said earnestly, "having the jury know a homicide detective was on Blaikie's case doesn't hurt, I have to tell you."

He nodded. "How are your daughters?"

"Good, good, thank you. You remember. Did you see Brooks inside?"

"Yeah," Maillet said, cocking his head toward the courtroom. "Pretty woman, all grown up."

"It's been a long time, hasn't it?" Smoki said unhappily.

"That it has," Maillet said, and he wished her good luck.

Ambling down the musty corridor of the genteel law school building, John Maillet thought about his own three daughters, all in their twenties now. He had never revealed that they and Ed Bacon's daughters were a big reason he had taken on the case ten years before. Nor had he ever spoken of his wife's death five months after Ed's.

John Maillet had never married again. No one but Colette could be the mother of their girls.

Planning a concise defense, Kemper's attorneys estimated for Judge Young the following Monday, February 4th, that their case would take no more than two days. The trial was entering its third week.

On an easel before the court was a photographic blowup of Bacon's so-called suicide note, "I CAN'T STAND IT ANYMORE." Using a slide-projector, a document examiner showed transparencies of Bacon's known hand-printing and compared them with the note. With a pointer she drew attention to what she described as features common to the exemplars and the note: the rounded top of the letter A, the horizontal line of the letter T not quite touching the vertical line and the curved strokes of the letter Y. These, she said, were characteristics of Bacon's normal writing style. Her conclusion was that the note showed no evidence of forgery and had been written by Edwin Bacon.

Always the weakest link in the case for murder, the "suicide note" had now reached judgment day. There was no way Masterman could evoke the opinion of

Bacon family members or investigators that if Bacon had written the note, it had been something other than a suicide message. All Masterman could do was stick to the evidence and point out that the note was neither signed nor dated.

Bringing to the witness stand a series of Kemper employees, Rooney attempted to establish that unfortunate as the loss of life was, Kemper was not responsible for the death of Edwin Bacon whether he had been murdered, or more likely, had committed suicide.

It was a challenging task, presenting company procedures and industry standards in the face of a human drama. Soldiering on, Rooney elicited testimony from the manager of the claims department, who quoted national statistics on causes of death among life insurance policyholders. She said that fewer than one percent of the deaths were homicides between 1973 and 1975, the years bracketing Bacon's death. The suicide rate among insured persons was twice as high in that three-year period; the accidental death rate six times as high.

The deposition of a former manager of client services, who was absent from court, indicated that he did not know of a single murder for insurance gain among Kemper clients in his sixteen years with the company.

If the jury were to decide Blaikie poisoned Bacon, Kemper hoped the infrequency of homicide supported its case. The company could not have foreseen that murder would be the result of approving the beneficiary application, which, in any event, it believed genuine.

Scheduled to give the final testimony in the eleven-day trial, Kemper's last witness took the stand on Tuesday, February 5, 1985. Ironically, she proved in Masterman's view to be the best rebuttal witness he could ask for.

Once head of Kemper's policyholder services, she testified under direct examination by Rooney that Bacon's beneficiary application had been processed like any other. A staff member had run a computer check of information on the policy and found no restriction against Blaikie becoming the beneficiary. Bacon's handwritten name had been compared to a signature in his file and the two had appeared to match. The application had then been approved. An acknowledgment of the change had been sent to the address under Bacon's name, his waterfront office.

Masterman rose to cross-examine her on the last in the series of events. Kemper had mailed the acknowledgment of the beneficiary change to Bacon five days before his death. Masterman, like the police and the Bacons, believed Ed never saw the acknowledgment, but that Blaikie had intercepted it.

In view of Blaikie's name as both witness and new beneficiary on the form, Masterman asked the witness why she or someone in her office had not informed Ed of the change personally, by telephone.

Bristling with impatience, she replied that office procedures had not called for telephoning acknowledgments.

In a voice etched with contempt, Masterman said, "Thank you," and strode back to his table.

With the agreement of attorneys on both sides, Judge Young empowered the twelve jurors and four alternates alike to reach a verdict. Unlike a jury in a criminal case, they did not have to arrive at a unanimous decision, but fourteen of them had to agree on a verdict.

The trial returned to the Suffolk County Courthouse in Boston, where the jury deliberated while Judge Young in his chambers completed work on other cases. *Bacon* vs *Kemper* was his last major case in the Superior Court, as he was slated for the federal bench later in the year.

On the third day of deliberation, a bitterly cold and snowy first Thursday in February, the jury came down the stairs from its third-floor room at eleven forty-five A.M., more than an hour before its scheduled one o'clock recess for lunch. The timing suggested a verdict might have been reached and Masterman hastened into the courtroom with Smoki and Brooks. Judge Young emerged from his chambers and the jury filed in with expressionless faces.

The Asian forewoman gave a note to the clerk who walked it over to the bench and handed it up to the judge.

The jury had not reached a verdict but drawn up what Judge Young termed a "decision tree" to organize their deliberations.

He pronounced their diagram accurate, stepped down from the bench, and stood before a portable blackboard next to the jury box. Consulting the jury's message, he replicated the "decision tree" with a piece of chalk.

If Jury Decides: The Verdict Is in Favor of:

1 BACON SUICIDE .... KEMPER
  BACON MURDERED BY BLAIKIE
     |
2. KEMPER HAD DUTY TO BACON?

     NO .... KEMPER
     YES
      |
3. KEMPER NEGLIGENT?

     NO .... KEMPER
     YES
      |
4. KEMPER NEGLIGENCE WAS
   PROXIMATE CAUSE OF MURDER?

     NO .... KEMPER
     YES .... BACONS
      |
5. AWARD DAMAGES TO BACONS?

Elaborating on the diagram, Judge Young emphasized that if the jury were to find Bacon a suicide, they would have reached a verdict in favor of Kemper and their deliberations would have ended.

If, on the other hand, murder by Blaikie were to be found, the jurors next would have to consider the question of *duty*. It meant a strictly legal obligation by Kemper to be reasonably certain the beneficiary-change application was genuine. If there had been that duty, had Kemper failed in the duty through *negligence?* If so, had that negligence been the *proximate cause* of Bacon's death? That meant the murder of Bacon on July 29, 1974 would not have occurred but for Kemper's negligence.

To win her case, Bacon had to have proved all four elements concerning the alleged murder. Then the jury had to decide whether a financial award for damages would be due to her and her daughters.

The jury also had a question, which Judge Young read. If the required majority of the jurors already believed that Kemper had not been the proximate cause of Bacon's death, was it necessary to decide whether the company had a duty to Bacon and had been negligent in that duty?

Judge Young replied no, adding that if Kemper had not caused Bacon's death, Kemper was to be acquitted.

Huddled with Brooks in a distant pew, Smoki turned a shade of white. "Dear," she whispered to her daughter, "it sounds as though they've already decided for Kemper, doesn't it?"

"Mother," Brooks scolded, firmly patting Smoki's hand, "don't be so pessimistic. They're still thinking about it. There's a lot to *think* about."

In the frigid lobby, Masterman in his elegant manner also put as happy a face on the episode as he could for his nerve-wracked client, but moments later he conceded privately to news reporters that the jury's question did not bode well for his case.

One of the defense attorneys telephoned word of the promising sign to Kemper headquarters in Illinois.

It was not until the following snow-lashed afternoon that the jury filed into the cramped courtroom shortly before four o'clock and announced it had reached a verdict. The forewoman handed the verdict card to the clerk. On Friday, February 8, 1985, after twenty hours of deliberation over a period of four days, the mystery of Edwin Bacon was to receive a solution in court after ten and a half years.

Judge Young inspected the jury's verdict and handed it back to the clerk, who stood before the bench and in a thick Boston accent briskly slurred the docket number of *Bacon* vs *Kemper* and then the verdict:

"The jury finds for the plaintiff."

The Bacons had won. For the wrongful death of Edwin Bacon and his conscious pain and suffering, the jury ordered Kemper to pay Smoki Bacon and her daughters $250,000 in damages. With interest over eight years from 1977, when the lawsuit was filed, the amount was nearly $600,000.

Amidst muted cries of relief and delight, Ed Masterman looked down from his height with veiled satisfaction and then accepted gracious if reserved congratulations from grim-faced opposing counsel.

Brooks tearfully reminded herself over and over again that her mother was the plaintiff and the family had proved its case. A jury had concluded that James Blaikie had murdered her father.

As she embraced her daughter, Smoki wept and thought, *Ed, I wasn't so bad after all, was I?*

Clasping Brooks's shoulders, she beamed happily for the first time in memory. "Let's go and telephone Hilary," Smoki whispered, and flanked by her daughter and her husband, she breezed out of the courtroom into the crowd.

Epilogue

Kemper appealed the case and two years later the Massachusetts Supreme Judicial Court reversed the 1985 jury verdict on one of its two elements.

In September 1987, the state's high court completely absolved Kemper of negligence. A majority of the justices found:

> There was no evidence which proved that Kemper knew or should have known that its acceptance and approval of the change of beneficiary request exposed Bacon to an unreasonable risk of harm from criminal conduct.

Referring to Blaikie's name as witness on the form, the court found the fact was "simply too innocuous to have aroused Kemper's suspicion that Bacon had not consented to the change of beneficiary."

Indeed, Massachusetts had no law requiring a third party to witness a beneficiary change.

The court thereby overturned the damage award and the Bacons received not a penny.

But the justices did uphold the jury's belief that Bacon died at Blaikie's hands. In a unanimous decision, they ruled:

> There was sufficient evidence to warrant a finding that Blaikie murdered Bacon.

It was what Alice Richmond had insisted to no avail as an assistant district attorney ten years before.

The case could be appealed no higher.

In addition to losing the damage award, Smoki Bacon found herself paying part of Kemper's legal costs.

Stunned and angered by the outcome, she and her daughters took consolation in the murder finding. Smoki also launched a campaign to tighten insurance-industry regulations. Sponsored by State Senator Paul Harold and State Representative Mark Roosevelt, an insurance fraud prevention bill passed the Massachusetts legislature in 1989.

In January 1990, nearly sixteen years after the death of Edwin Bacon, Governor Michael Dukakis signed the bill into law. It stated:

> No life insurance company shall accept or take action on any written request to change the designation of beneficiary under any policy of life or endowment insurance unless the signature of the person requesting the change is witnessed by a disinterested person. A disinterested person is one who is over eighteen years of age and not designated as a beneficiary in the requested change.

Since his 1976 conviction for the premeditated murder of David DeWilde, James Blaikie has remained incarcerated without furlough. His jobs have included work as an electrocardiogram technician and a maintenance man within prison confines. Continuing an interest begun while awaiting trial in the DeWilde case, he became a popular portrait artist in prison. He has frequently drawn fellow inmates and, working from photographs, chalked their loved ones into the pictures.

He became acquainted with a visiting social worker who observed his crime-prevention program aimed at youths. She and Blaikie were married in a prison chapel in 1985.

Although a first degree murder conviction carries a life sentence without eligibility for parole in Massachusetts, state law does permit lifers to petition authorities for a commutation of sentence. If such a request is approved by the governor and other officials, the sentence is reduced to punishment for second-degree murder: imprisonment with eligibility for parole after fifteen years.

By the end of 1990, James Blaikie had served that many years with a record of good behavior but had not applied for a commutation of sentence.

In an interview he continued to maintain he shot David DeWilde in self-defense. However, he said that with the help of psychological counseling he had come to accept responsibility for confronting David with a gun. Blaikie said that since killing DeWilde he has had a recurring nightmare about shooting him. The dream is vivid, he said, awakening him in icy terror with a feeling of helpless remorse.

James Blaikie denied accusations made in court that he murdered his parents. He reiterated statements made to police after his mother's death that he was not in her presence when she died of a gunshot wound. He claimed not to have visited his father in a VA hospital on the day the elder Blaikie died of double pneumonia according to his death certificate.

Blaikie has never been charged by authorities in connection with either death.

He denied killing Edwin Bacon and spoke of him as a valued friend.

MURDEROUS MINDS